CASTLE

RICHARD CASTLE'S

STORM SEASON

A DERRICK STORM MYSTERY

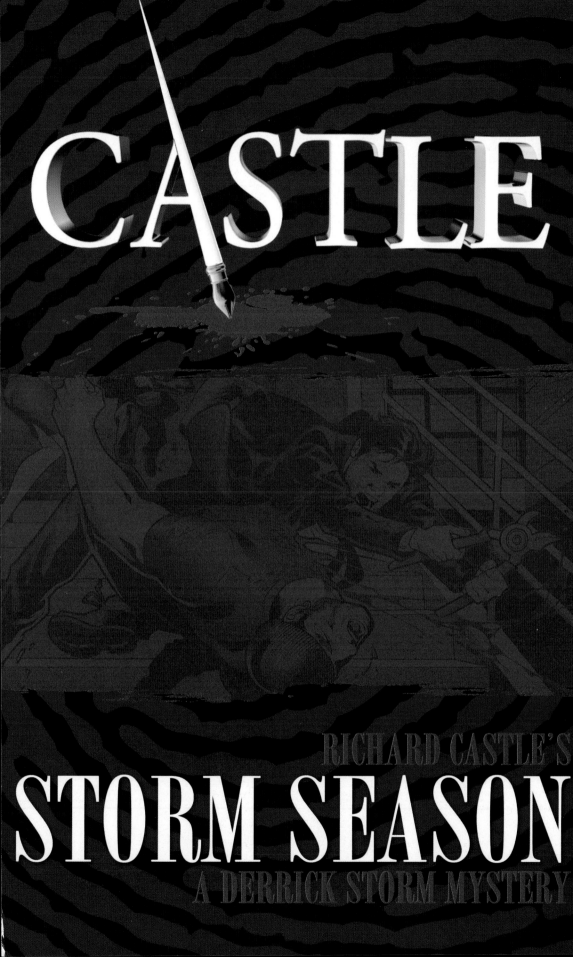

KELLY SUE DECONNICK &
BRIAN MICHAEL BENDIS

PENCILS
EMANUELA LUPACCHINO

INKS
GUILLERMO ORTEGO

COLORIST
MATT MILLA

LETTERER
VIRTUAL CALLIGRAPHY'S CORY PETIT

DUSTIN WEAVER & MARTE GRACIA

ASSISTANT EDITORS
ELLIE PYLE & JON MOISAN

EDITOR
SANA AMANAT

Special Thanks To:
Andrew Marlowe, Lisa Schomas, Cooper McMains,
Grace Yang and Rosalie Villapando

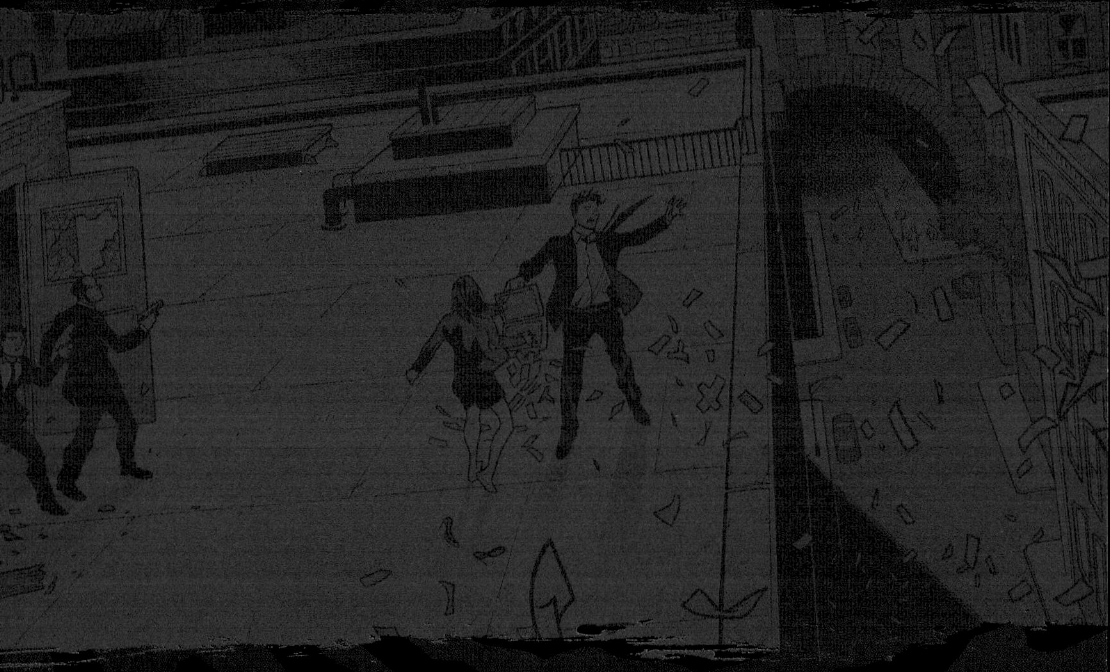

Collection Editor **Jennifer Grünwald** Assistant Editors **Alex Starbuck & Nelson Ribeiro**
Editor, Special Projects **Mark D. Beazley** Senior Editor, Special Projects **Jeff Youngquist** Senior Vice President of Sales **David Gabriel**
SVP of Brand Planning & Communications **Michael Pasciullo** Book Design **Jeff Powell**
Editor in Chief **Axel Alonso** Chief Creative Officer **Joe Quesada** Publisher **Dan Buckley**

CASTLE

STORM SEASON

A DERRICK STORM MYSTERY

INTRODUCTION

s a best-selling novelist, I'm often asked where my ideas come from. Usually, I give my standard smart-ass answer — I buy them from a homeless gentleman down on the Bowery. But the truth is, most ideas rarely have one source. They usually arise from the combination of many different influences. The same is true for Derrick Storm. But I do think I know where my journey started.

When I was seven years old, I ran away from home. I can't remember why, some petty slight of childhood involving uneaten vegetables, no doubt. My departure carried with it the requisite door slamming and grand pronouncements that ended with me fleeing the apartment and spilling out onto the hot city streets.

I didn't make it very far. After only a few minutes of walking the sidewalks in a teary rage of righteous indignation, I'd already become hot, sweaty and tired, though barely a few blocks from home. (In my defense, New York's a big city and I had much shorter legs at the time.) Yet as weary as I was, I knew returning after such a brief time would be nothing short of humiliating. I'd told my mother she'd be sorry and I'd hardly even given her enough time to put on make-up before coming to look for me. So, needing to kill time and wanting to escape the heat, I went to the movies.

There was an old revival house near our apartment that showed second-run films, usually a double feature. This was well before the VHS explosion, when if you wanted to see a movie you had to go to the theater. That day an old Disney movie was playing. Figuring two hours would be time enough for Mother to learn her lesson, I fished some money out of my pocket and slipped inside the palace of darkness.

Time has stolen the memory of what that first movie was. All I remember is that it was animated, and it held my childish attention. When it was over, I sat there for a bit contemplating the consequences of returning home. By the time I got out of my seat, the other movie was just about to start. I was halfway up the aisle when I heard it — one the coolest sounds in the world.

Dum-dah-dah-dum Dum-Dum-Dum-Dum-dah-dah-dum Dum-dum-dum Dah-wah Duh-nuh-nuh.

The film was *Goldfinger*. The sound was the Bond theme.

As I watched the screen turn blood red from Bond's gunshot, I was undeniably hooked. In that moment, I'd forgotten that I'd run away. I'd forgotten that someone was waiting for me. I'd forgotten everything. I sat hypnotized for the next two hours, watching as Bond battled bad guys and seduced women with ease, all while delivering bad-ass one liners. When it was over, I knew what I was going to be when I grew up. I was going to be a spy.

Well, I didn't become a spy, but I did become the next best thing — a spy novelist. Along the way I've even managed to save the world a couple of times, not to mention seduce a woman or two. No doubt there have been other influences that helped shape Derrick Storm — from the edgy and gruff Private Eyes of Raymond Chandler and Mickey Spillane, to Jim Steranko's bold and brassy take on Nick Fury — but I really believe that it all started on one hot summer day in the temple of imagination when a seven-year-old learned what it meant to be cool.

I must admit, to see Derrick Storm brought to life again in graphic novel form gives me quite a thrill. I am indebted to Kelly Sue DeConnick along with Brian Michael Bendis for the extraordinary care and creative passion they've brought to this project. They're both true super heroes of the Marvel Universe. Thanks also to Emanuela Lupacchino for bringing such a dynamic artistic vision to the pages you're about to read. And to the enormously talented Dustin Weaver, your cover is the distillation of pure excitement. It's like a window into the unbridled adrenaline-fueled adolescent part of my brain. To all you folks, and to the entire Marvel team, I am humbled and grateful.

Oh, by the way, in case you're curious, there was hell to pay when I finally got home. But thanks to Bond, I rode out my mother's blustery fury with the coolness of a double O being interrogated by enemy agents. In the end, I was grounded for six weeks with no TV. But I didn't really care. As far as I was concerned, it was well worth it. And it gave me time to catch up on my comic books.

Richard Castle
New York, 2012

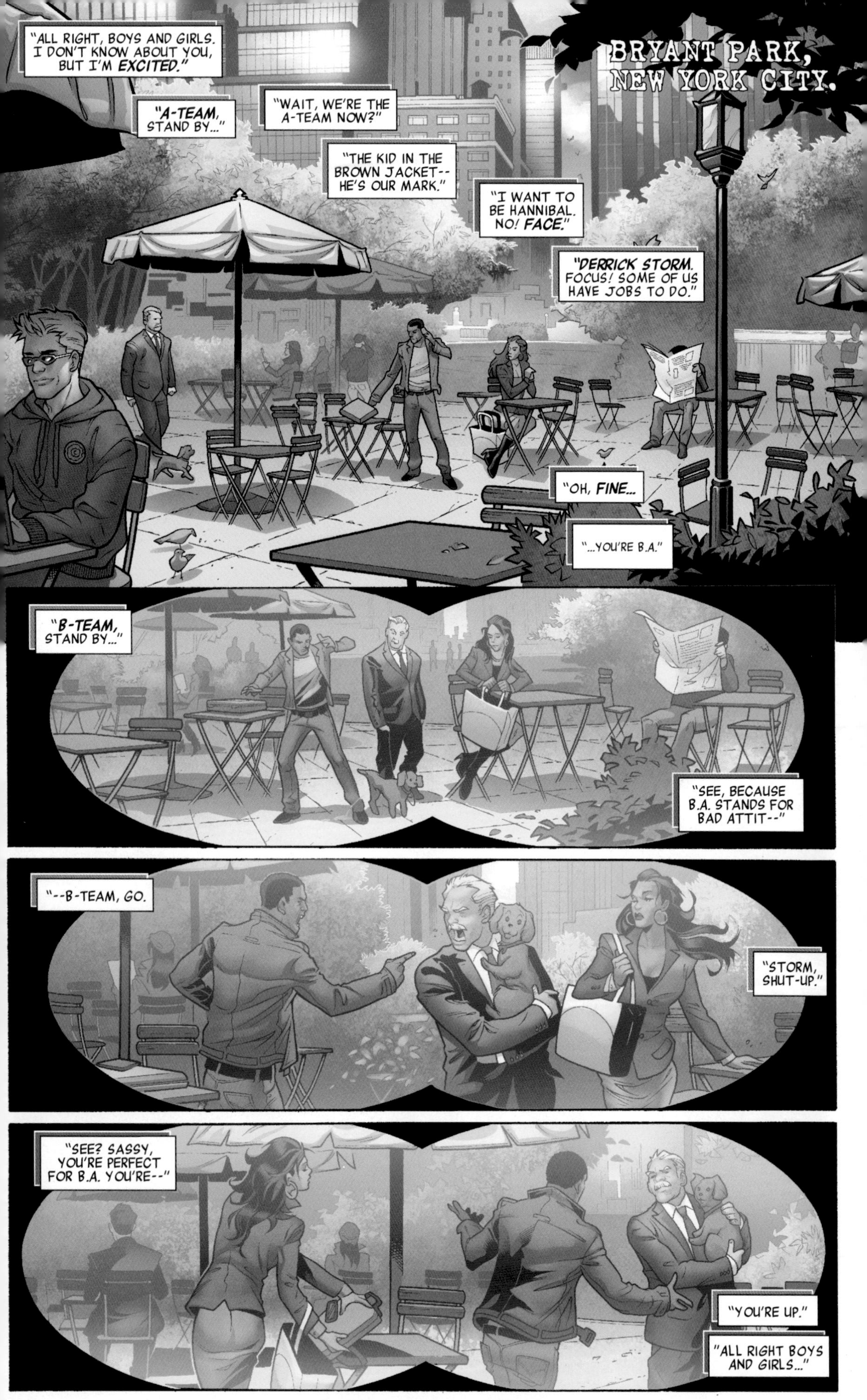
"ALL RIGHT, BOYS AND GIRLS. I DON'T KNOW ABOUT YOU, BUT I'M EXCITED."
BRYANT PARK, NEW YORK CITY.
"A-TEAM, STAND BY..."
"WAIT, WE'RE THE A-TEAM NOW?"
"THE KID IN THE BROWN JACKET-- HE'S OUR MARK."
"I WANT TO BE HANNIBAL. NO! FACE."
"DERRICK STORM. FOCUS! SOME OF US HAVE JOBS TO DO."
"OH, FINE...
"...YOU'RE B.A."
"B-TEAM, STAND BY..."
"SEE, BECAUSE B.A. STANDS FOR BAD ATTIT--"
"--B-TEAM, GO.
"STORM, SHUT-UP."
"SEE? SASSY, YOU'RE PERFECT FOR B.A. YOU'RE--"
"YOU'RE UP."
"ALL RIGHT BOYS AND GIRLS..."

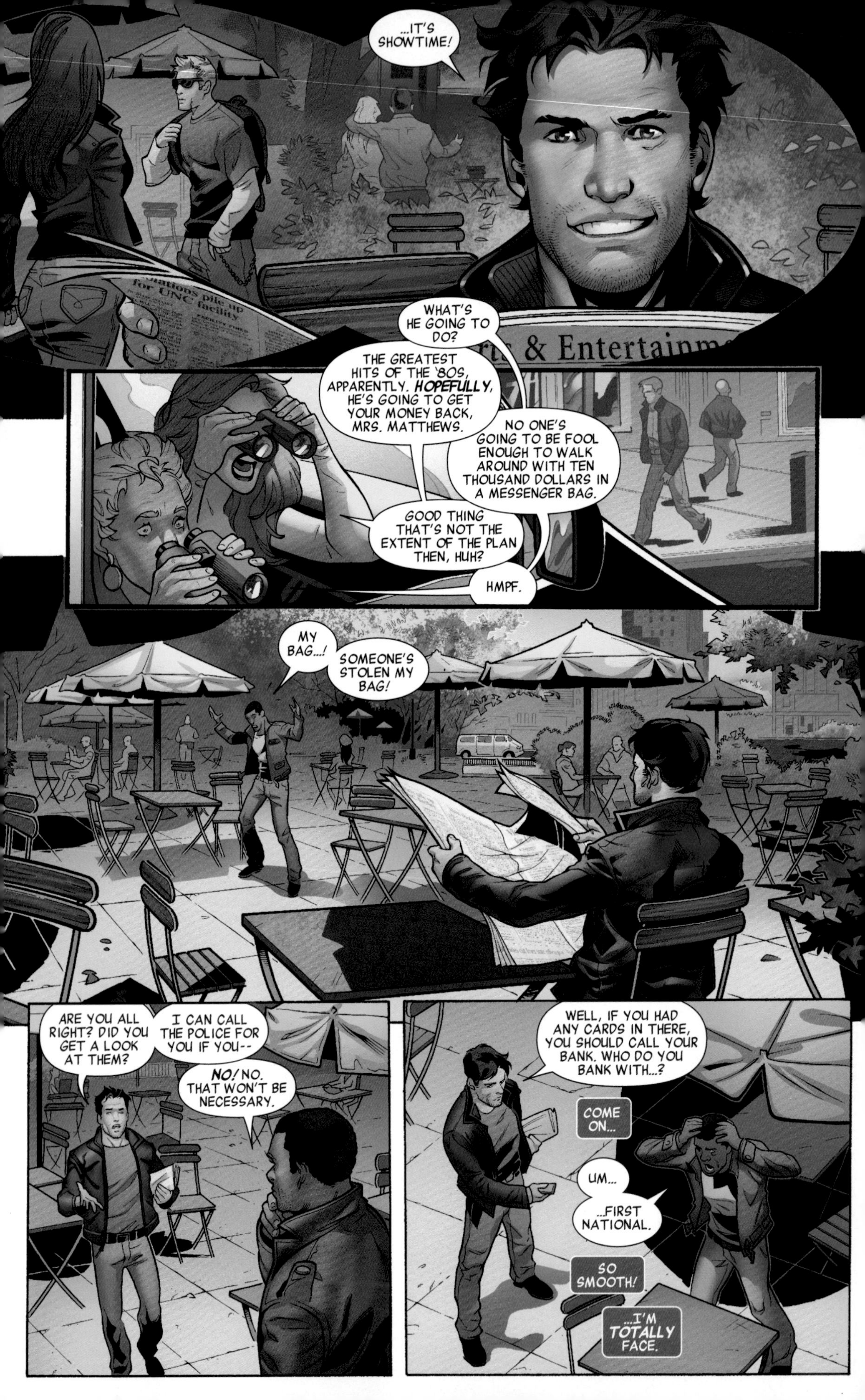
...IT'S SHOWTIME!
Arts & Entertainm
WHAT'S HE GOING TO DO?
THE GREATEST HITS OF THE '80S, APPARENTLY. HOPEFULLY, HE'S GOING TO GET YOUR MONEY BACK, MRS. MATTHEWS.
NO ONE'S GOING TO BE FOOL ENOUGH TO WALK AROUND WITH TEN THOUSAND DOLLARS IN A MESSENGER BAG.
GOOD THING THAT'S NOT THE EXTENT OF THE PLAN THEN, HUH?
HMPF.
MY BAG...!
SOMEONE'S STOLEN MY BAG!
ARE YOU ALL RIGHT? DID YOU GET A LOOK AT THEM?
I CAN CALL THE POLICE FOR YOU IF YOU--
NO! NO. THAT WON'T BE NECESSARY.
WELL, IF YOU HAD ANY CARDS IN THERE, YOU SHOULD CALL YOUR BANK. WHO DO YOU BANK WITH...?
COME ON...
UM...
...FIRST NATIONAL.
SO SMOOTH!
...I'M TOTALLY FACE.

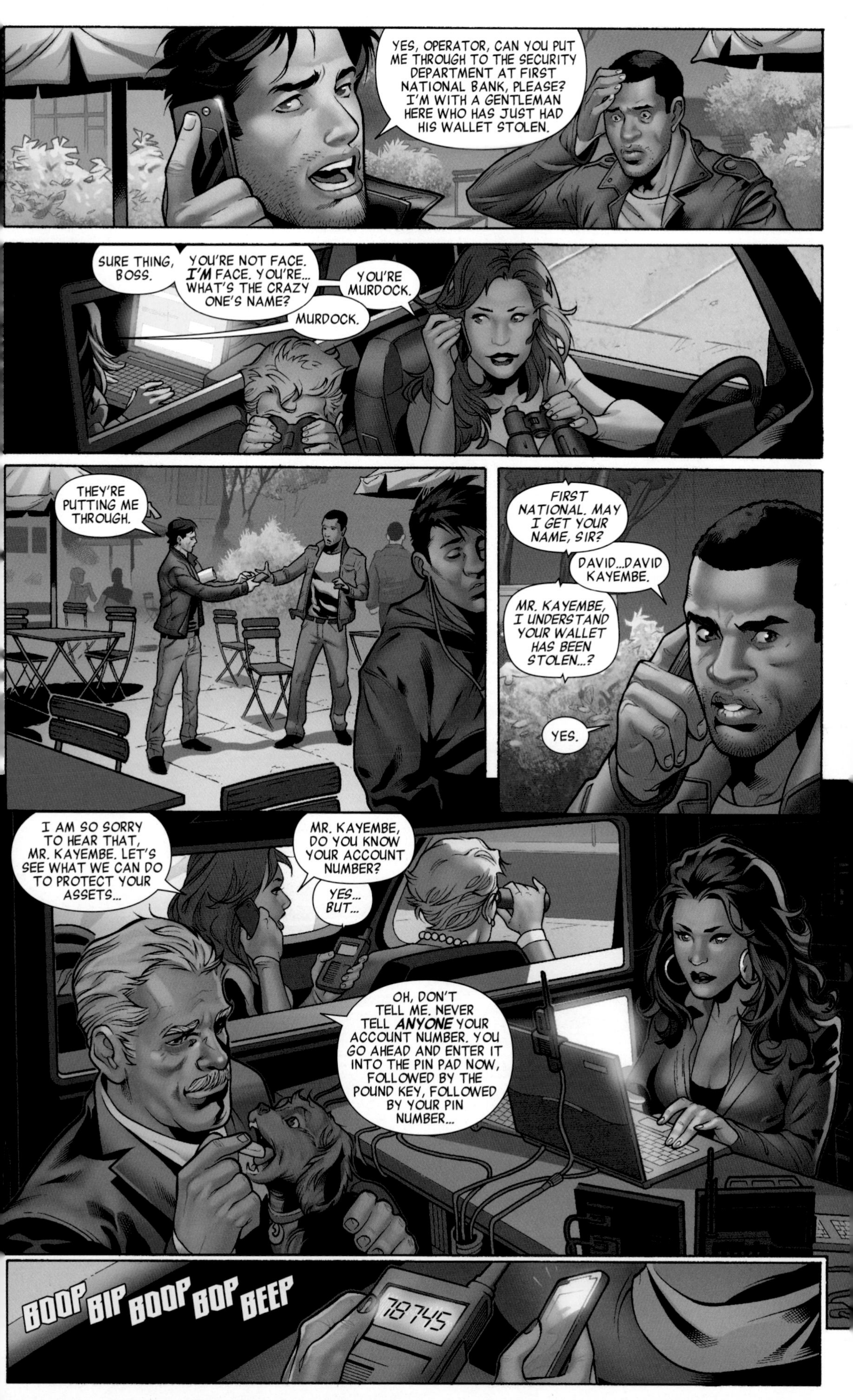
YES, OPERATOR, CAN YOU PUT ME THROUGH TO THE SECURITY DEPARTMENT AT FIRST NATIONAL BANK, PLEASE? I'M WITH A GENTLEMAN HERE WHO HAS JUST HAD HIS WALLET STOLEN.
SURE THING, BOSS.
YOU'RE NOT FACE. I'M FACE. YOU'RE... WHAT'S THE CRAZY ONE'S NAME?
YOU'RE MURDOCK.
MURDOCK.
THEY'RE PUTTING ME THROUGH.
FIRST NATIONAL. MAY I GET YOUR NAME, SIR?
DAVID...DAVID KAYEMBE.
MR. KAYEMBE, I UNDERSTAND YOUR WALLET HAS BEEN STOLEN...?
YES.
I AM SO SORRY TO HEAR THAT, MR. KAYEMBE. LET'S SEE WHAT WE CAN DO TO PROTECT YOUR ASSETS...
MR. KAYEMBE, DO YOU KNOW YOUR ACCOUNT NUMBER?
YES... BUT...
OH, DON'T TELL ME. NEVER TELL ANYONE YOUR ACCOUNT NUMBER. YOU GO AHEAD AND ENTER IT INTO THE PIN PAD NOW, FOLLOWED BY THE POUND KEY, FOLLOWED BY YOUR PIN NUMBER...
BOOP BIP BOOP BOP BEEP
78745

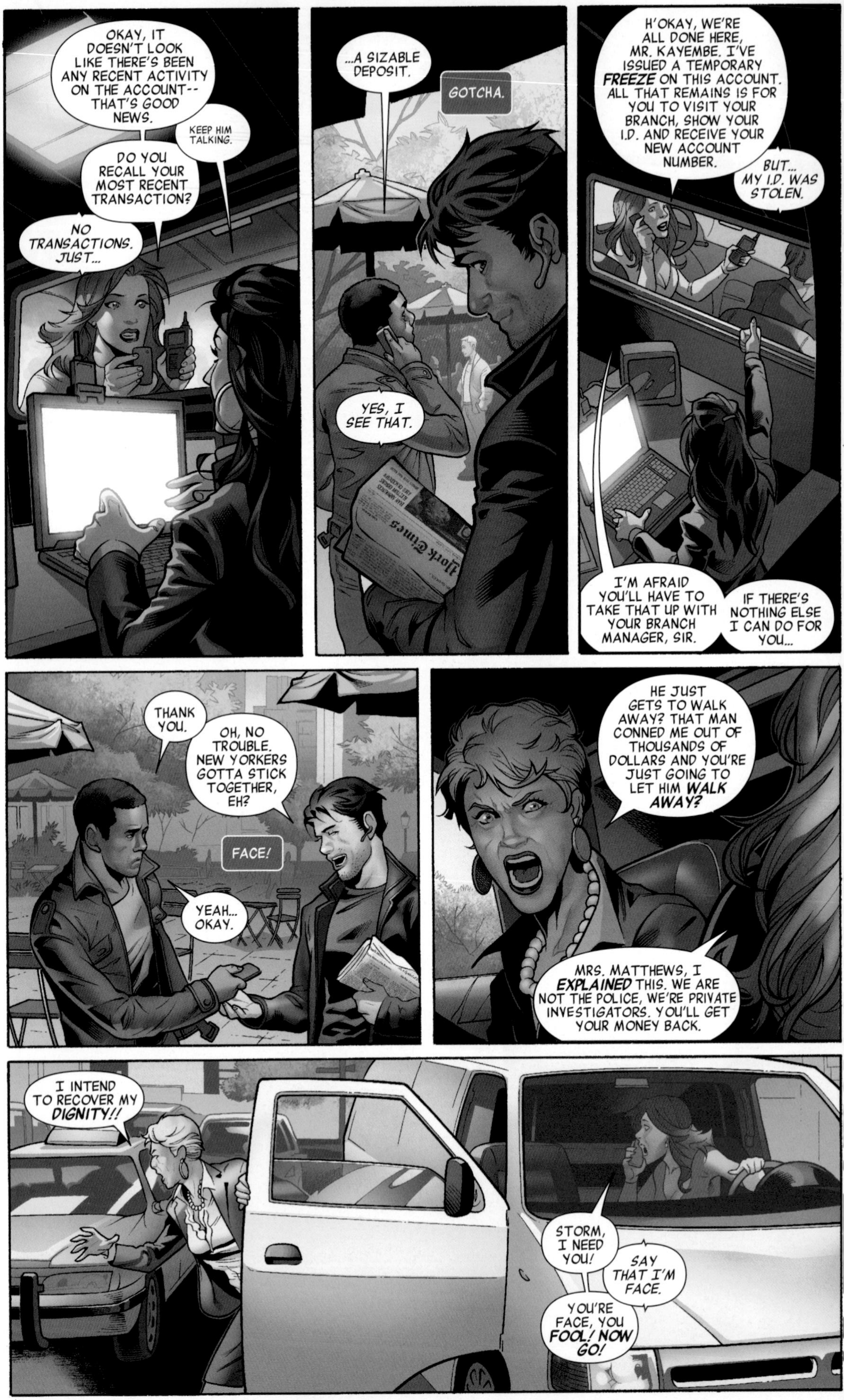

OKAY, IT DOESN'T LOOK LIKE THERE'S BEEN ANY RECENT ACTIVITY ON THE ACCOUNT-- THAT'S GOOD NEWS.
KEEP HIM TALKING.
DO YOU RECALL YOUR MOST RECENT TRANSACTION?
NO TRANSACTIONS. JUST...
...A SIZABLE DEPOSIT.
GOTCHA.
YES, I SEE THAT.
H'OKAY, WE'RE ALL DONE HERE, MR. KAYEMBE. I'VE ISSUED A TEMPORARY FREEZE ON THIS ACCOUNT. ALL THAT REMAINS IS FOR YOU TO VISIT YOUR BRANCH, SHOW YOUR I.D. AND RECEIVE YOUR NEW ACCOUNT NUMBER.
BUT... MY I.D. WAS STOLEN.
I'M AFRAID YOU'LL HAVE TO TAKE THAT UP WITH YOUR BRANCH MANAGER, SIR.
IF THERE'S NOTHING ELSE I CAN DO FOR YOU...
THANK YOU.
OH, NO TROUBLE. NEW YORKERS GOTTA STICK TOGETHER, EH?
FACE!
YEAH... OKAY.
HE JUST GETS TO WALK AWAY? THAT MAN CONNED ME OUT OF THOUSANDS OF DOLLARS AND YOU'RE JUST GOING TO LET HIM WALK AWAY?
MRS. MATTHEWS, I EXPLAINED THIS. WE ARE NOT THE POLICE, WE'RE PRIVATE INVESTIGATORS. YOU'LL GET YOUR MONEY BACK.
I INTEND TO RECOVER MY DIGNITY!!
STORM, I NEED YOU!
SAY THAT I'M FACE.
YOU'RE FACE, YOU FOOL! NOW GO!

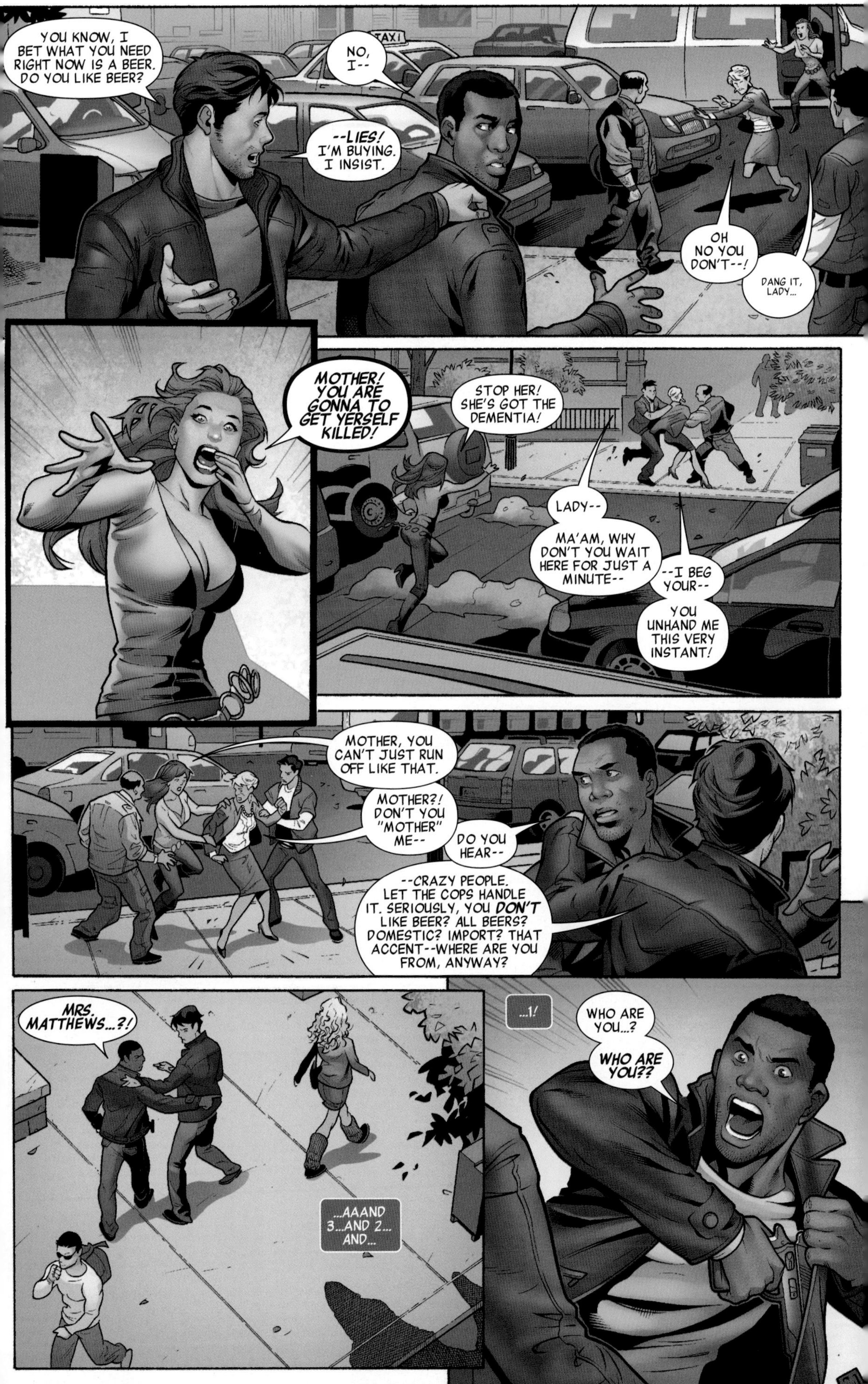

YOU KNOW, I BET WHAT YOU NEED RIGHT NOW IS A BEER. DO YOU LIKE BEER?
NO, I--
--LIES! I'M BUYING. I INSIST.
OH NO YOU DON'T--!
DANG IT, LADY...
MOTHER! YOU ARE GONNA TO GET YERSELF KILLED!
STOP HER! SHE'S GOT THE DEMENTIA!
LADY--
MA'AM, WHY DON'T YOU WAIT HERE FOR JUST A MINUTE--
--I BEG YOUR--
YOU UNHAND ME THIS VERY INSTANT!
MOTHER, YOU CAN'T JUST RUN OFF LIKE THAT.
MOTHER?! DON'T YOU "MOTHER" ME--
DO YOU HEAR--
--CRAZY PEOPLE. LET THE COPS HANDLE IT. SERIOUSLY, YOU DON'T LIKE BEER? ALL BEERS? DOMESTIC? IMPORT? THAT ACCENT--WHERE ARE YOU FROM, ANYWAY?
MRS. MATTHEWS...?!
...AAAND 3...AND 2... AND...
...1!
WHO ARE YOU...?
WHO ARE YOU??

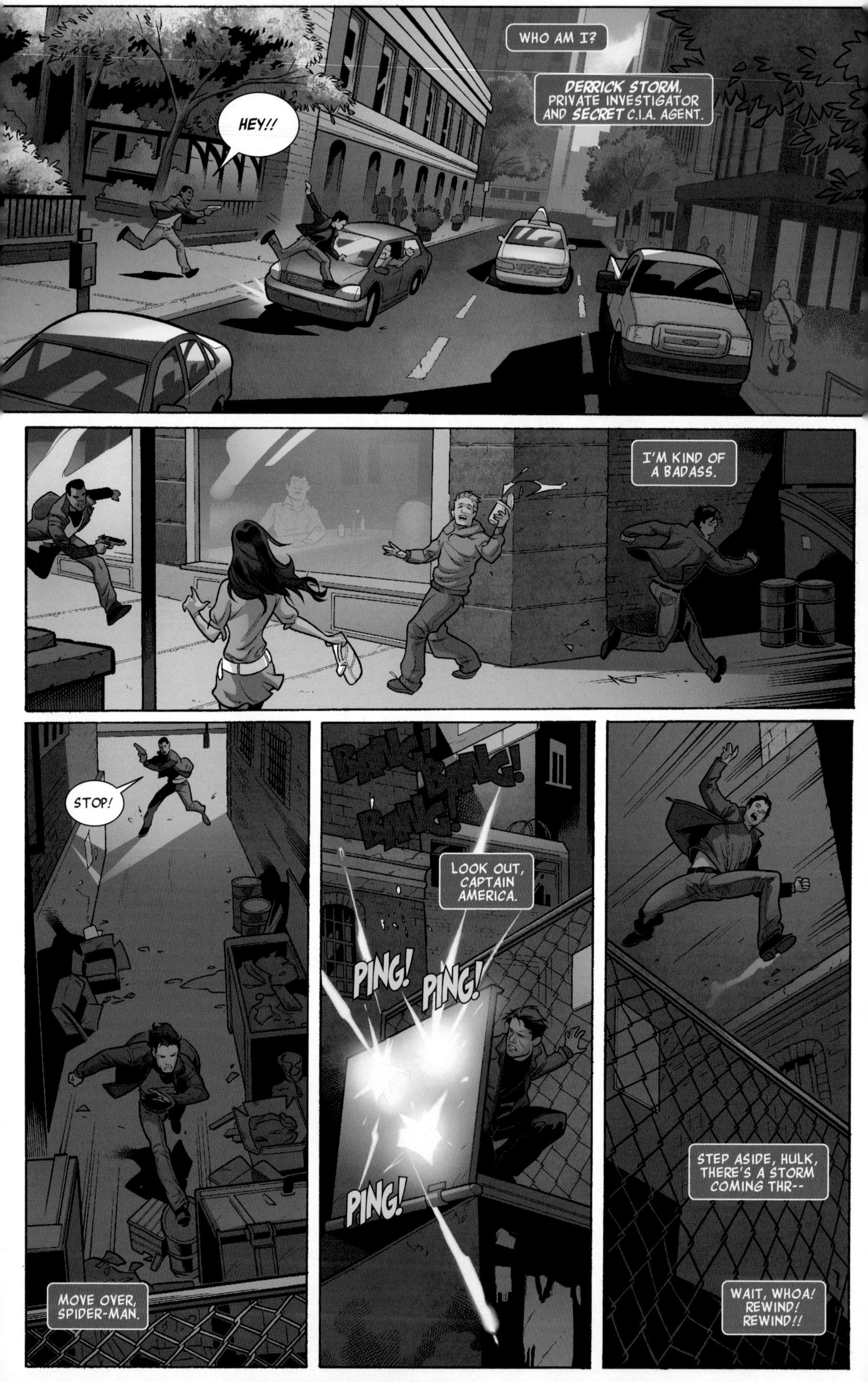
WHO AM I?
DERRICK STORM, PRIVATE INVESTIGATOR AND SECRET C.I.A. AGENT.
HEY!!
I'M KIND OF A BADASS.
STOP!
MOVE OVER, SPIDER-MAN.
BANG! BANG! BANG!
LOOK OUT, CAPTAIN AMERICA.
PING!
PING!
PING!
STEP ASIDE, HULK, THERE'S A STORM COMING THR--
WAIT, WHOA! REWIND! REWIND!!

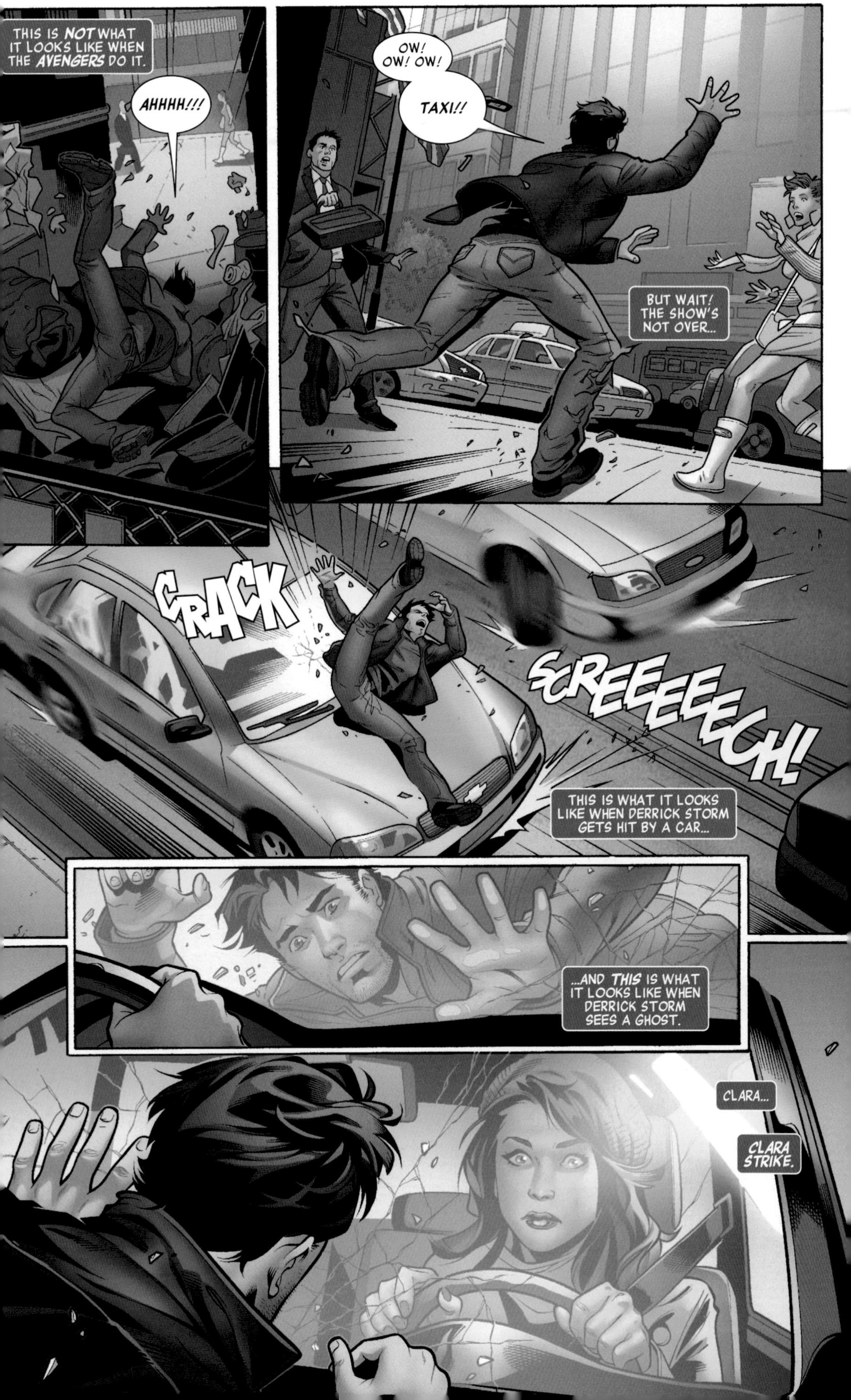

THIS IS NOT WHAT IT LOOKS LIKE WHEN THE AVENGERS DO IT.
AHHHH!!!
OW! OW! OW!
TAXI!!
BUT WAIT! THE SHOW'S NOT OVER...
CRACK
SCREEEEECH!
THIS IS WHAT IT LOOKS LIKE WHEN DERRICK STORM GETS HIT BY A CAR...
...AND THIS IS WHAT IT LOOKS LIKE WHEN DERRICK STORM SEES A GHOST.
CLARA...
CLARA STRIKE.

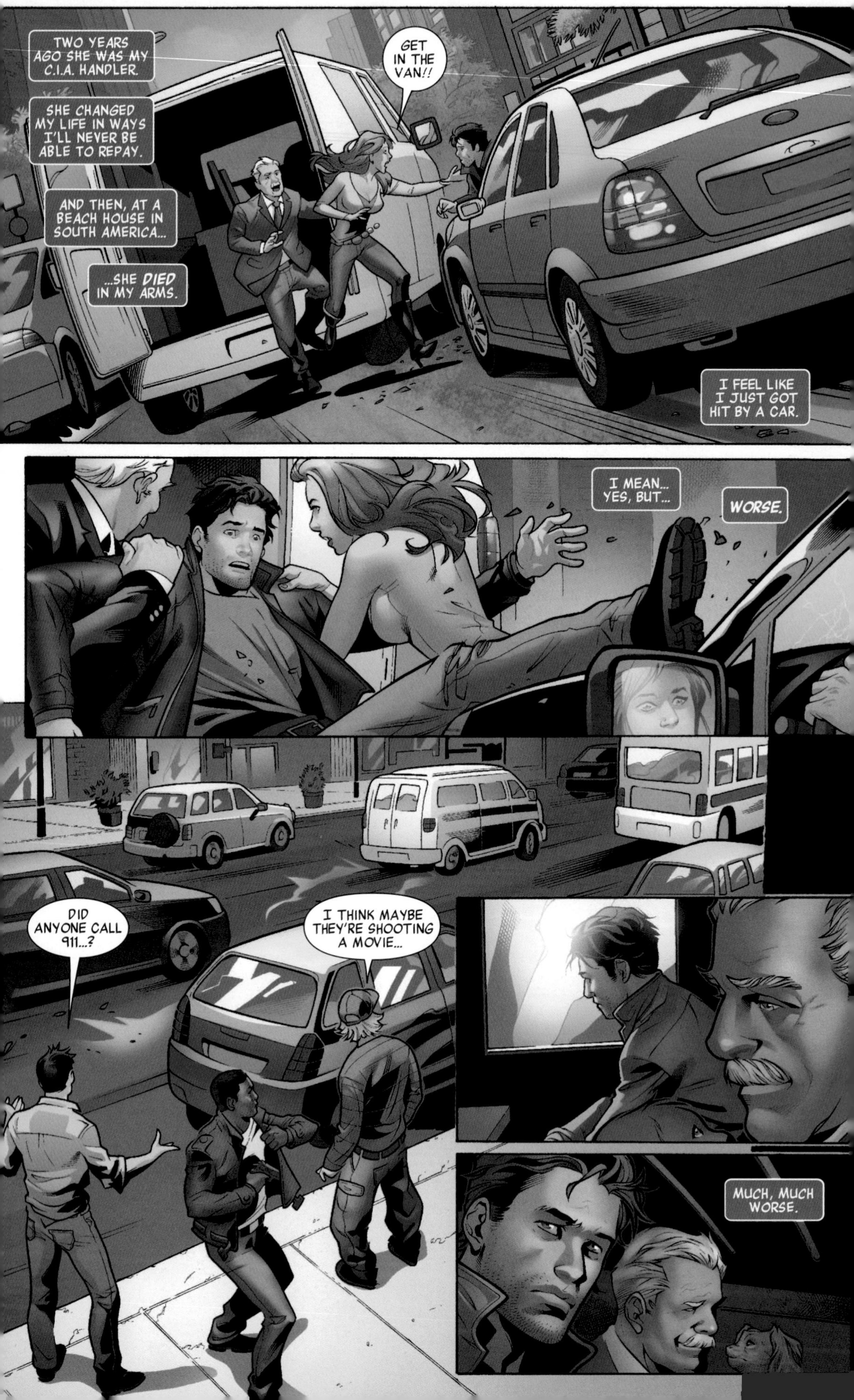
TWO YEARS AGO SHE WAS MY C.I.A. HANDLER.
GET IN THE VAN!!
SHE CHANGED MY LIFE IN WAYS I'LL NEVER BE ABLE TO REPAY.
AND THEN, AT A BEACH HOUSE IN SOUTH AMERICA...
...SHE *DIED* IN MY ARMS.
I FEEL LIKE I JUST GOT HIT BY A CAR.
I MEAN... YES, BUT...
WORSE.
DID ANYONE CALL 911...?
I THINK MAYBE THEY'RE SHOOTING A MOVIE...
MUCH, MUCH WORSE.

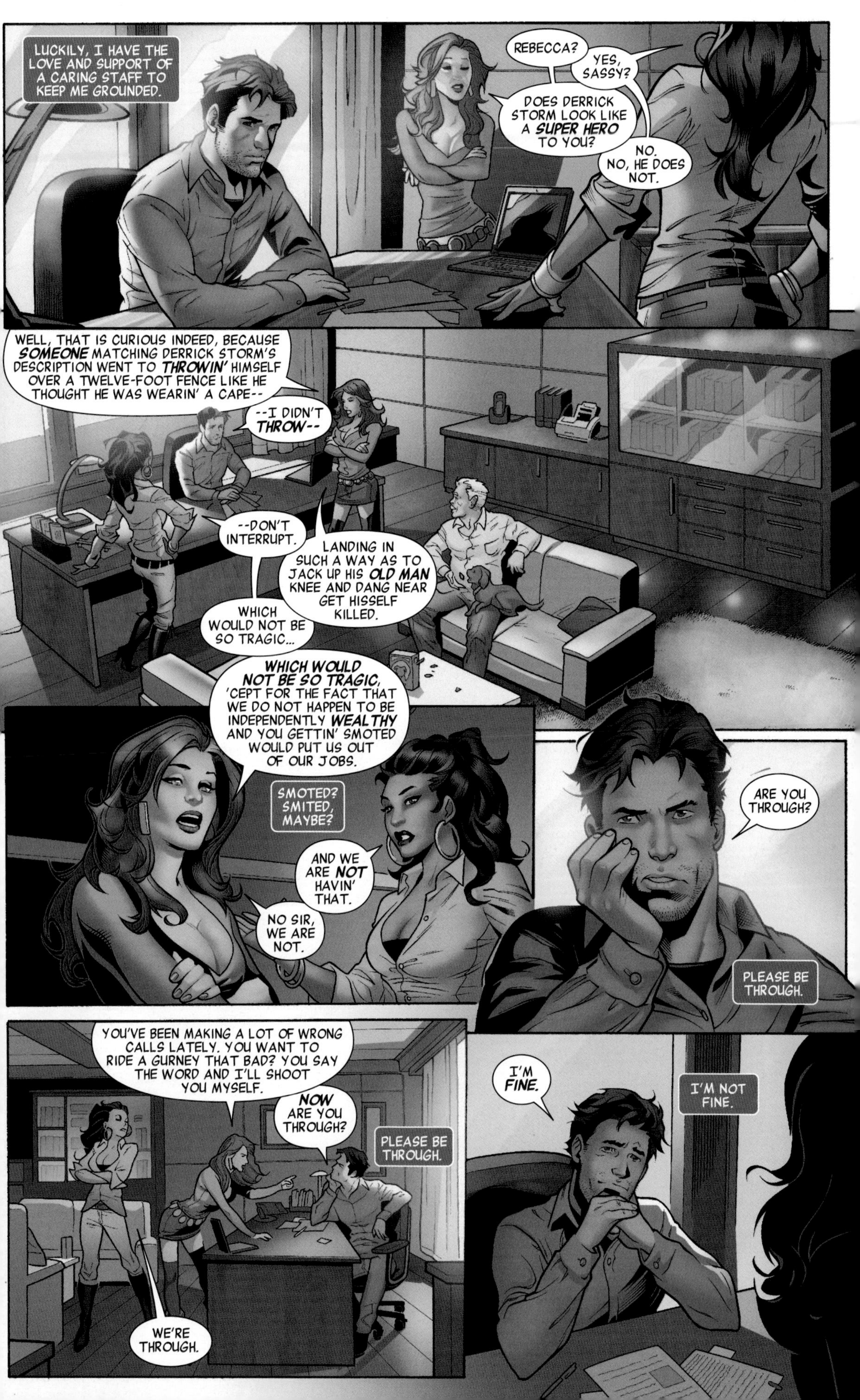

LUCKILY, I HAVE THE LOVE AND SUPPORT OF A CARING STAFF TO KEEP ME GROUNDED.
REBECCA?
YES, SASSY?
DOES DERRICK STORM LOOK LIKE A SUPER HERO TO YOU?
NO. NO, HE DOES NOT.
WELL, THAT IS CURIOUS INDEED, BECAUSE SOMEONE MATCHING DERRICK STORM'S DESCRIPTION WENT TO THROWIN' HIMSELF OVER A TWELVE-FOOT FENCE LIKE HE THOUGHT HE WAS WEARIN' A CAPE--
--I DIDN'T THROW--
--DON'T INTERRUPT.
LANDING IN SUCH A WAY AS TO JACK UP HIS OLD MAN KNEE AND DANG NEAR GET HISSELF KILLED.
WHICH WOULD NOT BE SO TRAGIC...
WHICH WOULD NOT BE SO TRAGIC, 'CEPT FOR THE FACT THAT WE DO NOT HAPPEN TO BE INDEPENDENTLY WEALTHY AND YOU GETTIN' SMOTED WOULD PUT US OUT OF OUR JOBS.
SMOTED? SMITED, MAYBE?
AND WE ARE NOT HAVIN' THAT.
NO SIR, WE ARE NOT.
ARE YOU THROUGH?
PLEASE BE THROUGH.
YOU'VE BEEN MAKING A LOT OF WRONG CALLS LATELY. YOU WANT TO RIDE A GURNEY THAT BAD? YOU SAY THE WORD AND I'LL SHOOT YOU MYSELF.
NOW ARE YOU THROUGH?
PLEASE BE THROUGH.
WE'RE THROUGH.
I'M FINE.
I'M NOT FINE.

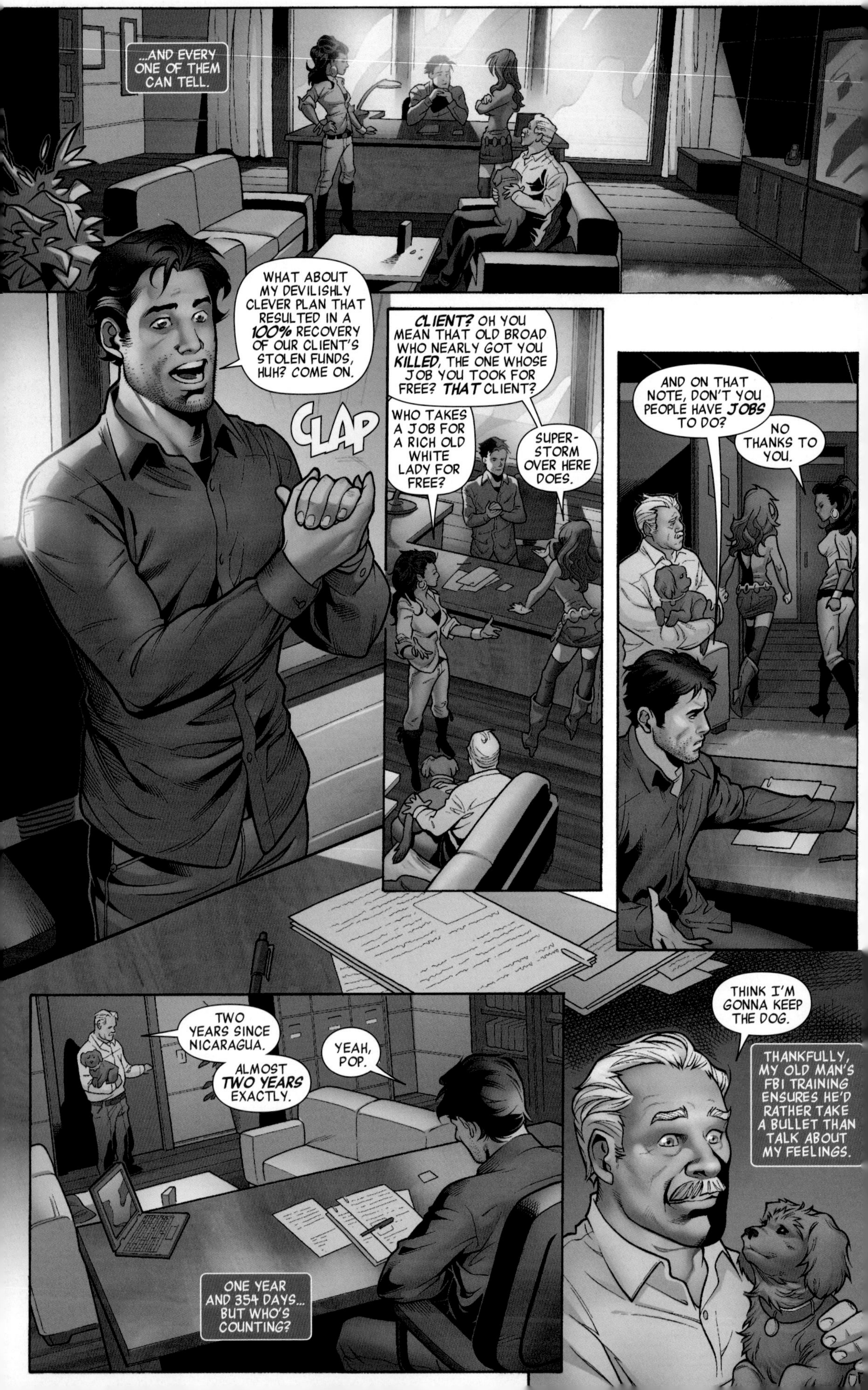
...AND EVERY ONE OF THEM CAN TELL.
WHAT ABOUT MY DEVILISHLY CLEVER PLAN THAT RESULTED IN A 100% RECOVERY OF OUR CLIENT'S STOLEN FUNDS, HUH? COME ON.
CLAP
CLIENT? OH YOU MEAN THAT OLD BROAD WHO NEARLY GOT YOU KILLED, THE ONE WHOSE JOB YOU TOOK FOR FREE? THAT CLIENT?
WHO TAKES A JOB FOR A RICH OLD WHITE LADY FOR FREE?
SUPER-STORM OVER HERE DOES.
AND ON THAT NOTE, DON'T YOU PEOPLE HAVE JOBS TO DO?
NO THANKS TO YOU.
TWO YEARS SINCE NICARAGUA.
ALMOST TWO YEARS EXACTLY.
YEAH, POP.
ONE YEAR AND 354 DAYS... BUT WHO'S COUNTING?
THINK I'M GONNA KEEP THE DOG.
THANKFULLY, MY OLD MAN'S FBI TRAINING ENSURES HE'D RATHER TAKE A BULLET THAN TALK ABOUT MY FEELINGS.

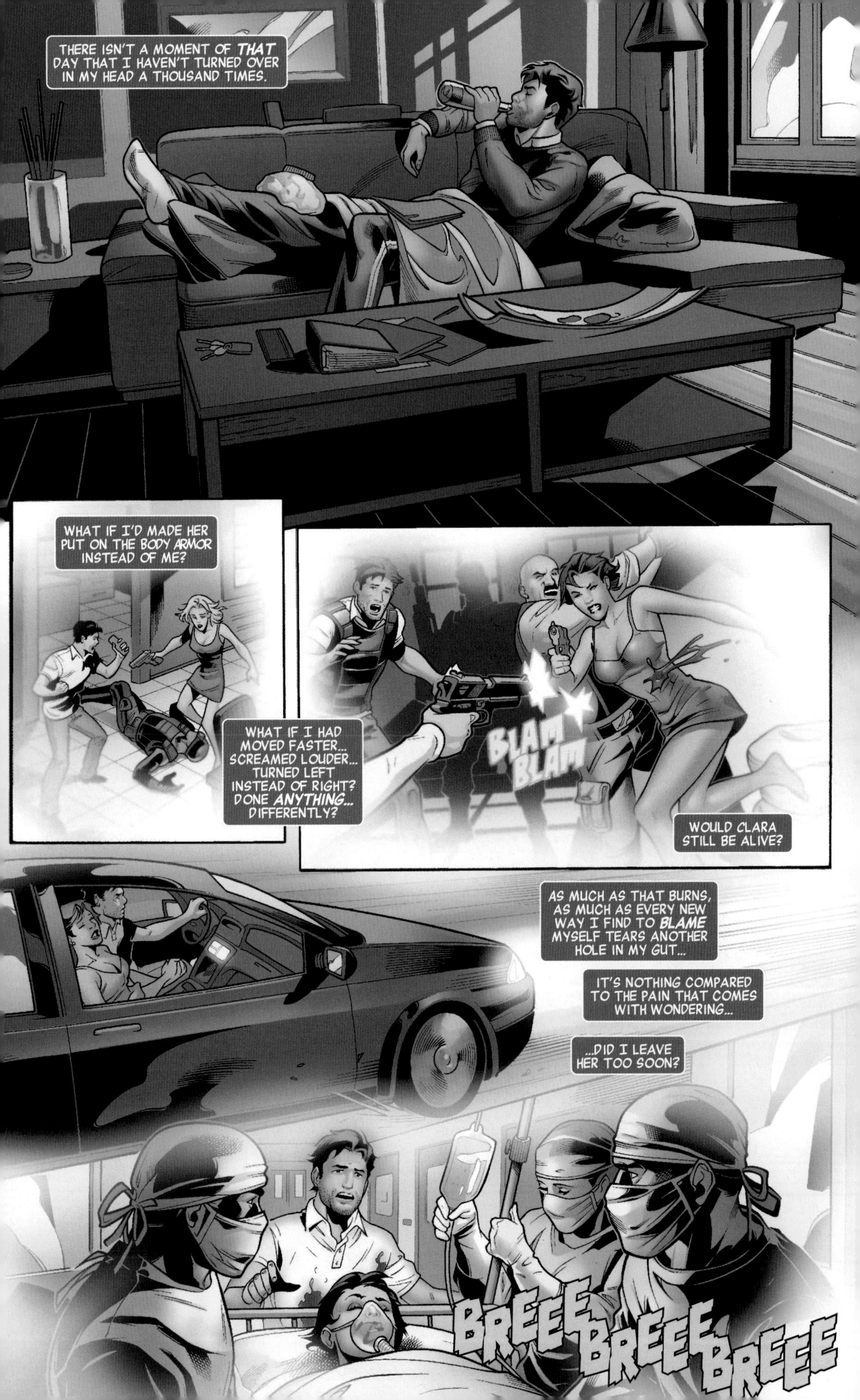
THERE ISN'T A MOMENT OF THAT DAY THAT I HAVEN'T TURNED OVER IN MY HEAD A THOUSAND TIMES.
WHAT IF I'D MADE HER PUT ON THE BODY ARMOR INSTEAD OF ME?
WHAT IF I HAD MOVED FASTER... SCREAMED LOUDER... TURNED LEFT INSTEAD OF RIGHT? DONE ANYTHING... DIFFERENTLY?
BLAM BLAM
WOULD CLARA STILL BE ALIVE?
AS MUCH AS THAT BURNS, AS MUCH AS EVERY NEW WAY I FIND TO BLAME MYSELF TEARS ANOTHER HOLE IN MY GUT...
IT'S NOTHING COMPARED TO THE PAIN THAT COMES WITH WONDERING...
...DID I LEAVE HER TOO SOON?
BREEE BREEE BREEE

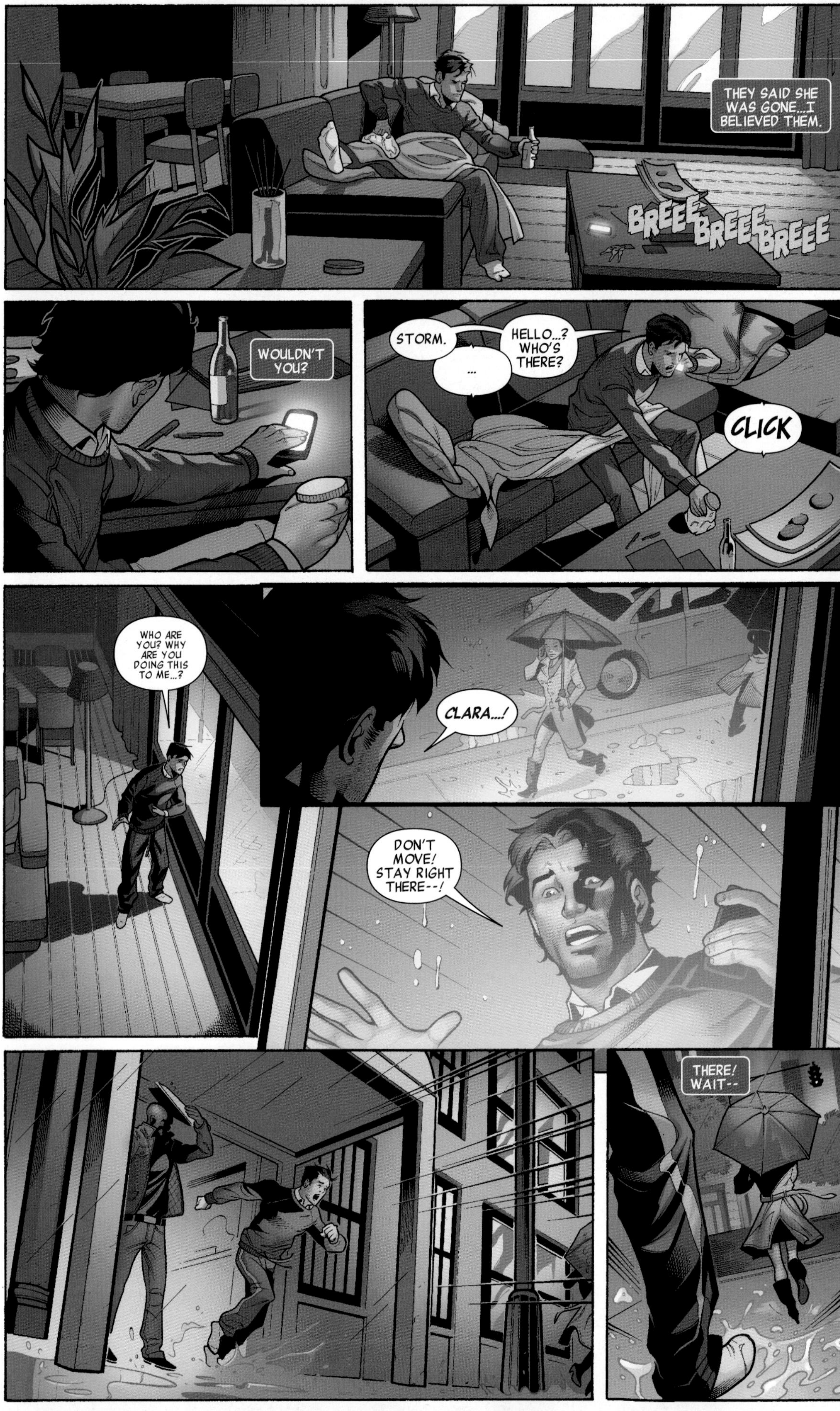
THEY SAID SHE WAS GONE...I BELIEVED THEM.
BREEE BREEE BREEE
WOULDN'T YOU?
HELLO...? WHO'S THERE?
STORM.
...
CLICK
WHO ARE YOU? WHY ARE YOU DOING THIS TO ME...?
CLARA...!
DON'T MOVE! STAY RIGHT THERE--!
THERE! WAIT--

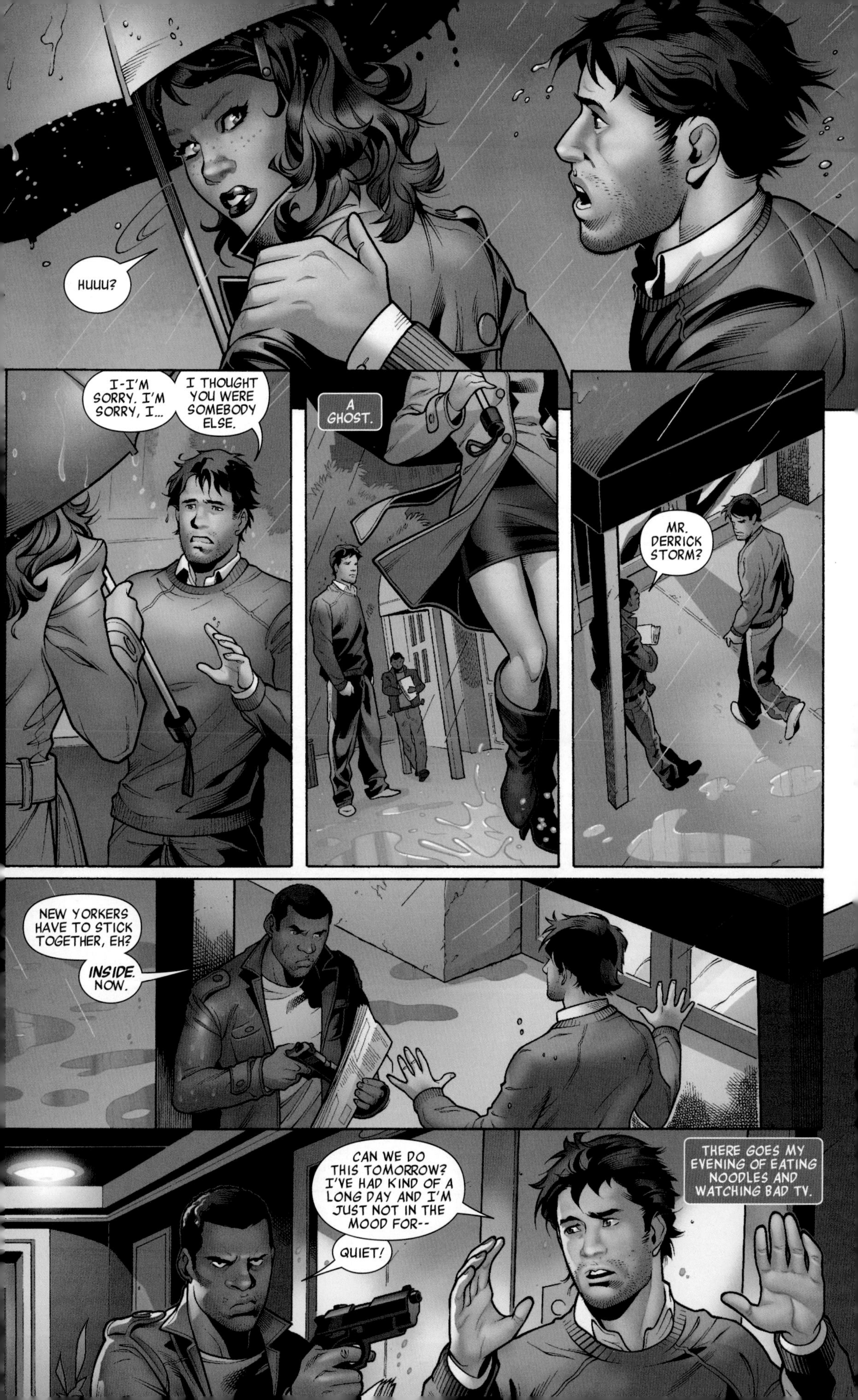
HUUU?
I-I'M SORRY. I'M SORRY, I...
I THOUGHT YOU WERE SOMEBODY ELSE.
A GHOST.
MR. DERRICK STORM?
NEW YORKERS HAVE TO STICK TOGETHER, EH?
INSIDE. NOW.
THERE GOES MY EVENING OF EATING NOODLES AND WATCHING BAD TV.
CAN WE DO THIS TOMORROW? I'VE HAD KIND OF A LONG DAY AND I'M JUST NOT IN THE MOOD FOR--
QUIET!

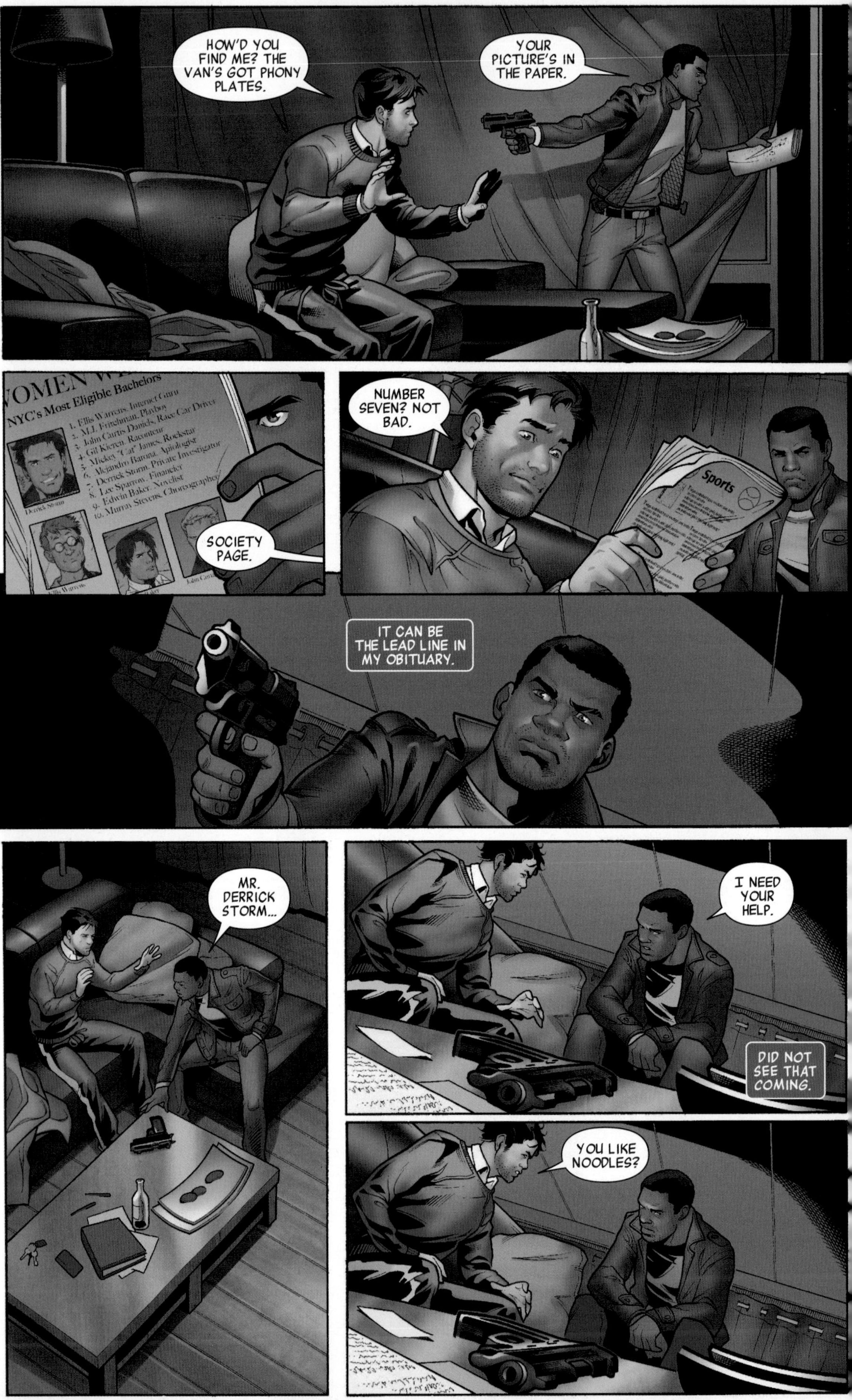
HOW'D YOU FIND ME? THE VAN'S GOT PHONY PLATES.
YOUR PICTURE'S IN THE PAPER.
NYC's Most Eligible Bachelors
1. Ellis Warrens, Internet Guru
2. M.J. Fritchman, Playboy
3. John Curtis Daniels, Race Car Driver
4. Gil Kieren, Raconteur
5. Mickey "Cat" James, Rockstar
6. Alejandro Barona, Apiologist
7. Derrick Storm, Private Investigator
8. Lee Sparrow, Financier
9. Edwin Baker, Novelist
10. Murray Stevens, Choreographer
Derrick Storm
SOCIETY PAGE.
NUMBER SEVEN? NOT BAD.
Sports
IT CAN BE THE LEAD LINE IN MY OBITUARY.
MR. DERRICK STORM...
I NEED YOUR HELP.
DID NOT SEE THAT COMING.
YOU LIKE NOODLES?

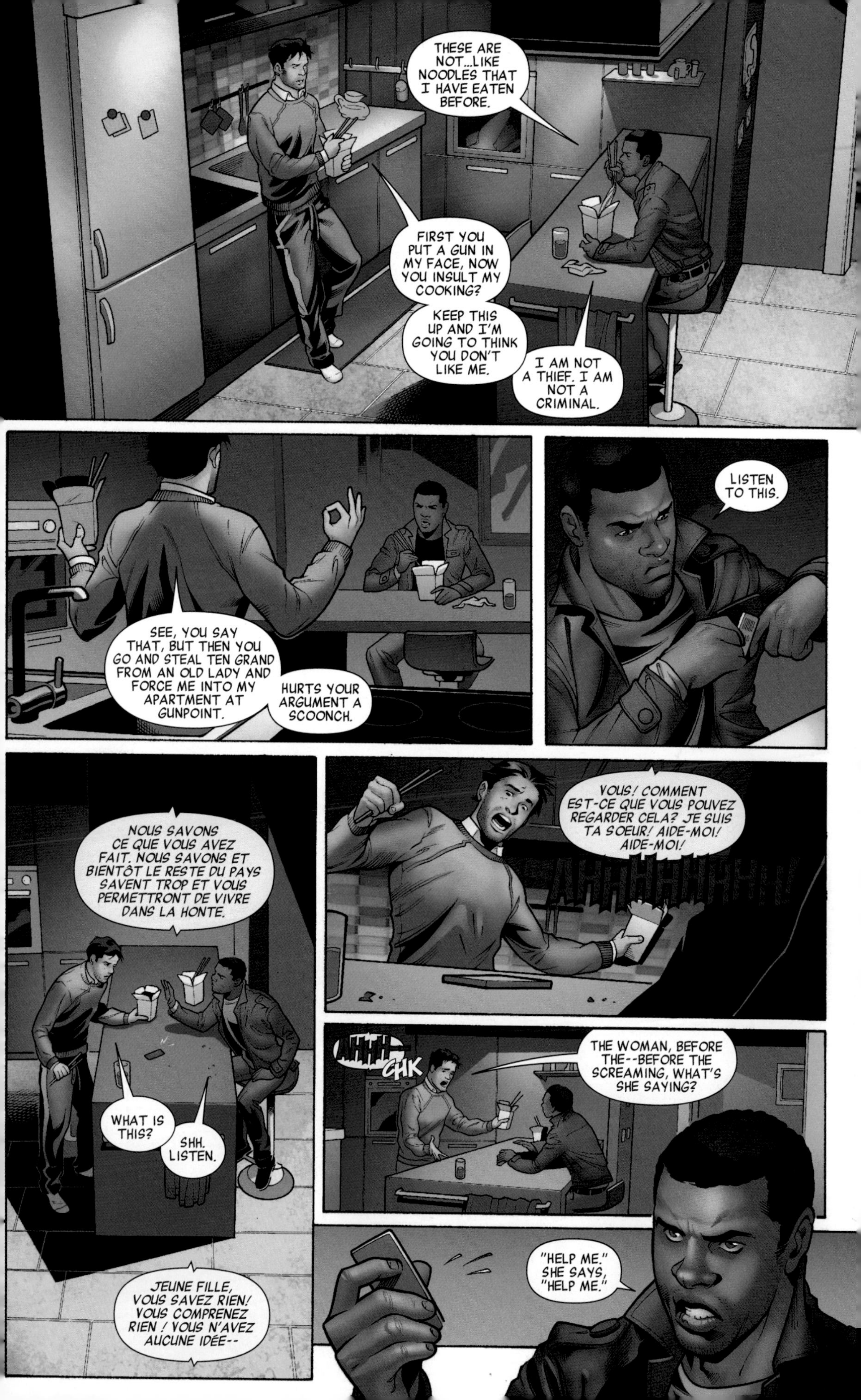
THESE ARE NOT...LIKE NOODLES THAT I HAVE EATEN BEFORE.
FIRST YOU PUT A GUN IN MY FACE, NOW YOU INSULT MY COOKING?
KEEP THIS UP AND I'M GOING TO THINK YOU DON'T LIKE ME.
I AM NOT A THIEF. I AM NOT A CRIMINAL.
SEE, YOU SAY THAT, BUT THEN YOU GO AND STEAL TEN GRAND FROM AN OLD LADY AND FORCE ME INTO MY APARTMENT AT GUNPOINT.
HURTS YOUR ARGUMENT A SCOONCH.
LISTEN TO THIS.
NOUS SAVONS CE QUE VOUS AVEZ FAIT. NOUS SAVONS ET BIENTÔT LE RESTE DU PAYS SAVENT TROP ET VOUS PERMETTRONT DE VIVRE DANS LA HONTE.
WHAT IS THIS?
SHH. LISTEN.
JEUNE FILLE, VOUS SAVEZ RIEN! VOUS COMPRENEZ RIEN ! VOUS N'AVEZ AUCUNE IDÉE--
VOUS! COMMENT EST-CE QUE VOUS POUVEZ REGARDER CELA? JE SUIS TA SOEUR! AIDE-MOI! AIDE-MOI!
AHHH-- CHK
THE WOMAN, BEFORE THE--BEFORE THE SCREAMING, WHAT'S SHE SAYING?
"HELP ME." SHE SAYS, "HELP ME."

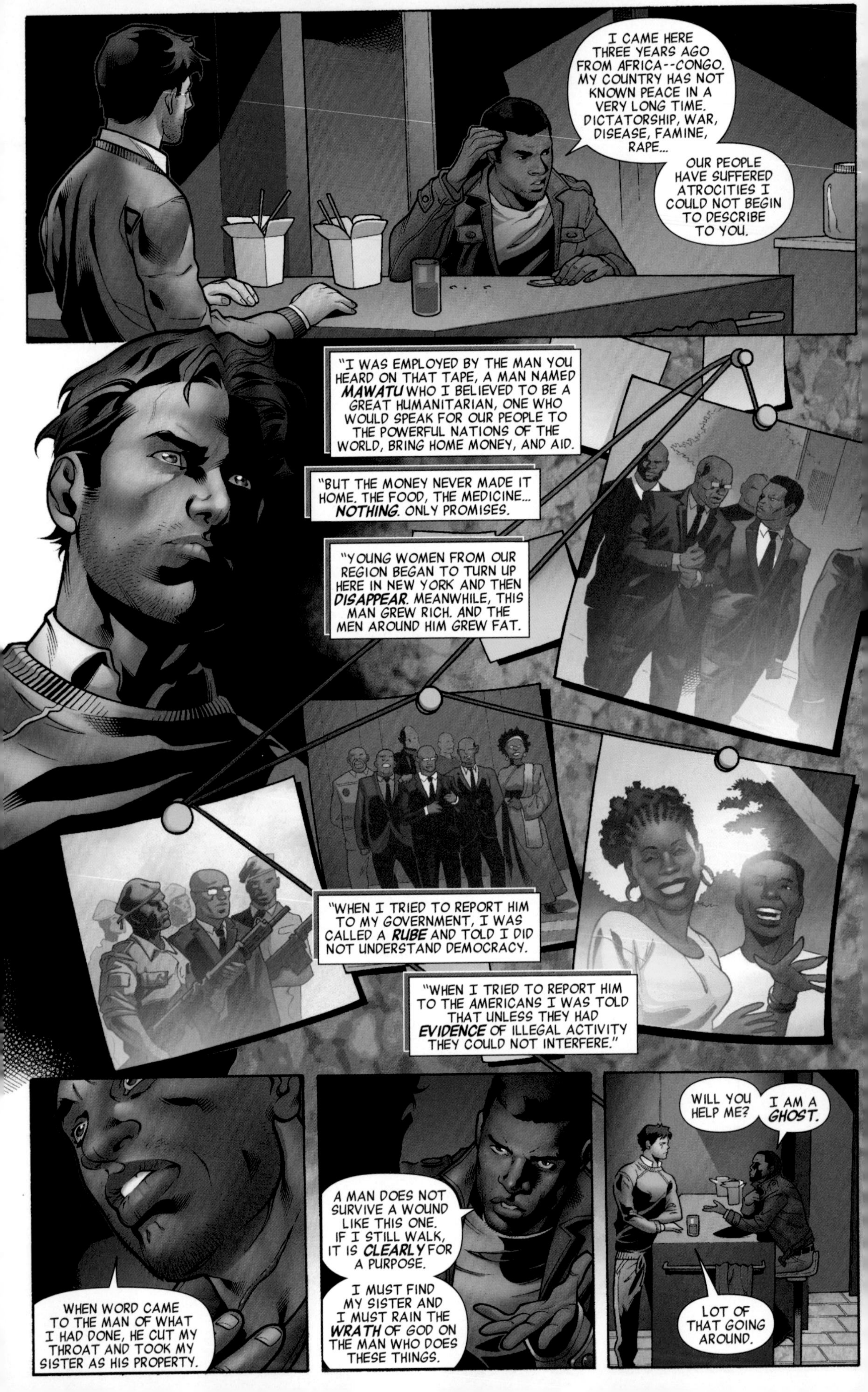
I CAME HERE THREE YEARS AGO FROM AFRICA--CONGO. MY COUNTRY HAS NOT KNOWN PEACE IN A VERY LONG TIME. DICTATORSHIP, WAR, DISEASE, FAMINE, RAPE...
OUR PEOPLE HAVE SUFFERED ATROCITIES I COULD NOT BEGIN TO DESCRIBE TO YOU.
"I WAS EMPLOYED BY THE MAN YOU HEARD ON THAT TAPE, A MAN NAMED MAWATU WHO I BELIEVED TO BE A GREAT HUMANITARIAN, ONE WHO WOULD SPEAK FOR OUR PEOPLE TO THE POWERFUL NATIONS OF THE WORLD, BRING HOME MONEY, AND AID.
"BUT THE MONEY NEVER MADE IT HOME. THE FOOD, THE MEDICINE... NOTHING. ONLY PROMISES.
"YOUNG WOMEN FROM OUR REGION BEGAN TO TURN UP HERE IN NEW YORK AND THEN DISAPPEAR. MEANWHILE, THIS MAN GREW RICH. AND THE MEN AROUND HIM GREW FAT.
"WHEN I TRIED TO REPORT HIM TO MY GOVERNMENT, I WAS CALLED A RUBE AND TOLD I DID NOT UNDERSTAND DEMOCRACY.
"WHEN I TRIED TO REPORT HIM TO THE AMERICANS I WAS TOLD THAT UNLESS THEY HAD EVIDENCE OF ILLEGAL ACTIVITY THEY COULD NOT INTERFERE."
WHEN WORD CAME TO THE MAN OF WHAT I HAD DONE, HE CUT MY THROAT AND TOOK MY SISTER AS HIS PROPERTY.
A MAN DOES NOT SURVIVE A WOUND LIKE THIS ONE. IF I STILL WALK, IT IS CLEARLY FOR A PURPOSE.
I MUST FIND MY SISTER AND I MUST RAIN THE WRATH OF GOD ON THE MAN WHO DOES THESE THINGS.
WILL YOU HELP ME?
I AM A GHOST.
LOT OF THAT GOING AROUND.

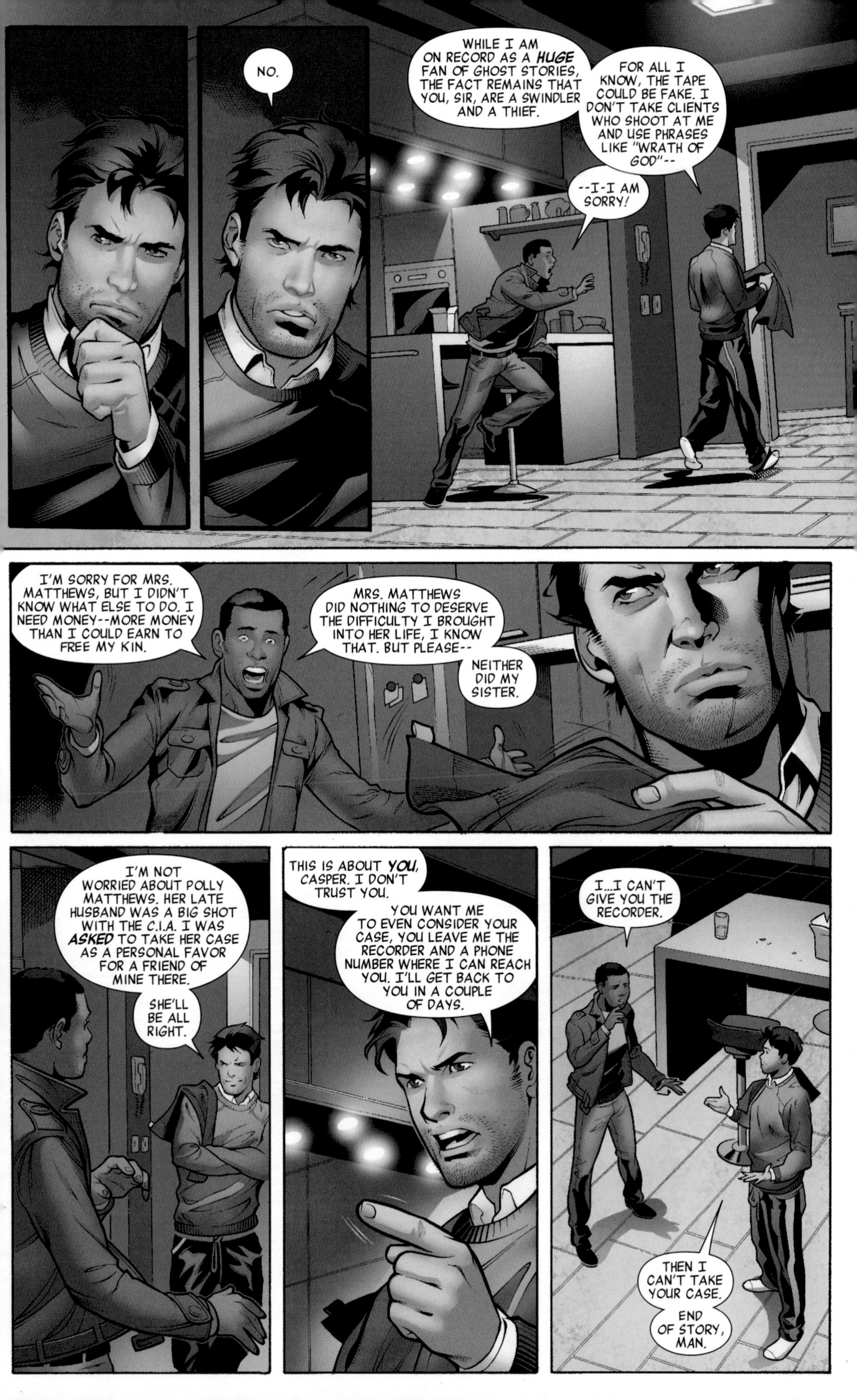
NO.
WHILE I AM ON RECORD AS A HUGE FAN OF GHOST STORIES, THE FACT REMAINS THAT YOU, SIR, ARE A SWINDLER AND A THIEF.
FOR ALL I KNOW, THE TAPE COULD BE FAKE. I DON'T TAKE CLIENTS WHO SHOOT AT ME AND USE PHRASES LIKE "WRATH OF GOD"--
--I-I AM SORRY!
I'M SORRY FOR MRS. MATTHEWS, BUT I DIDN'T KNOW WHAT ELSE TO DO. I NEED MONEY--MORE MONEY THAN I COULD EARN TO FREE MY KIN.
MRS. MATTHEWS DID NOTHING TO DESERVE THE DIFFICULTY I BROUGHT INTO HER LIFE, I KNOW THAT. BUT PLEASE--
NEITHER DID MY SISTER.
I'M NOT WORRIED ABOUT POLLY MATTHEWS. HER LATE HUSBAND WAS A BIG SHOT WITH THE C.I.A. I WAS ASKED TO TAKE HER CASE AS A PERSONAL FAVOR FOR A FRIEND OF MINE THERE.
SHE'LL BE ALL RIGHT.
THIS IS ABOUT YOU, CASPER. I DON'T TRUST YOU.
YOU WANT ME TO EVEN CONSIDER YOUR CASE, YOU LEAVE ME THE RECORDER AND A PHONE NUMBER WHERE I CAN REACH YOU. I'LL GET BACK TO YOU IN A COUPLE OF DAYS.
I...I CAN'T GIVE YOU THE RECORDER.
THEN I CAN'T TAKE YOUR CASE.
END OF STORY, MAN.

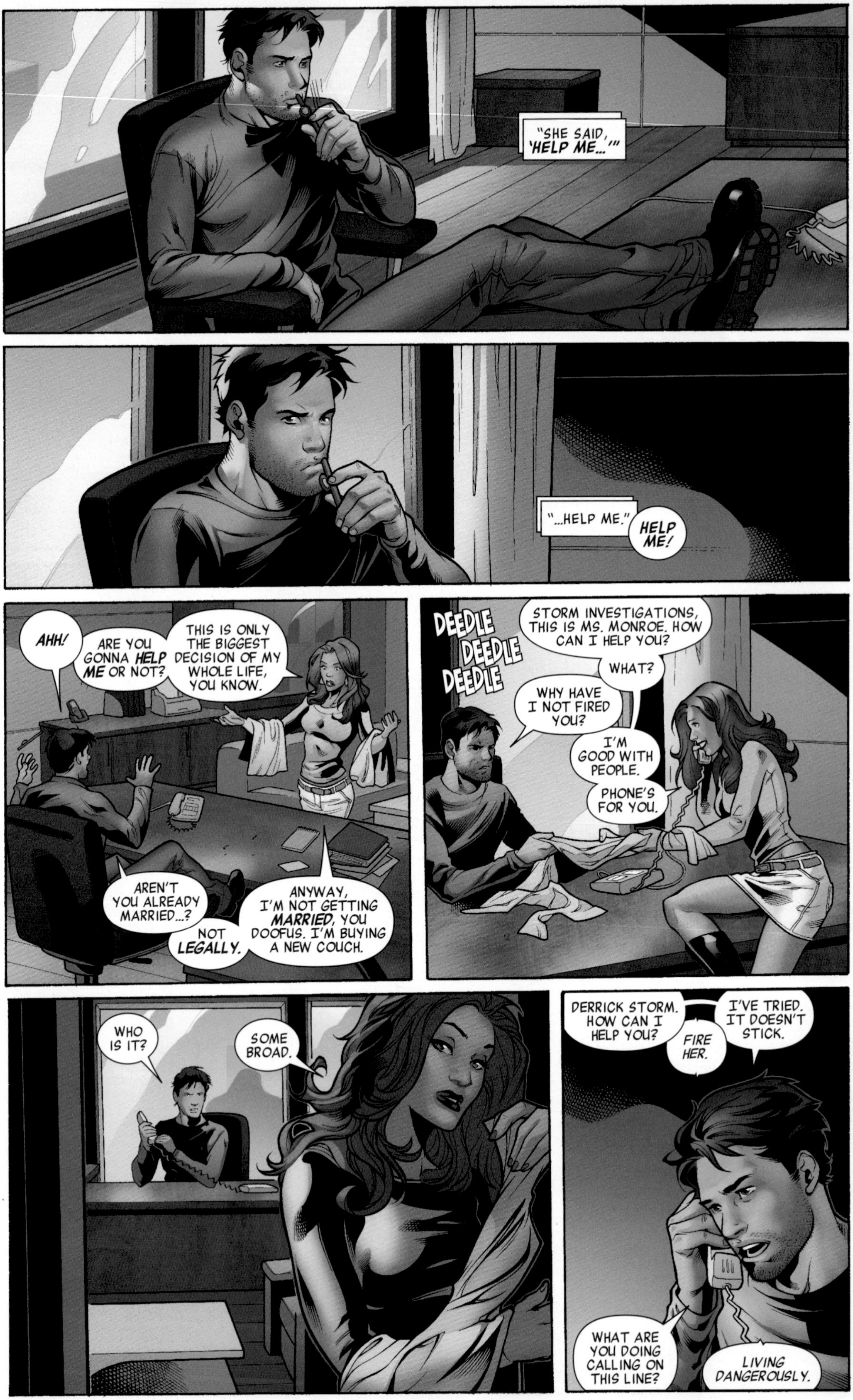

"SHE SAID, 'HELP ME...'"
"...HELP ME."
HELP ME!
AHH!
ARE YOU GONNA HELP ME OR NOT?
THIS IS ONLY THE BIGGEST DECISION OF MY WHOLE LIFE, YOU KNOW.
AREN'T YOU ALREADY MARRIED...?
NOT LEGALLY.
ANYWAY, I'M NOT GETTING MARRIED, YOU DOOFUS. I'M BUYING A NEW COUCH.
DEEDLE DEEDLE DEEDLE
STORM INVESTIGATIONS, THIS IS MS. MONROE. HOW CAN I HELP YOU?
WHAT?
WHY HAVE I NOT FIRED YOU?
I'M GOOD WITH PEOPLE.
PHONE'S FOR YOU.
WHO IS IT?
SOME BROAD.
DERRICK STORM. HOW CAN I HELP YOU?
FIRE HER.
I'VE TRIED. IT DOESN'T STICK.
WHAT ARE YOU DOING CALLING ON THIS LINE?
LIVING DANGEROUSLY.

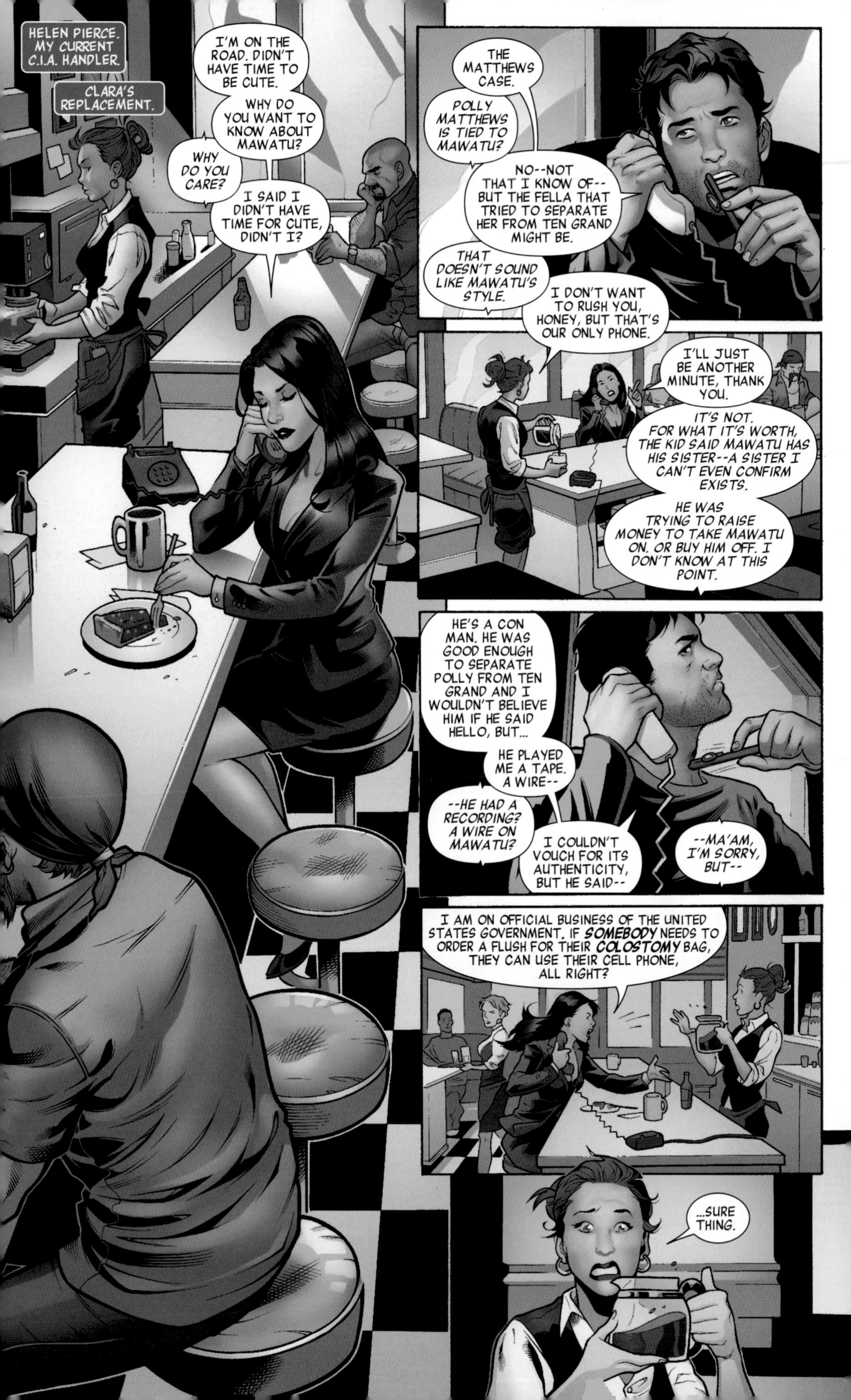

HELEN PIERCE. MY CURRENT C.I.A. HANDLER.
CLARA'S REPLACEMENT.
I'M ON THE ROAD. DIDN'T HAVE TIME TO BE CUTE.
WHY DO YOU WANT TO KNOW ABOUT MAWATU?
WHY DO YOU CARE?
I SAID I DIDN'T HAVE TIME FOR CUTE, DIDN'T I?
THE MATTHEWS CASE.
POLLY MATTHEWS IS TIED TO MAWATU?
NO--NOT THAT I KNOW OF--BUT THE FELLA THAT TRIED TO SEPARATE HER FROM TEN GRAND MIGHT BE.
THAT DOESN'T SOUND LIKE MAWATU'S STYLE.
I DON'T WANT TO RUSH YOU, HONEY, BUT THAT'S OUR ONLY PHONE.
I'LL JUST BE ANOTHER MINUTE, THANK YOU.
IT'S NOT. FOR WHAT IT'S WORTH, THE KID SAID MAWATU HAS HIS SISTER--A SISTER I CAN'T EVEN CONFIRM EXISTS.
HE WAS TRYING TO RAISE MONEY TO TAKE MAWATU ON. OR BUY HIM OFF. I DON'T KNOW AT THIS POINT.
HE'S A CON MAN. HE WAS GOOD ENOUGH TO SEPARATE POLLY FROM TEN GRAND AND I WOULDN'T BELIEVE HIM IF HE SAID HELLO, BUT...
HE PLAYED ME A TAPE. A WIRE--
--HE HAD A RECORDING? A WIRE ON MAWATU?
I COULDN'T VOUCH FOR ITS AUTHENTICITY, BUT HE SAID--
--MA'AM, I'M SORRY, BUT--
I AM ON OFFICIAL BUSINESS OF THE UNITED STATES GOVERNMENT. IF SOMEBODY NEEDS TO ORDER A FLUSH FOR THEIR COLOSTOMY BAG, THEY CAN USE THEIR CELL PHONE, ALL RIGHT?
...SURE THING.

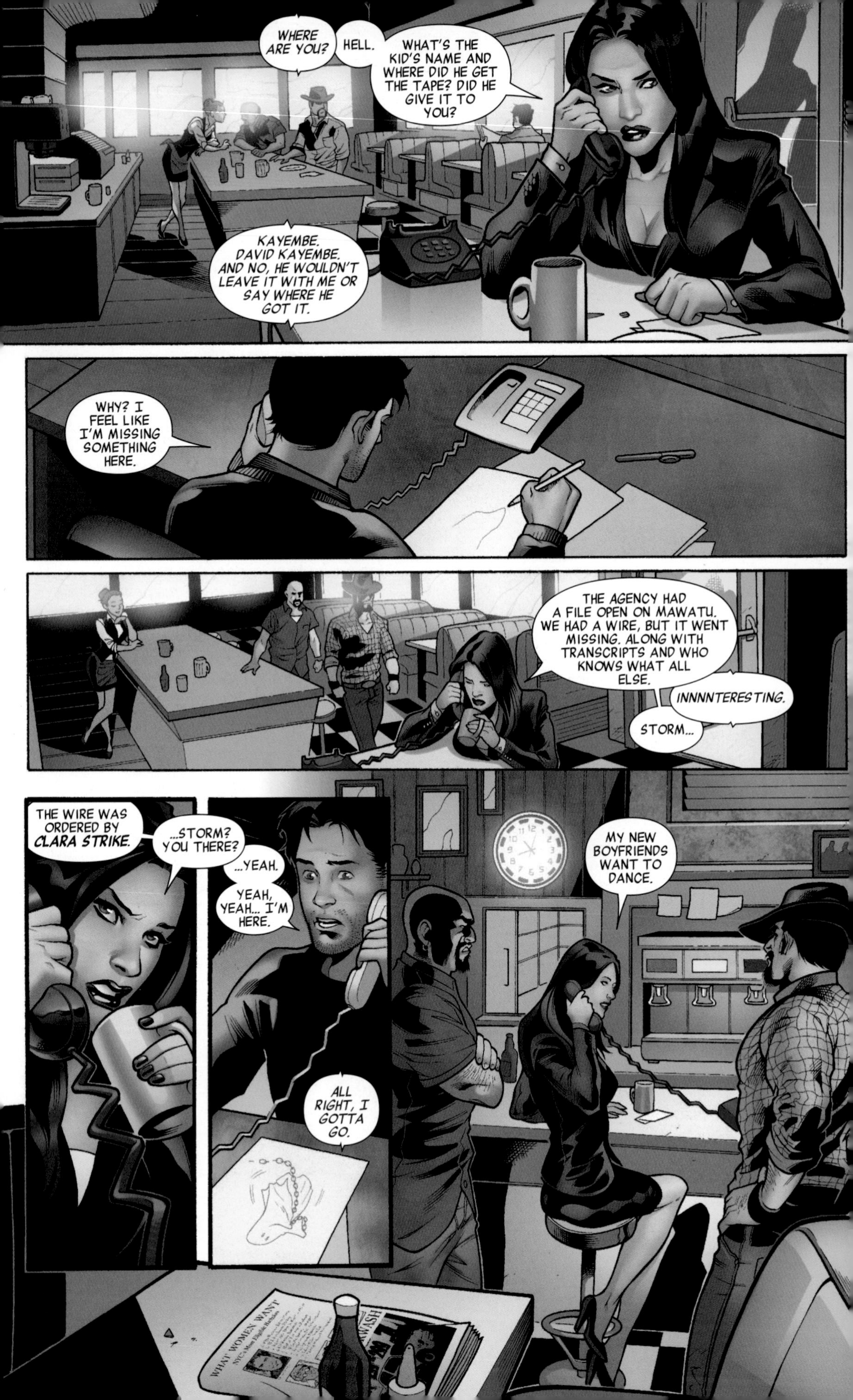
WHERE ARE YOU?
HELL.
WHAT'S THE KID'S NAME AND WHERE DID HE GET THE TAPE? DID HE GIVE IT TO YOU?
KAYEMBE. DAVID KAYEMBE. AND NO, HE WOULDN'T LEAVE IT WITH ME OR SAY WHERE HE GOT IT.
WHY? I FEEL LIKE I'M MISSING SOMETHING HERE.
THE AGENCY HAD A FILE OPEN ON MAWATU. WE HAD A WIRE, BUT IT WENT MISSING. ALONG WITH TRANSCRIPTS AND WHO KNOWS WHAT ALL ELSE.
INNNNTERESTING.
STORM...
THE WIRE WAS ORDERED BY CLARA STRIKE.
...STORM? YOU THERE?
...YEAH.
YEAH, YEAH... I'M HERE.
ALL RIGHT, I GOTTA GO.
MY NEW BOYFRIENDS WANT TO DANCE.
WHAT WOMEN WANT

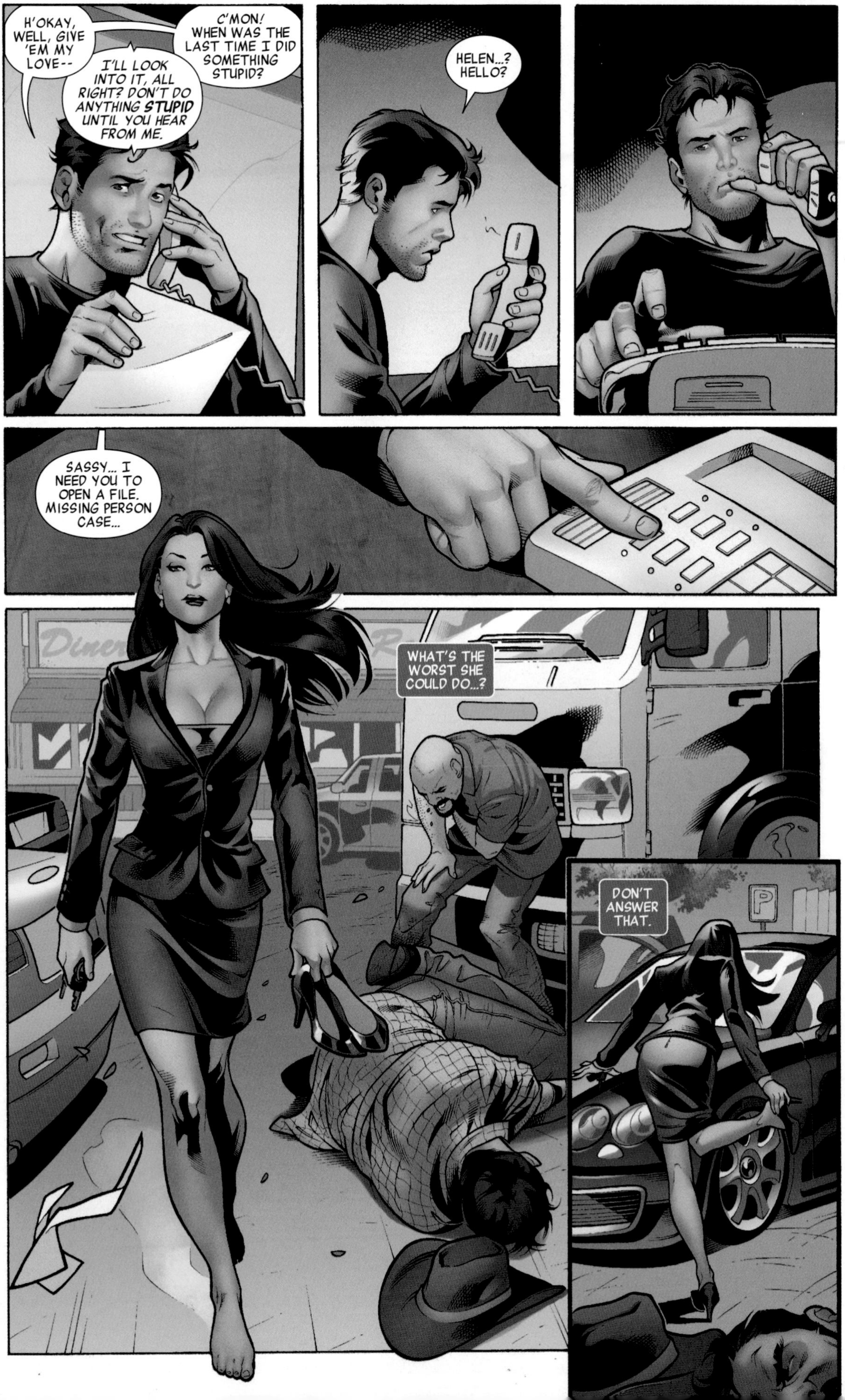
H'OKAY, WELL, GIVE 'EM MY LOVE--
I'LL LOOK INTO IT, ALL RIGHT? DON'T DO ANYTHING STUPID UNTIL YOU HEAR FROM ME.
C'MON! WHEN WAS THE LAST TIME I DID SOMETHING STUPID?
HELEN...? HELLO?
SASSY... I NEED YOU TO OPEN A FILE. MISSING PERSON CASE...
Diner
WHAT'S THE WORST SHE COULD DO...?
DON'T ANSWER THAT.
P

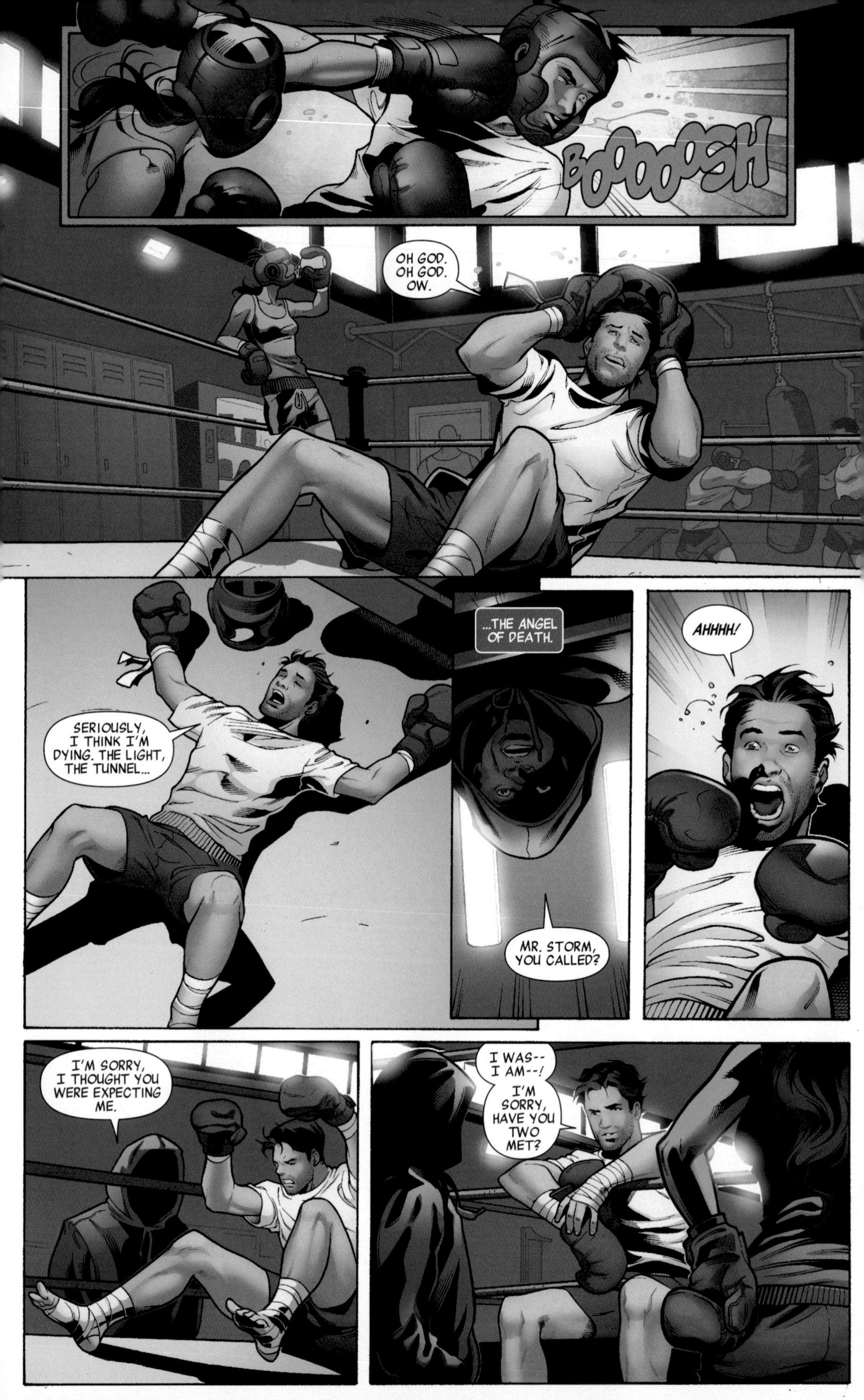
BOOOOOSH
OH GOD. OH GOD. OW.
SERIOUSLY, I THINK I'M DYING. THE LIGHT, THE TUNNEL...
...THE ANGEL OF DEATH.
MR. STORM, YOU CALLED?
AHHHH!
I'M SORRY, I THOUGHT YOU WERE EXPECTING ME.
I WAS-- I AM--!
I'M SORRY, HAVE YOU TWO MET?

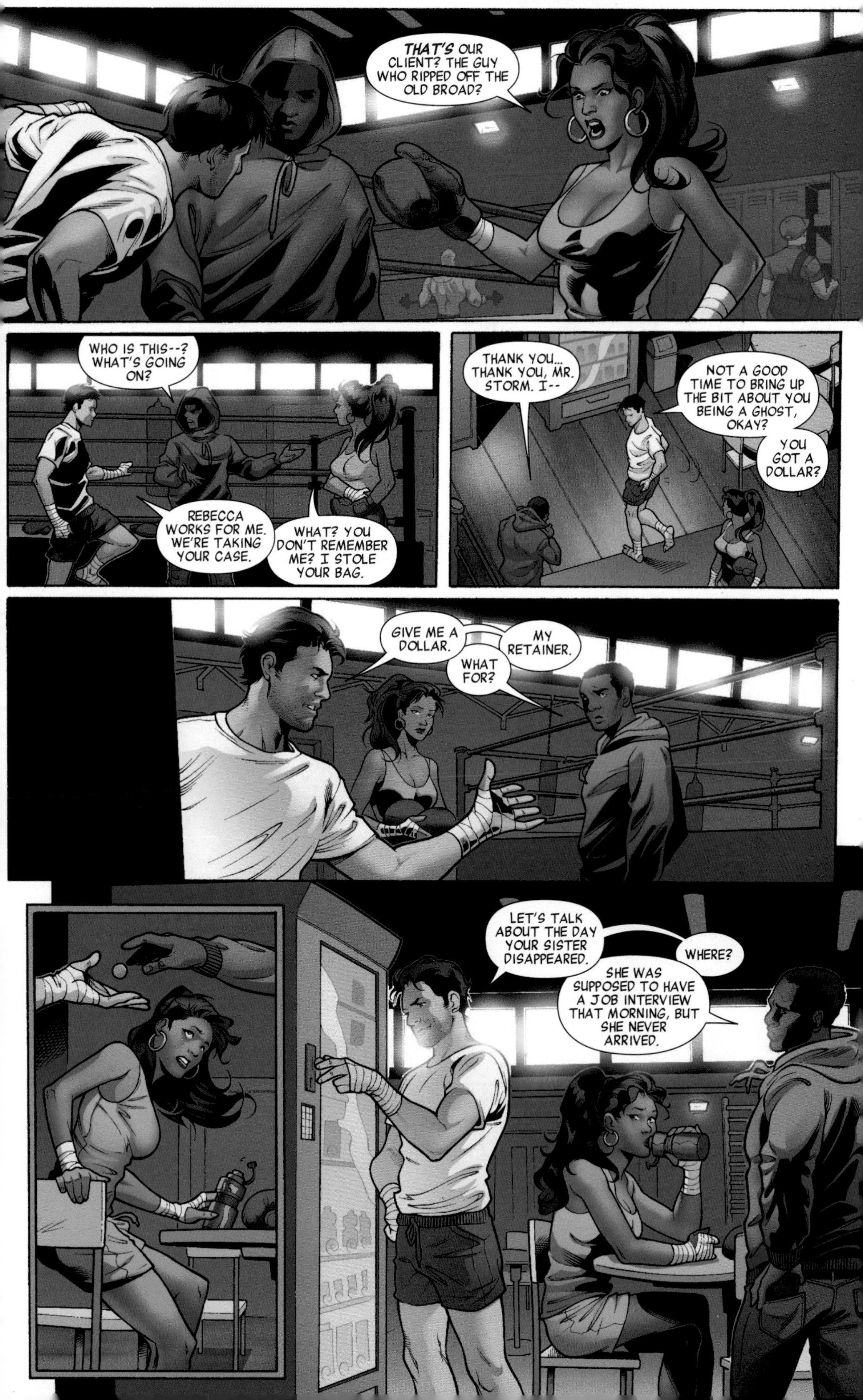
THAT'S OUR CLIENT? THE GUY WHO RIPPED OFF THE OLD BROAD?
WHO IS THIS--? WHAT'S GOING ON?
REBECCA WORKS FOR ME. WE'RE TAKING YOUR CASE.
WHAT? YOU DON'T REMEMBER ME? I STOLE YOUR BAG.
THANK YOU... THANK YOU, MR. STORM. I--
NOT A GOOD TIME TO BRING UP THE BIT ABOUT YOU BEING A GHOST, OKAY?
YOU GOT A DOLLAR?
GIVE ME A DOLLAR.
WHAT FOR?
MY RETAINER.
LET'S TALK ABOUT THE DAY YOUR SISTER DISAPPEARED.
WHERE?
SHE WAS SUPPOSED TO HAVE A JOB INTERVIEW THAT MORNING, BUT SHE NEVER ARRIVED.

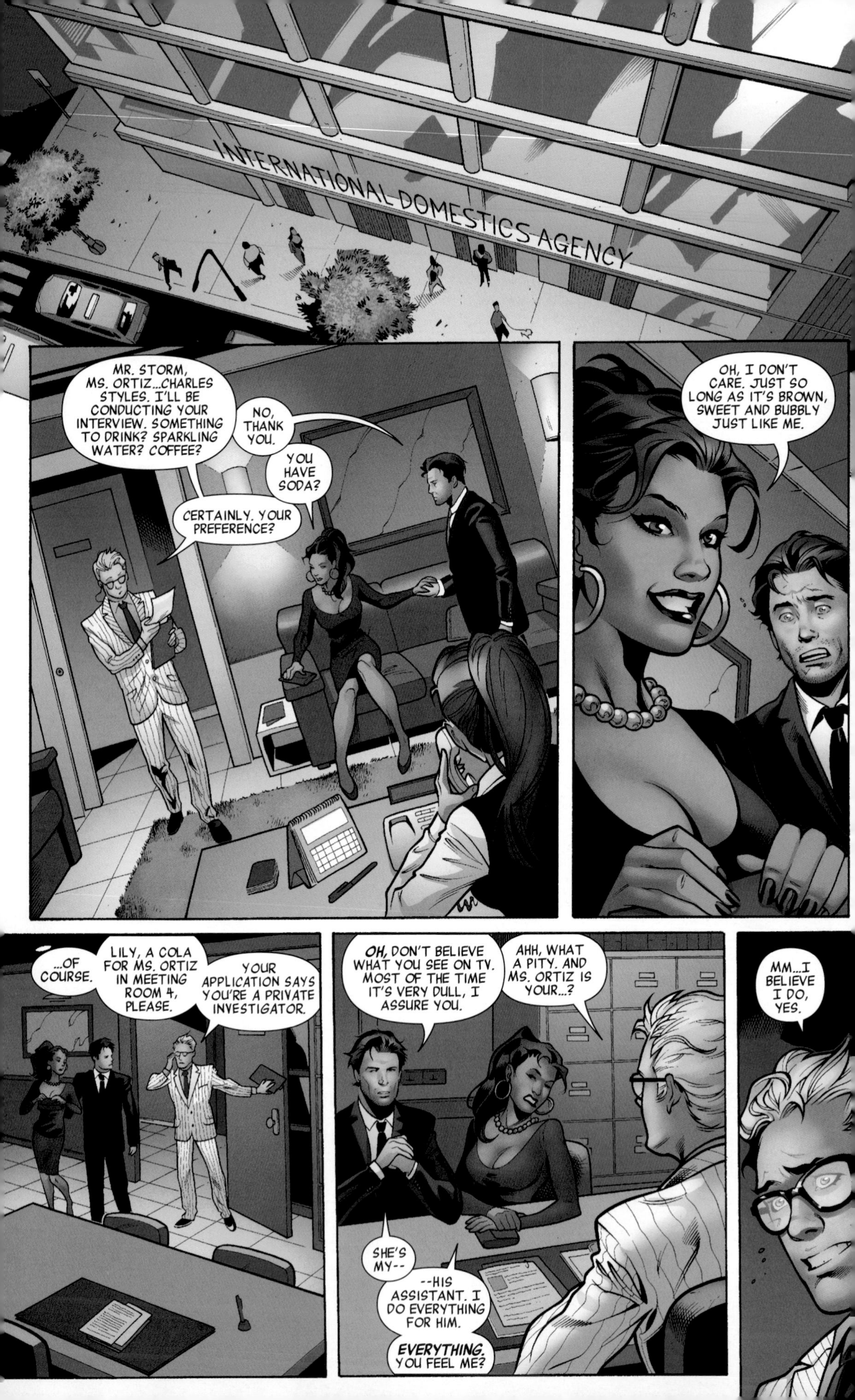
INTERNATIONAL DOMESTICS AGENCY
MR. STORM, MS. ORTIZ...CHARLES STYLES. I'LL BE CONDUCTING YOUR INTERVIEW. SOMETHING TO DRINK? SPARKLING WATER? COFFEE?
NO, THANK YOU.
YOU HAVE SODA?
CERTAINLY. YOUR PREFERENCE?
OH, I DON'T CARE. JUST SO LONG AS IT'S BROWN, SWEET AND BUBBLY JUST LIKE ME.
...OF COURSE.
LILY, A COLA FOR MS. ORTIZ IN MEETING ROOM 4, PLEASE.
YOUR APPLICATION SAYS YOU'RE A PRIVATE INVESTIGATOR.
OH, DON'T BELIEVE WHAT YOU SEE ON TV. MOST OF THE TIME IT'S VERY DULL, I ASSURE YOU.
AHH, WHAT A PITY. AND MS. ORTIZ IS YOUR...?
SHE'S MY--
--HIS ASSISTANT. I DO EVERYTHING FOR HIM.
EVERYTHING. YOU FEEL ME?
MM...I BELIEVE I DO, YES.

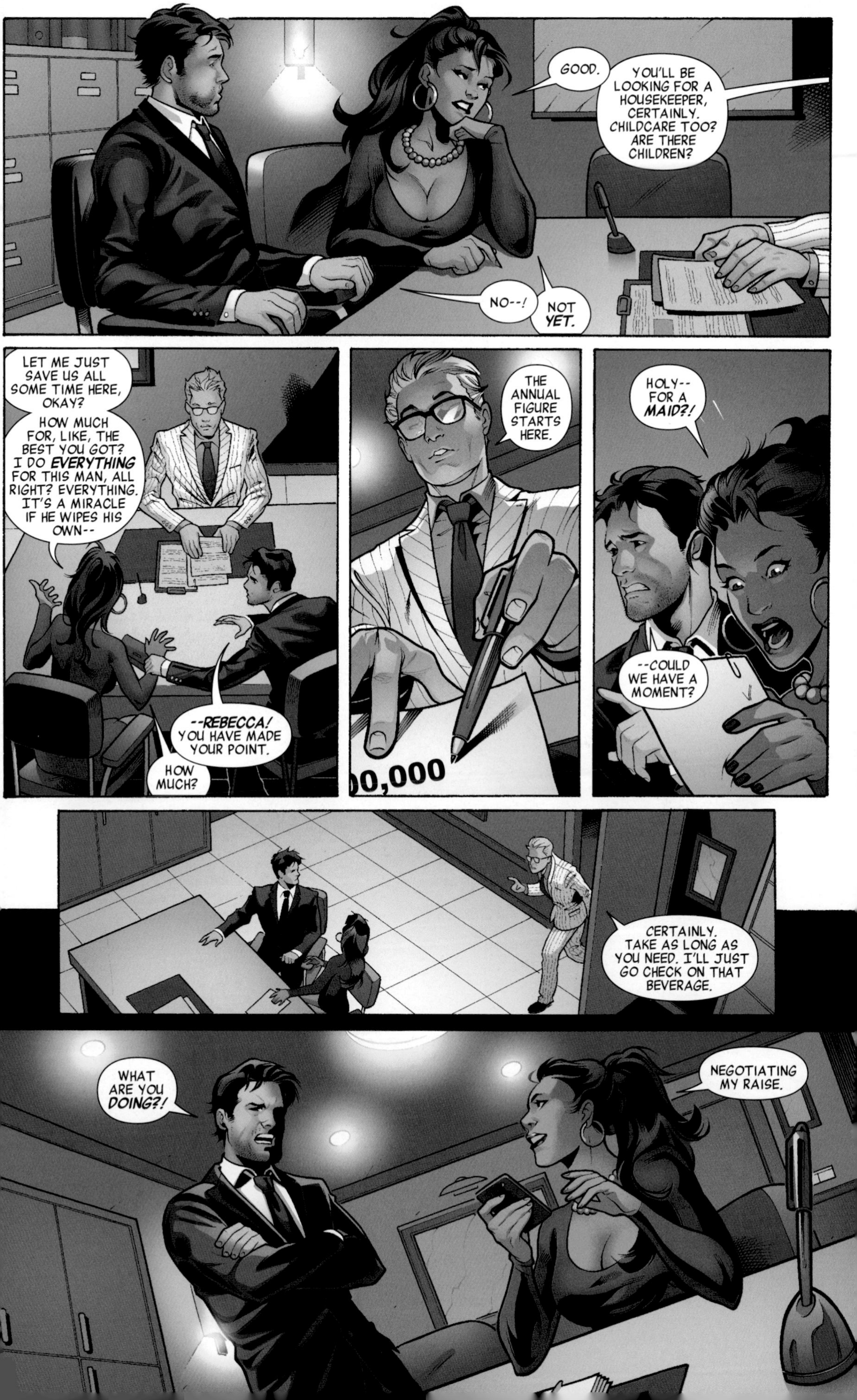
GOOD.
YOU'LL BE LOOKING FOR A HOUSEKEEPER, CERTAINLY. CHILDCARE TOO? ARE THERE CHILDREN?
NO--!
NOT YET.
LET ME JUST SAVE US ALL SOME TIME HERE, OKAY?
HOW MUCH FOR, LIKE, THE BEST YOU GOT? I DO EVERYTHING FOR THIS MAN, ALL RIGHT? EVERYTHING. IT'S A MIRACLE IF HE WIPES HIS OWN--
--REBECCA! YOU HAVE MADE YOUR POINT.
HOW MUCH?
THE ANNUAL FIGURE STARTS HERE.
00,000
HOLY-- FOR A MAID?!
--COULD WE HAVE A MOMENT?
CERTAINLY. TAKE AS LONG AS YOU NEED. I'LL JUST GO CHECK ON THAT BEVERAGE.
WHAT ARE YOU DOING?!
NEGOTIATING MY RAISE.

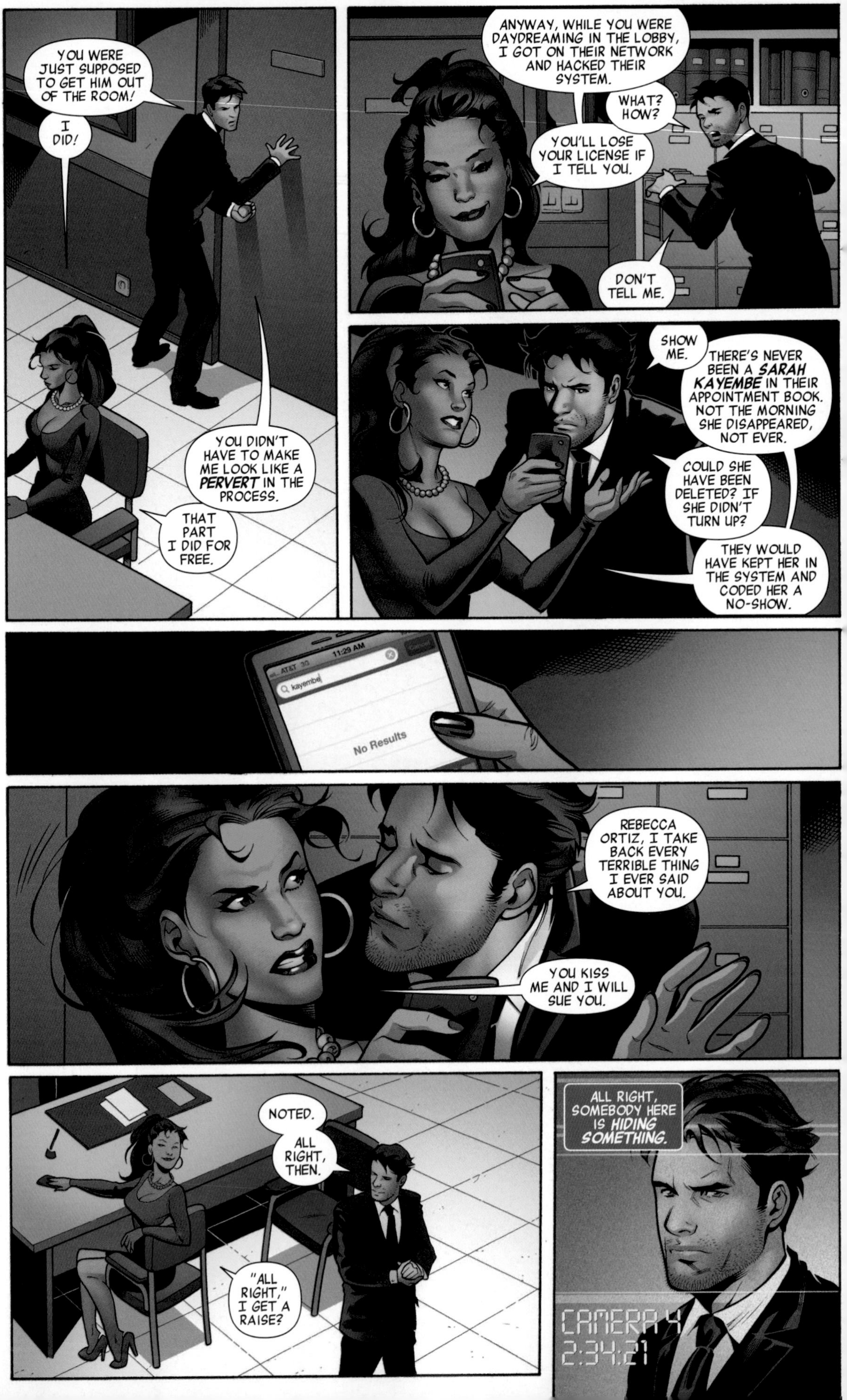
YOU WERE JUST SUPPOSED TO GET HIM OUT OF THE ROOM!
I DID!
YOU DIDN'T HAVE TO MAKE ME LOOK LIKE A PERVERT IN THE PROCESS.
THAT PART I DID FOR FREE.
ANYWAY, WHILE YOU WERE DAYDREAMING IN THE LOBBY, I GOT ON THEIR NETWORK AND HACKED THEIR SYSTEM.
WHAT? HOW?
YOU'LL LOSE YOUR LICENSE IF I TELL YOU.
DON'T TELL ME.
SHOW ME.
THERE'S NEVER BEEN A SARAH KAYEMBE IN THEIR APPOINTMENT BOOK. NOT THE MORNING SHE DISAPPEARED, NOT EVER.
COULD SHE HAVE BEEN DELETED? IF SHE DIDN'T TURN UP?
THEY WOULD HAVE KEPT HER IN THE SYSTEM AND CODED HER A NO-SHOW.
11:29 AM
kayembe
No Results
REBECCA ORTIZ, I TAKE BACK EVERY TERRIBLE THING I EVER SAID ABOUT YOU.
YOU KISS ME AND I WILL SUE YOU.
NOTED.
ALL RIGHT, THEN.
"ALL RIGHT," I GET A RAISE?
ALL RIGHT, SOMEBODY HERE IS HIDING SOMETHING.
CAMERA 4
2:34:21

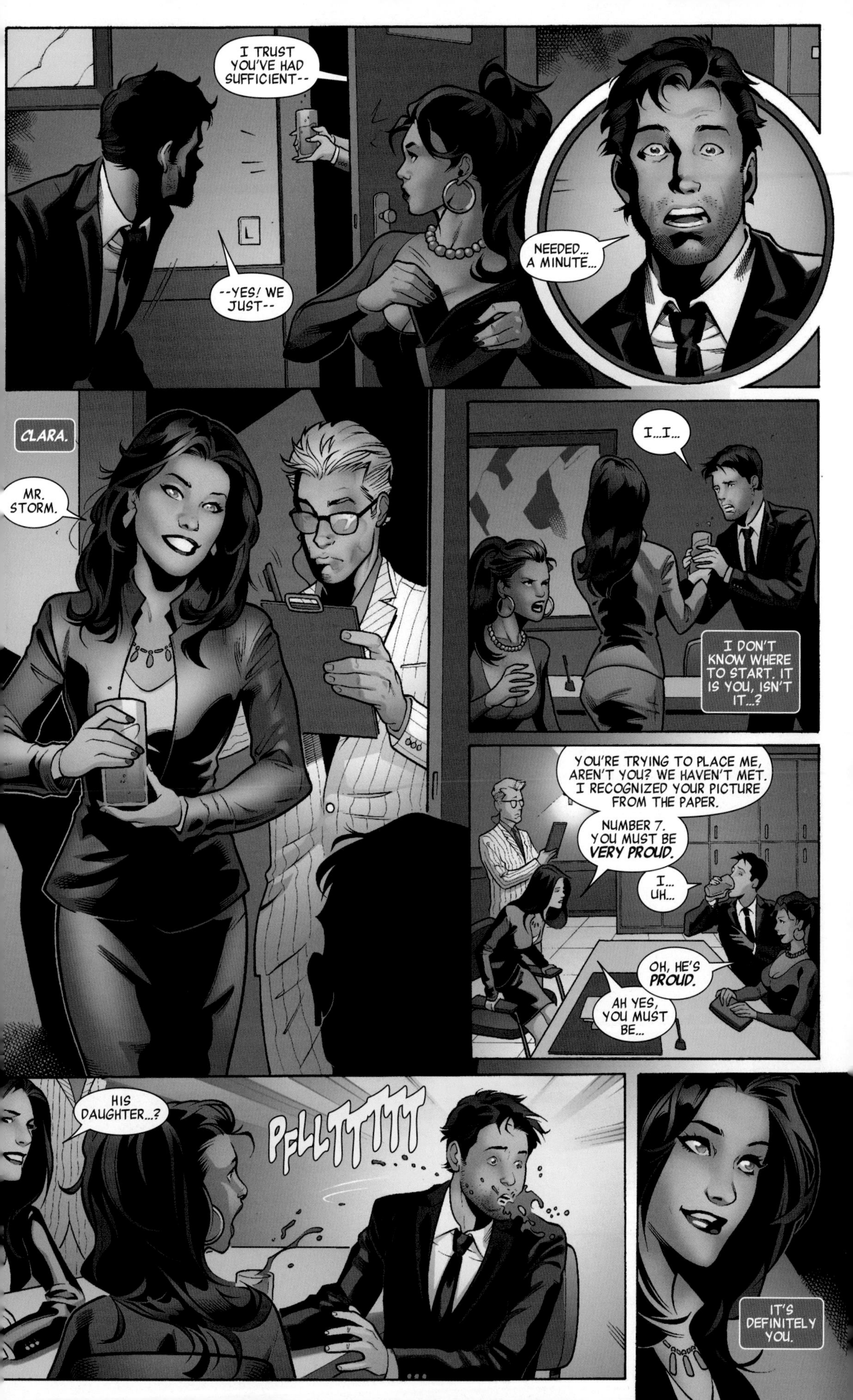

I TRUST YOU'VE HAD SUFFICIENT--
--YES! WE JUST--
NEEDED... A MINUTE...
CLARA.
MR. STORM.
I...I...
I DON'T KNOW WHERE TO START. IT IS YOU, ISN'T IT...?
YOU'RE TRYING TO PLACE ME, AREN'T YOU? WE HAVEN'T MET. I RECOGNIZED YOUR PICTURE FROM THE PAPER.
NUMBER 7. YOU MUST BE VERY PROUD.
I... UH...
OH, HE'S PROUD.
AH YES, YOU MUST BE...
HIS DAUGHTER...?
PFLLTTTTT
IT'S DEFINITELY YOU.

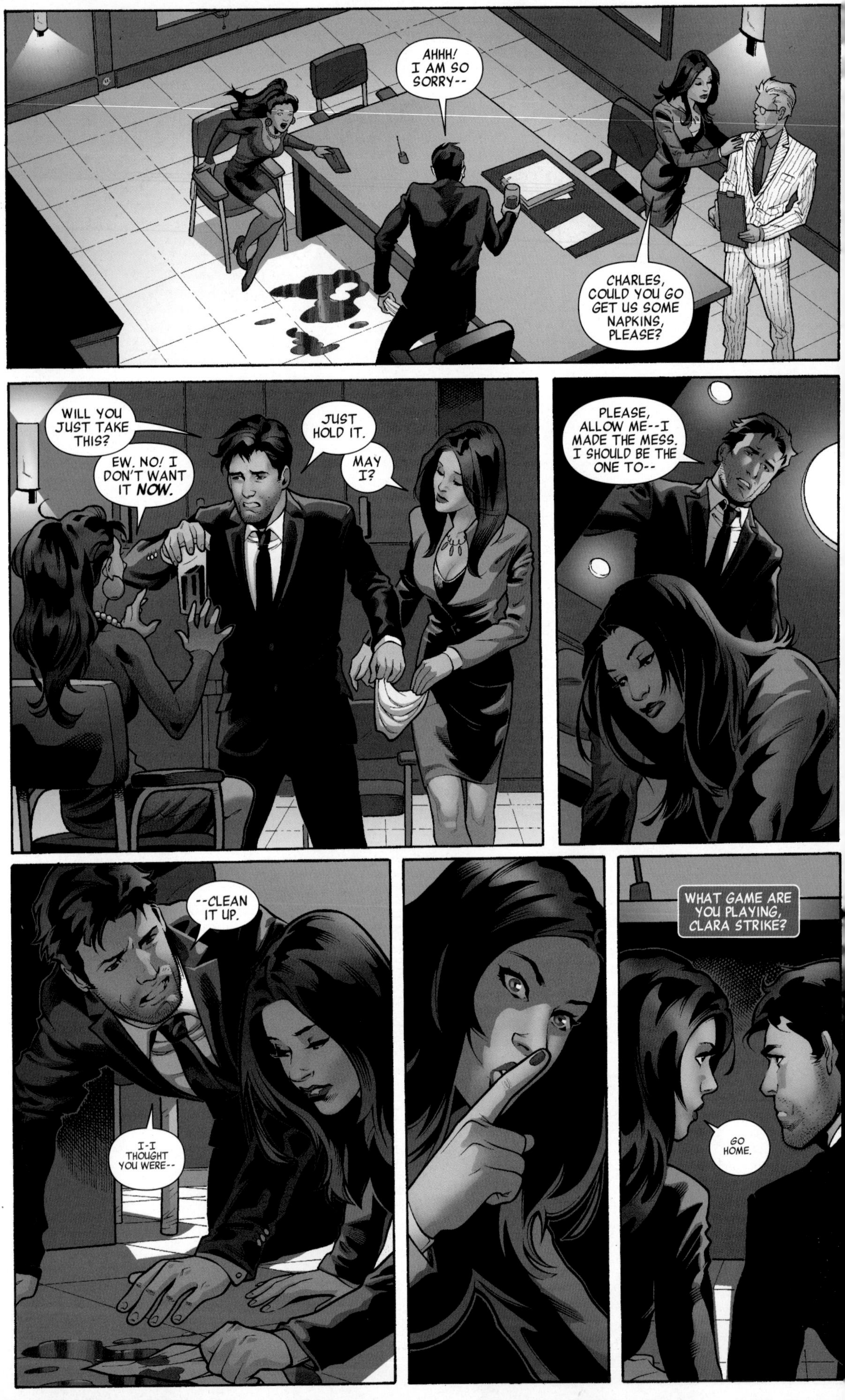
AHHH! I AM SO SORRY--
CHARLES, COULD YOU GO GET US SOME NAPKINS, PLEASE?
WILL YOU JUST TAKE THIS?
EW. NO! I DON'T WANT IT **NOW.**
JUST HOLD IT.
MAY I?
PLEASE, ALLOW ME--I MADE THE MESS. I SHOULD BE THE ONE TO--
--CLEAN IT UP.
I-I THOUGHT YOU WERE--
WHAT GAME ARE YOU PLAYING, CLARA STRIKE?
GO HOME.

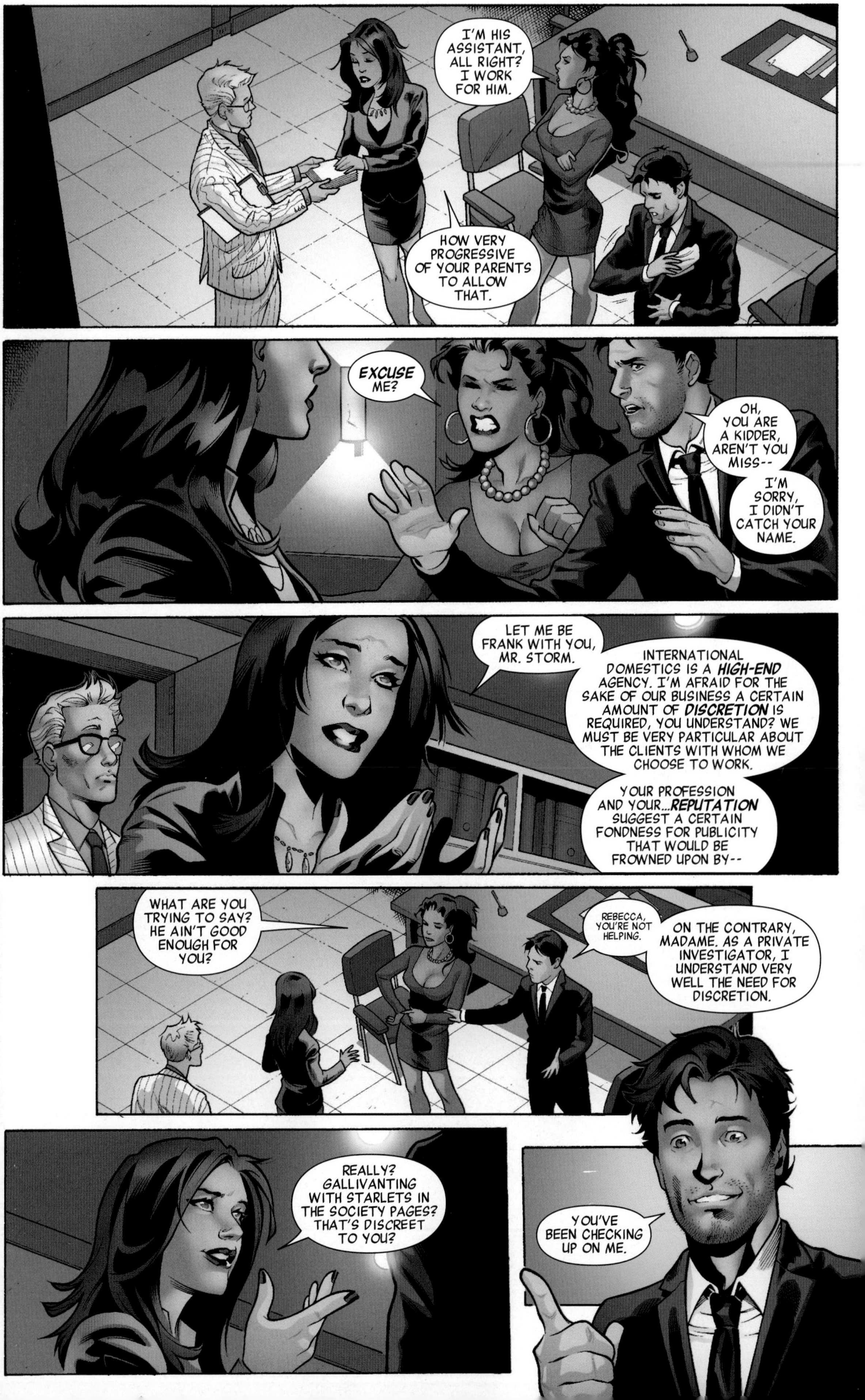
I'M HIS ASSISTANT, ALL RIGHT? I WORK FOR HIM.
HOW VERY PROGRESSIVE OF YOUR PARENTS TO ALLOW THAT.
EXCUSE ME?
OH, YOU ARE A KIDDER, AREN'T YOU MISS--
I'M SORRY, I DIDN'T CATCH YOUR NAME.
LET ME BE FRANK WITH YOU, MR. STORM.
INTERNATIONAL DOMESTICS IS A HIGH-END AGENCY. I'M AFRAID FOR THE SAKE OF OUR BUSINESS A CERTAIN AMOUNT OF DISCRETION IS REQUIRED, YOU UNDERSTAND? WE MUST BE VERY PARTICULAR ABOUT THE CLIENTS WITH WHOM WE CHOOSE TO WORK.
YOUR PROFESSION AND YOUR...REPUTATION SUGGEST A CERTAIN FONDNESS FOR PUBLICITY THAT WOULD BE FROWNED UPON BY--
WHAT ARE YOU TRYING TO SAY? HE AIN'T GOOD ENOUGH FOR YOU?
REBECCA, YOU'RE NOT HELPING.
ON THE CONTRARY, MADAME. AS A PRIVATE INVESTIGATOR, I UNDERSTAND VERY WELL THE NEED FOR DISCRETION.
REALLY? GALLIVANTING WITH STARLETS IN THE SOCIETY PAGES? THAT'S DISCREET TO YOU?
YOU'VE BEEN CHECKING UP ON ME.

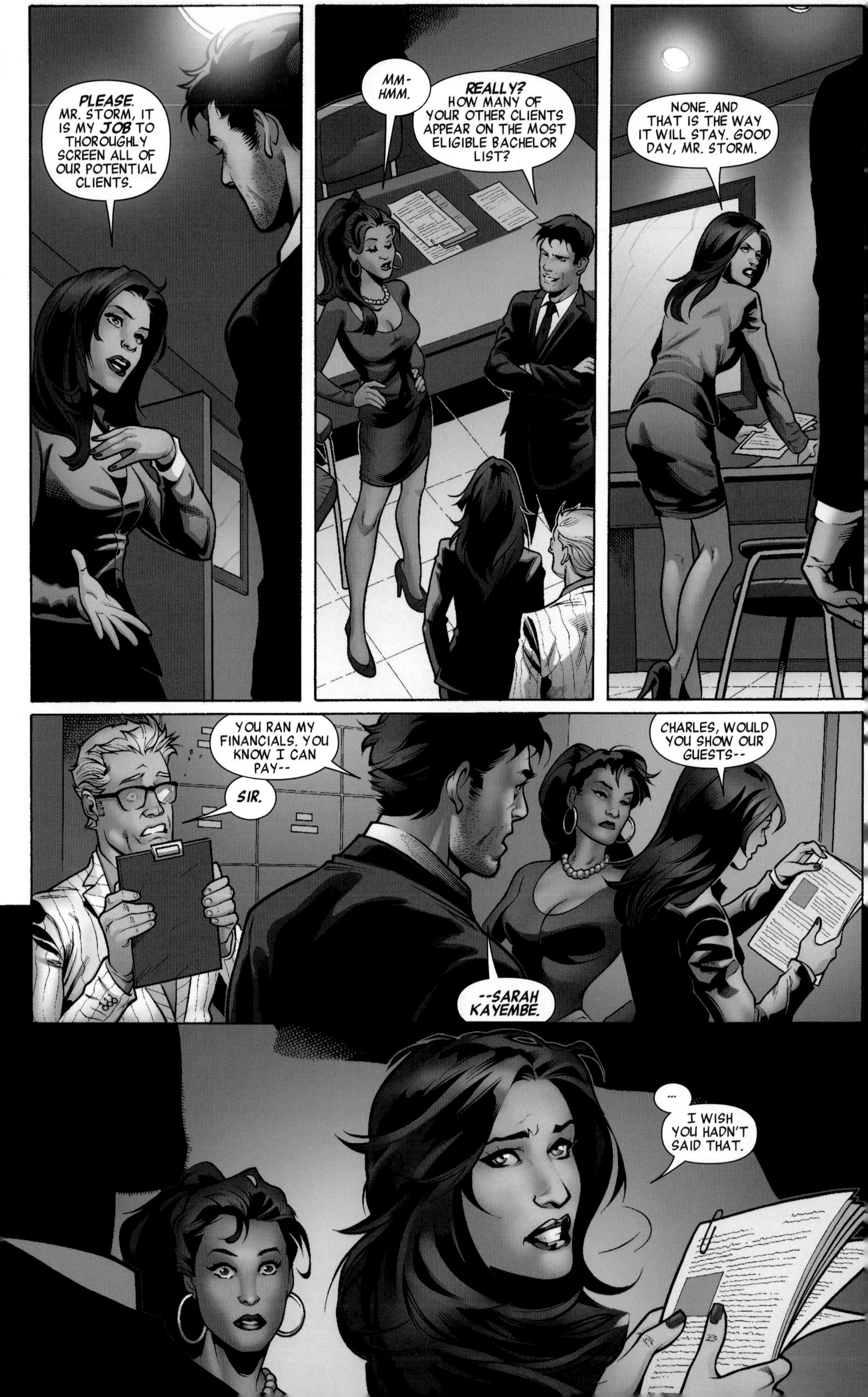
PLEASE. MR. STORM, IT IS MY JOB TO THOROUGHLY SCREEN ALL OF OUR POTENTIAL CLIENTS.
MM-HMM.
REALLY? HOW MANY OF YOUR OTHER CLIENTS APPEAR ON THE MOST ELIGIBLE BACHELOR LIST?
NONE. AND THAT IS THE WAY IT WILL STAY. GOOD DAY, MR. STORM.
YOU RAN MY FINANCIALS. YOU KNOW I CAN PAY--
SIR.
CHARLES, WOULD YOU SHOW OUR GUESTS--
--SARAH KAYEMBE.
...
I WISH YOU HADN'T SAID THAT.

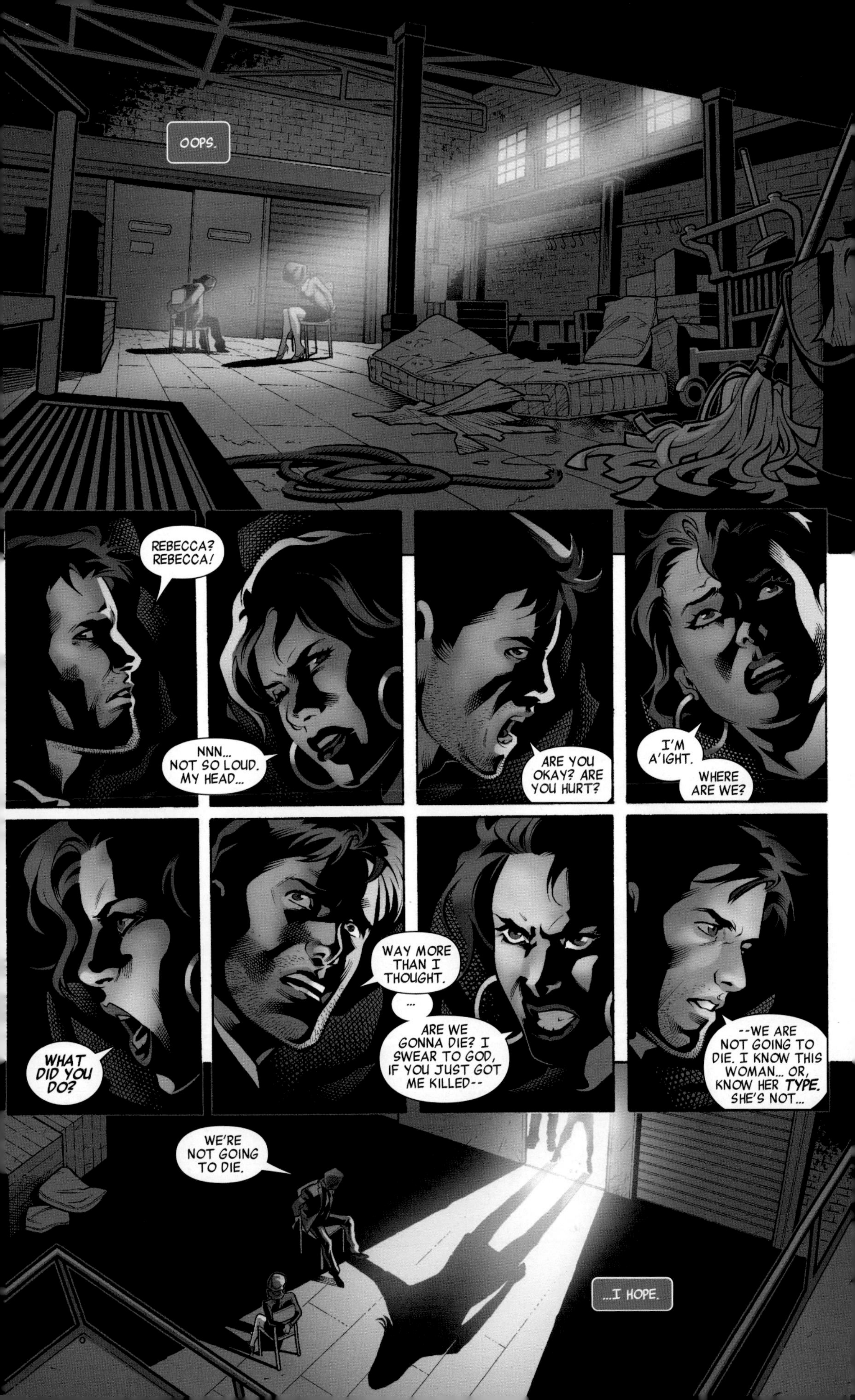
OOPS.
REBECCA? REBECCA!
NNN... NOT SO LOUD. MY HEAD...
ARE YOU OKAY? ARE YOU HURT?
I'M A'IGHT.
WHERE ARE WE?
WHAT DID YOU DO?
WAY MORE THAN I THOUGHT.
...
ARE WE GONNA DIE? I SWEAR TO GOD, IF YOU JUST GOT ME KILLED--
--WE ARE NOT GOING TO DIE. I KNOW THIS WOMAN... OR, KNOW HER TYPE. SHE'S NOT...
WE'RE NOT GOING TO DIE.
...I HOPE.

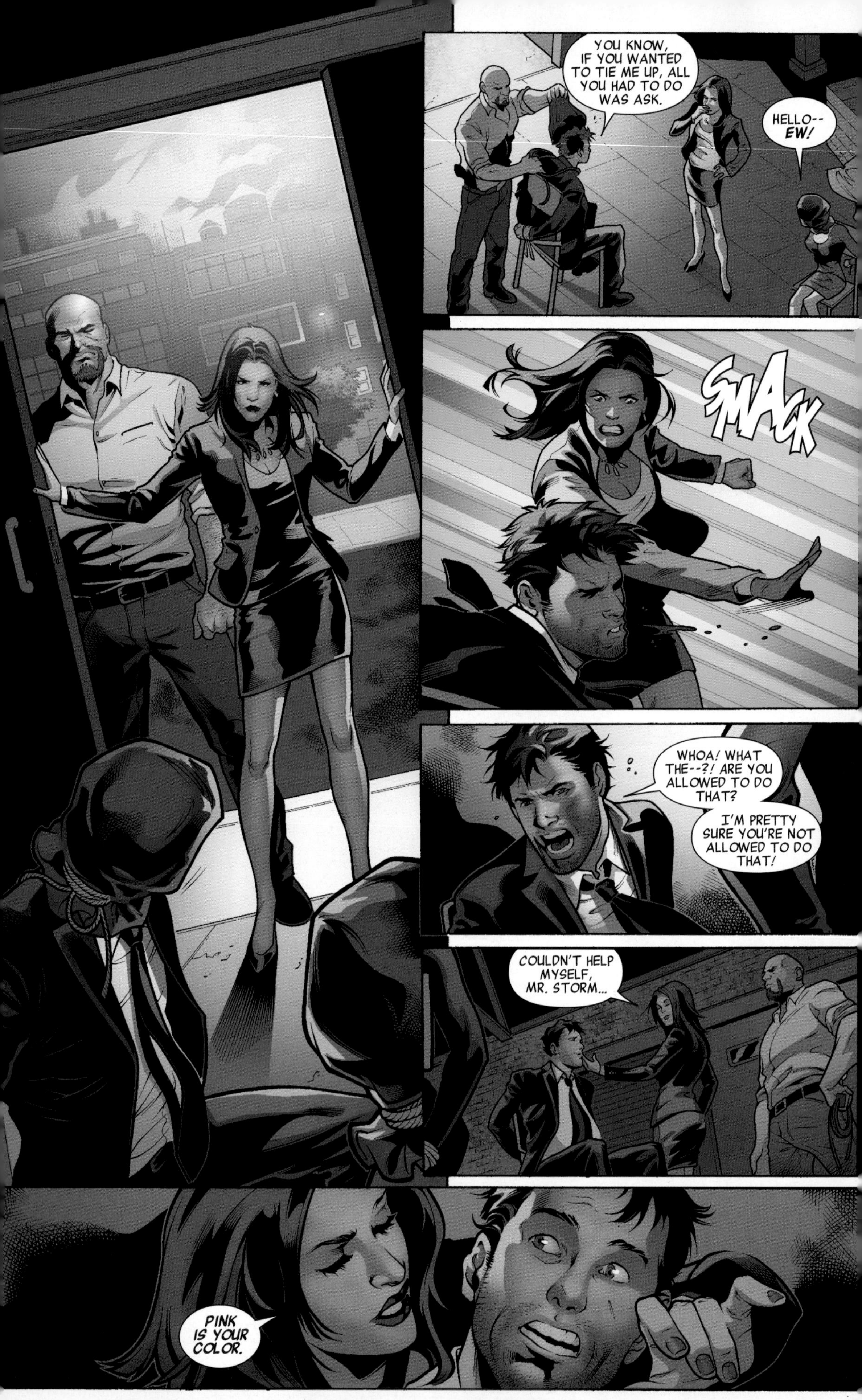
YOU KNOW, IF YOU WANTED TO TIE ME UP, ALL YOU HAD TO DO WAS ASK.
HELLO-- EW!
SMACK
WHOA! WHAT THE--?! ARE YOU ALLOWED TO DO THAT?
I'M PRETTY SURE YOU'RE NOT ALLOWED TO DO THAT!
COULDN'T HELP MYSELF, MR. STORM...
PINK IS YOUR COLOR.

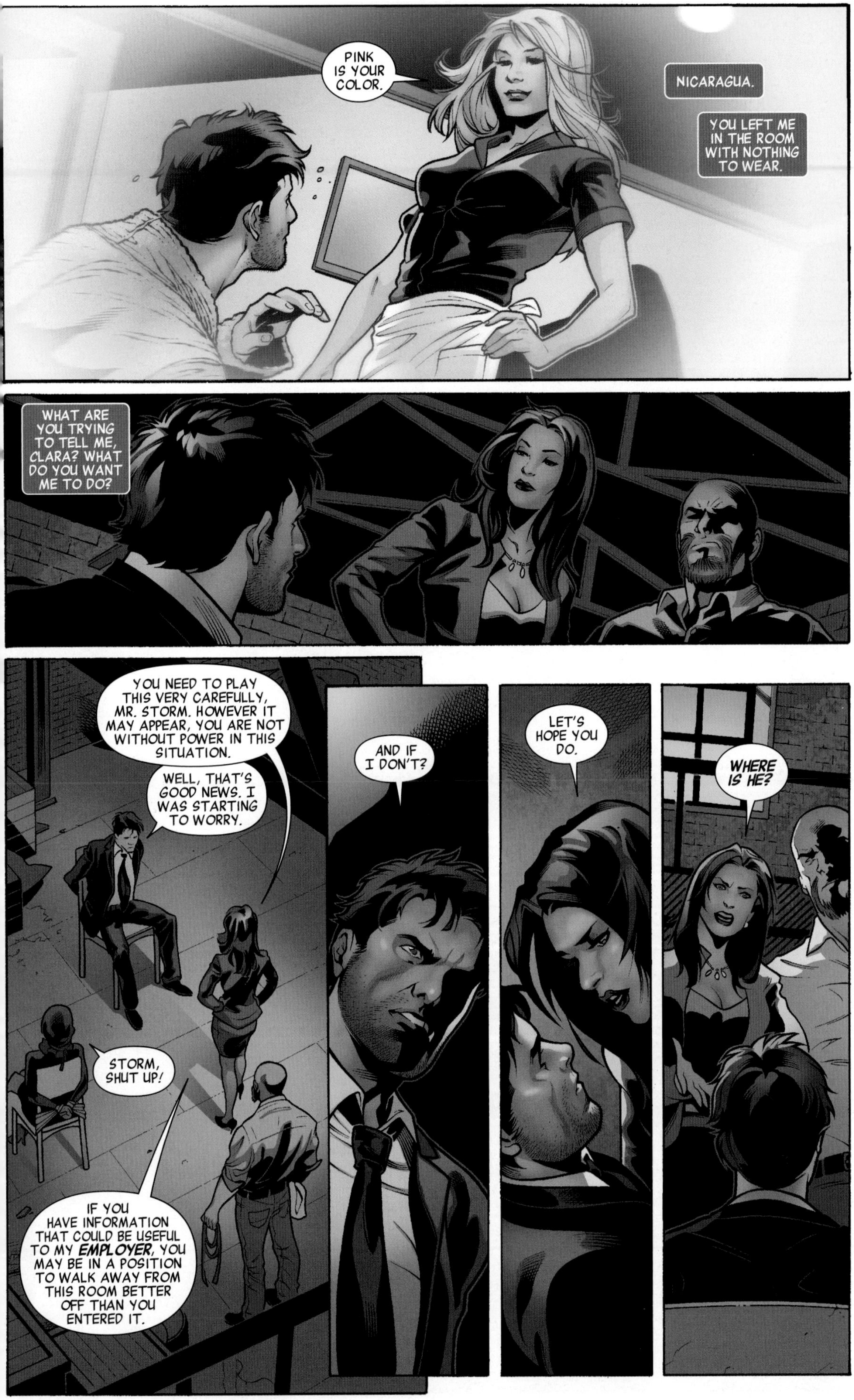
PINK IS YOUR COLOR.
NICARAGUA.
YOU LEFT ME IN THE ROOM WITH NOTHING TO WEAR.
WHAT ARE YOU TRYING TO TELL ME, CLARA? WHAT DO YOU WANT ME TO DO?
YOU NEED TO PLAY THIS VERY CAREFULLY, MR. STORM. HOWEVER IT MAY APPEAR, YOU ARE NOT WITHOUT POWER IN THIS SITUATION.
WELL, THAT'S GOOD NEWS. I WAS STARTING TO WORRY.
STORM, SHUT UP!
IF YOU HAVE INFORMATION THAT COULD BE USEFUL TO MY ***EMPLOYER***, YOU MAY BE IN A POSITION TO WALK AWAY FROM THIS ROOM BETTER OFF THAN YOU ENTERED IT.
AND IF I DON'T?
LET'S HOPE YOU DO.
WHERE IS HE?

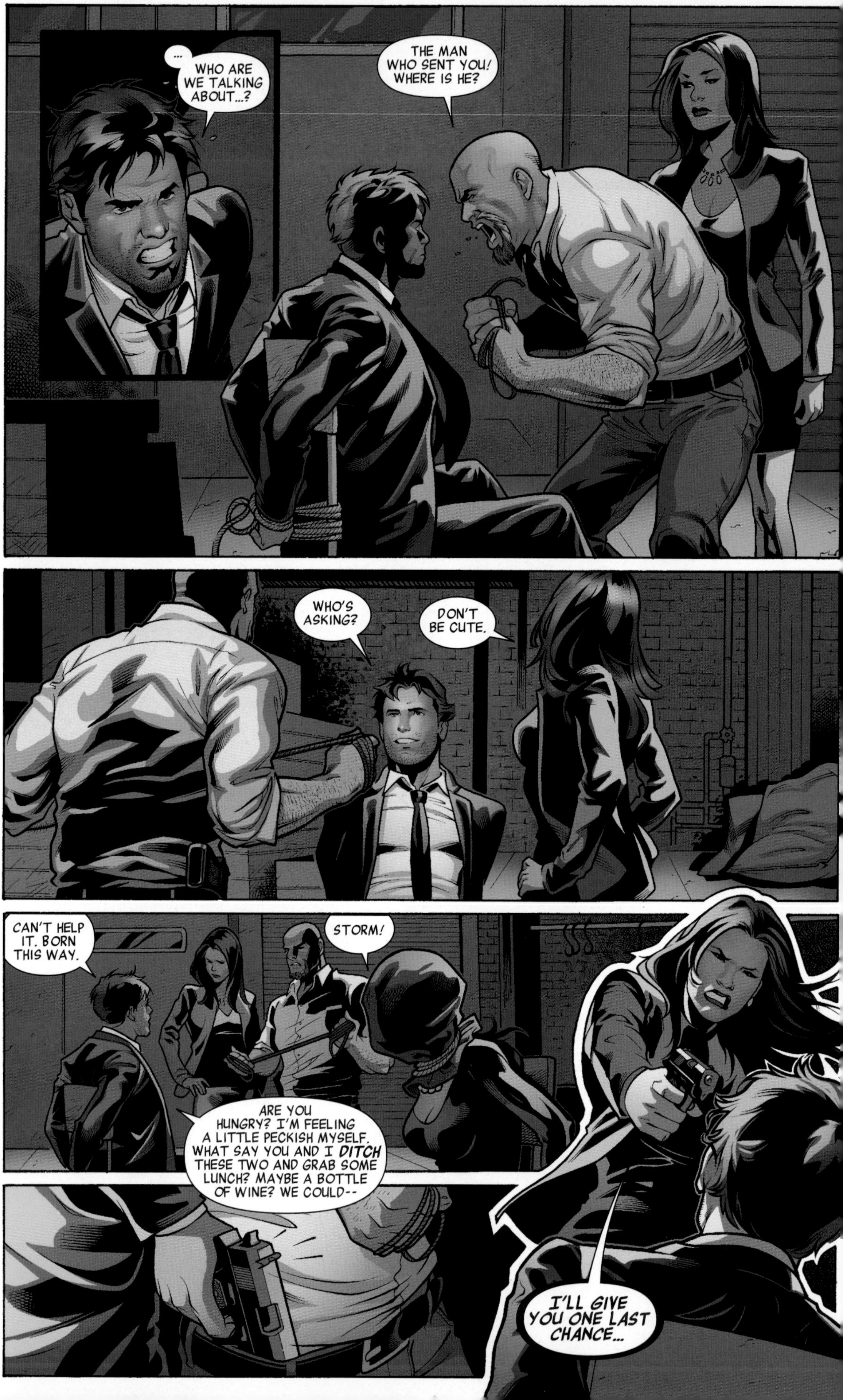
...
WHO ARE WE TALKING ABOUT...?
THE MAN WHO SENT YOU! WHERE IS HE?
WHO'S ASKING?
DON'T BE CUTE.
CAN'T HELP IT. BORN THIS WAY.
STORM!
ARE YOU HUNGRY? I'M FEELING A LITTLE PECKISH MYSELF. WHAT SAY YOU AND I DITCH THESE TWO AND GRAB SOME LUNCH? MAYBE A BOTTLE OF WINE? WE COULD--
I'LL GIVE YOU ONE LAST CHANCE...

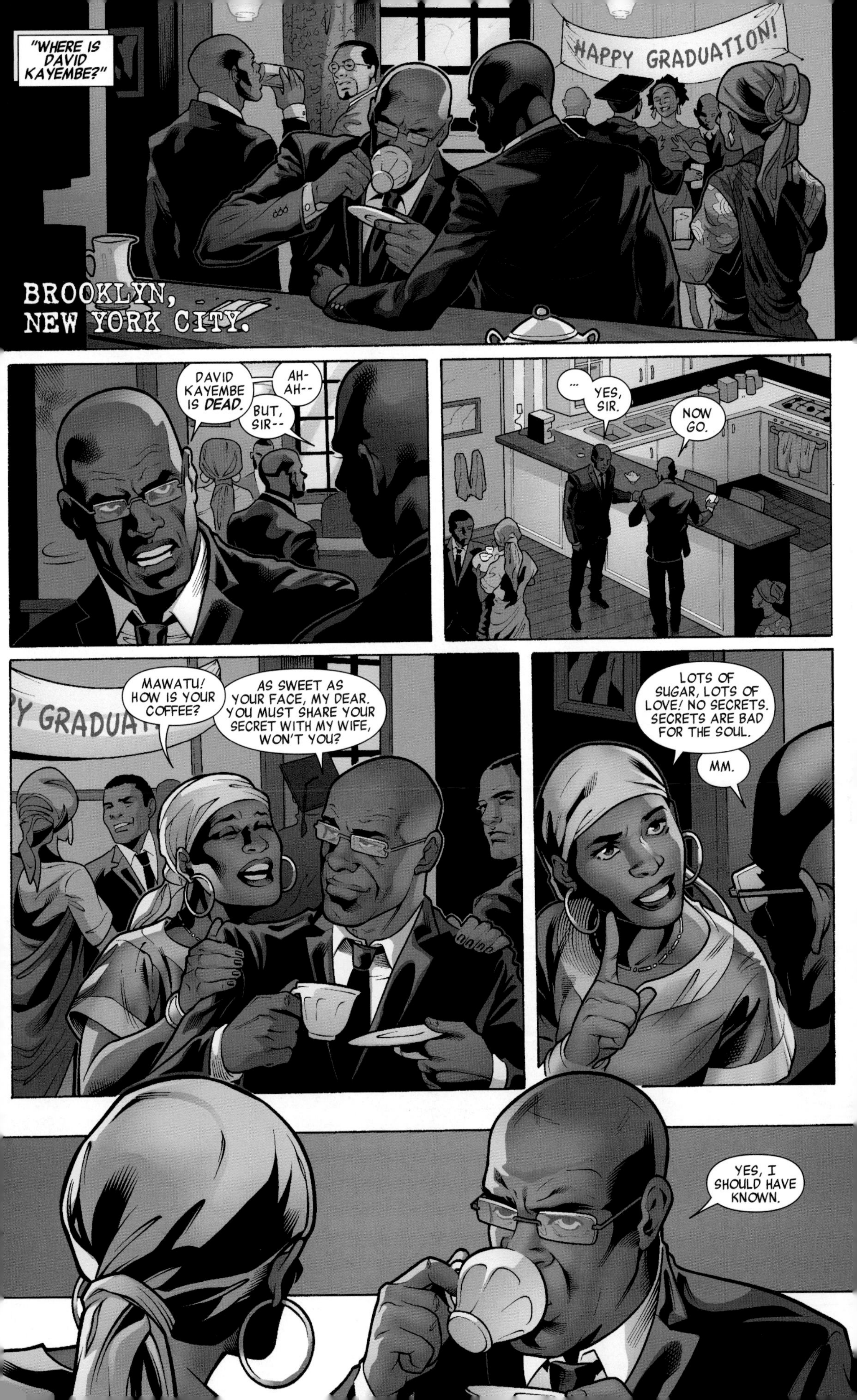
"WHERE IS DAVID KAYEMBE?"
HAPPY GRADUATION!
BROOKLYN, NEW YORK CITY.
DAVID KAYEMBE IS DEAD.
AH-AH--
BUT, SIR--
...
YES, SIR.
NOW GO.
MAWATU! HOW IS YOUR COFFEE?
AS SWEET AS YOUR FACE, MY DEAR. YOU MUST SHARE YOUR SECRET WITH MY WIFE, WON'T YOU?
LOTS OF SUGAR, LOTS OF LOVE! NO SECRETS. SECRETS ARE BAD FOR THE SOUL.
MM.
YES, I SHOULD HAVE KNOWN.

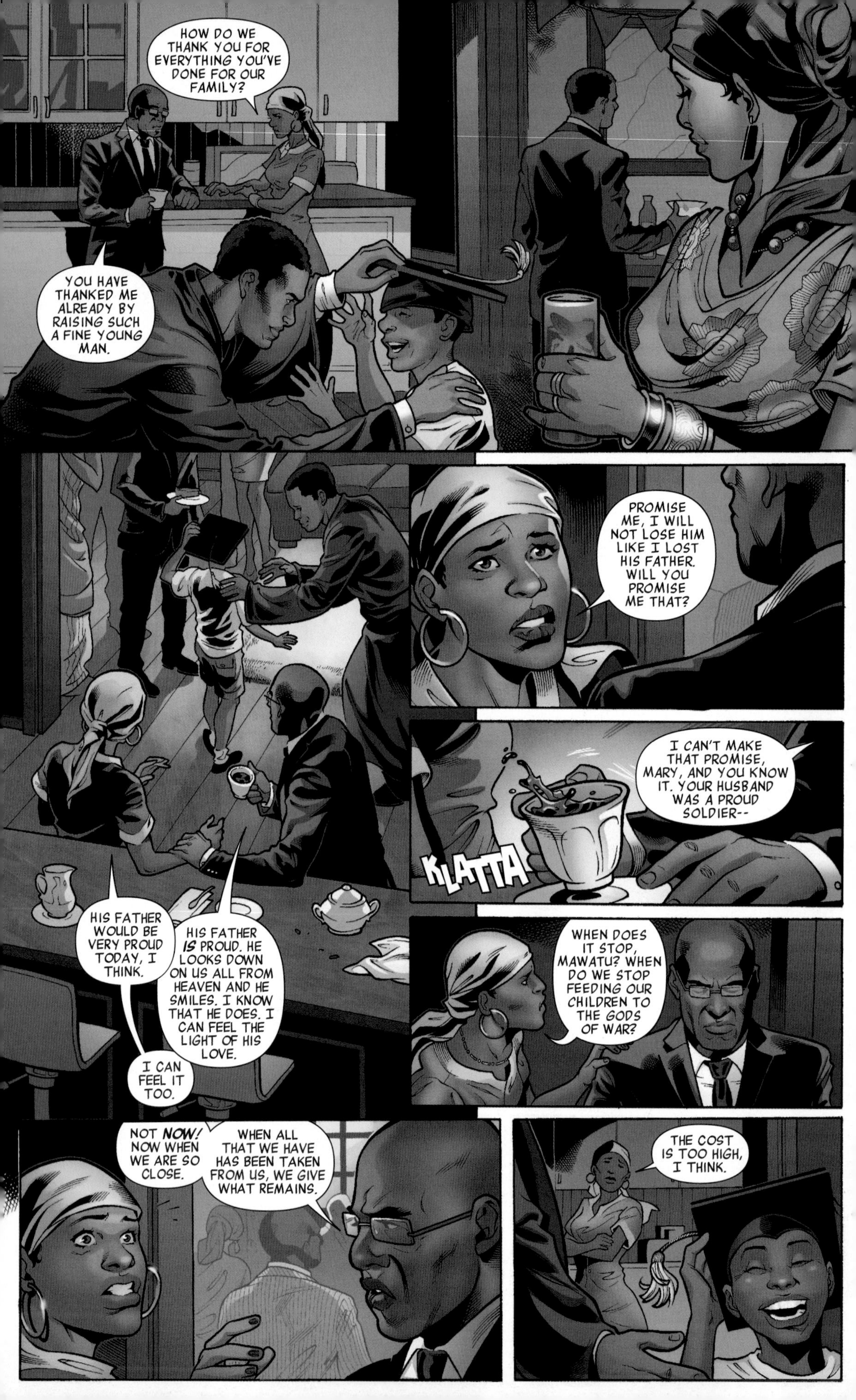
HOW DO WE THANK YOU FOR EVERYTHING YOU'VE DONE FOR OUR FAMILY?
YOU HAVE THANKED ME ALREADY BY RAISING SUCH A FINE YOUNG MAN.
PROMISE ME, I WILL NOT LOSE HIM LIKE I LOST HIS FATHER. WILL YOU PROMISE ME THAT?
I CAN'T MAKE THAT PROMISE, MARY, AND YOU KNOW IT. YOUR HUSBAND WAS A PROUD SOLDIER--
KLATTA
HIS FATHER WOULD BE VERY PROUD TODAY, I THINK.
HIS FATHER IS PROUD. HE LOOKS DOWN ON US ALL FROM HEAVEN AND HE SMILES. I KNOW THAT HE DOES. I CAN FEEL THE LIGHT OF HIS LOVE.
I CAN FEEL IT TOO.
WHEN DOES IT STOP, MAWATU? WHEN DO WE STOP FEEDING OUR CHILDREN TO THE GODS OF WAR?
NOT NOW! NOW WHEN WE ARE SO CLOSE.
WHEN ALL THAT WE HAVE HAS BEEN TAKEN FROM US, WE GIVE WHAT REMAINS.
THE COST IS TOO HIGH, I THINK.

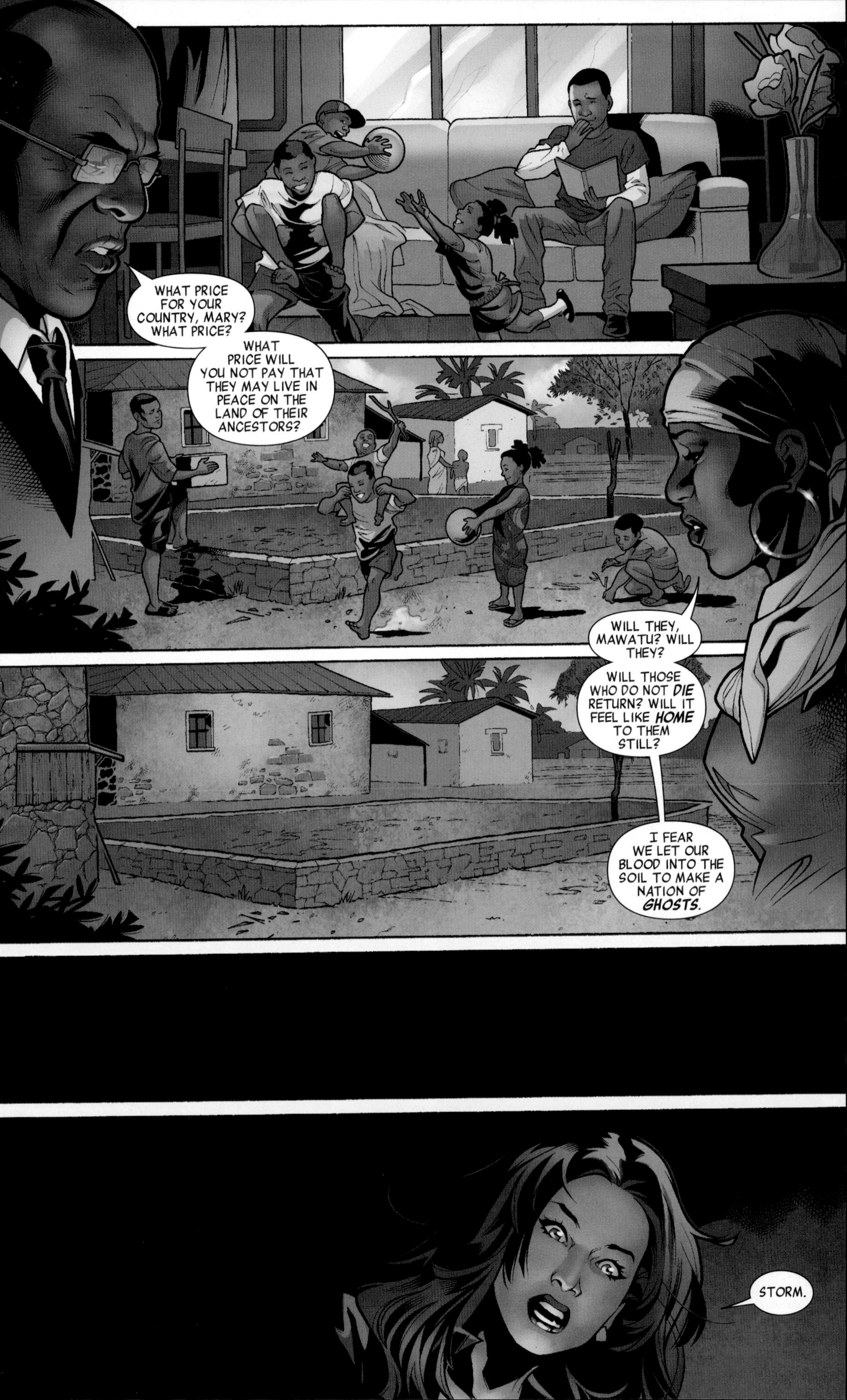
WHAT PRICE FOR YOUR COUNTRY, MARY? WHAT PRICE?
WHAT PRICE WILL YOU NOT PAY THAT THEY MAY LIVE IN PEACE ON THE LAND OF THEIR ANCESTORS?
WILL THEY, MAWATU? WILL THEY?
WILL THOSE WHO DO NOT DIE RETURN? WILL IT FEEL LIKE HOME TO THEM STILL?
I FEAR WE LET OUR BLOOD INTO THE SOIL TO MAKE A NATION OF GHOSTS.
STORM.

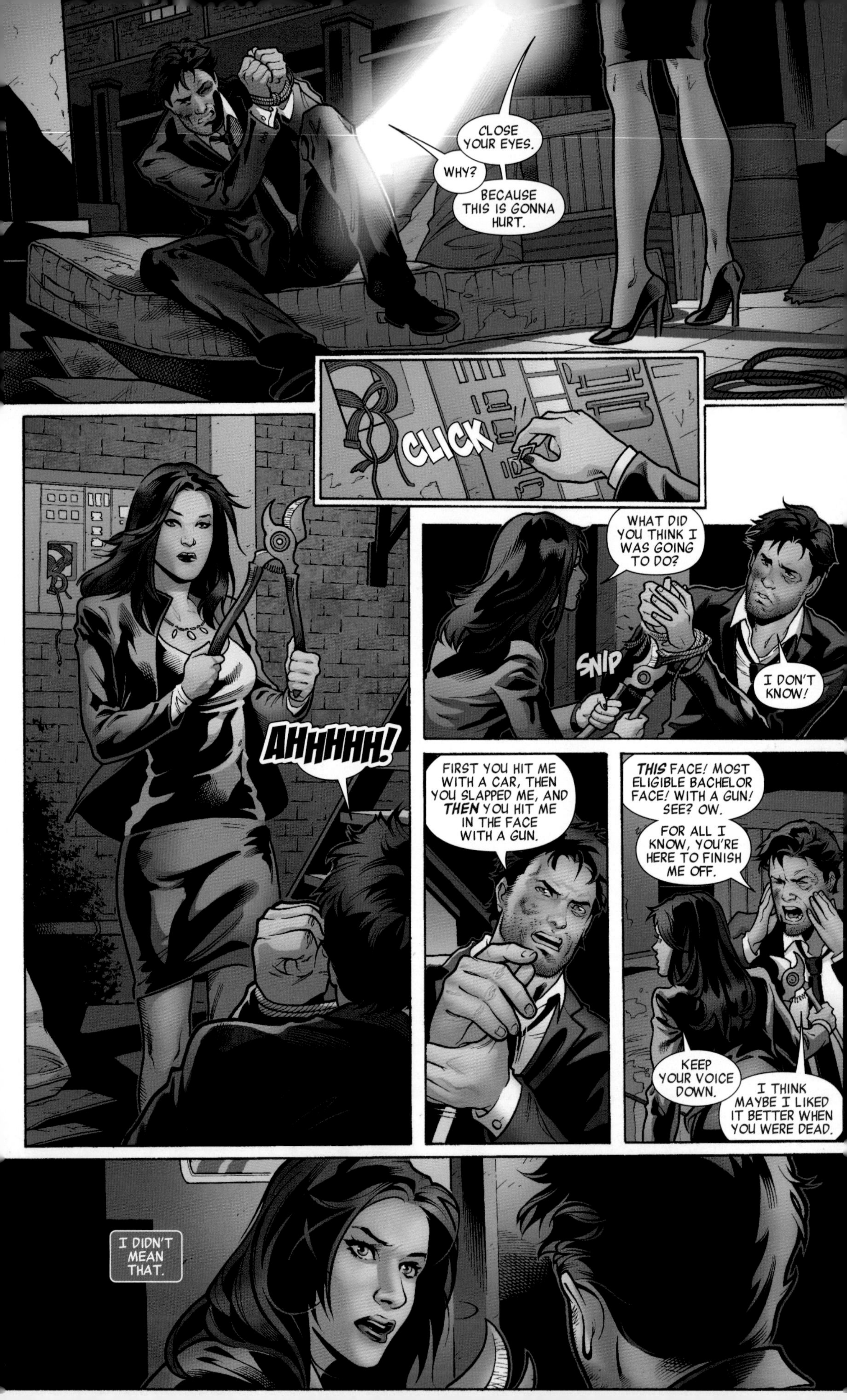
CLOSE YOUR EYES.
WHY?
BECAUSE THIS IS GONNA HURT.
CLICK
AHHHHH!
WHAT DID YOU THINK I WAS GOING TO DO?
SNIP
I DON'T KNOW!
FIRST YOU HIT ME WITH A CAR, THEN YOU SLAPPED ME, AND THEN YOU HIT ME IN THE FACE WITH A GUN.
THIS FACE! MOST ELIGIBLE BACHELOR FACE! WITH A GUN! SEE? OW.
FOR ALL I KNOW, YOU'RE HERE TO FINISH ME OFF.
KEEP YOUR VOICE DOWN.
I THINK MAYBE I LIKED IT BETTER WHEN YOU WERE DEAD.
I DIDN'T MEAN THAT.

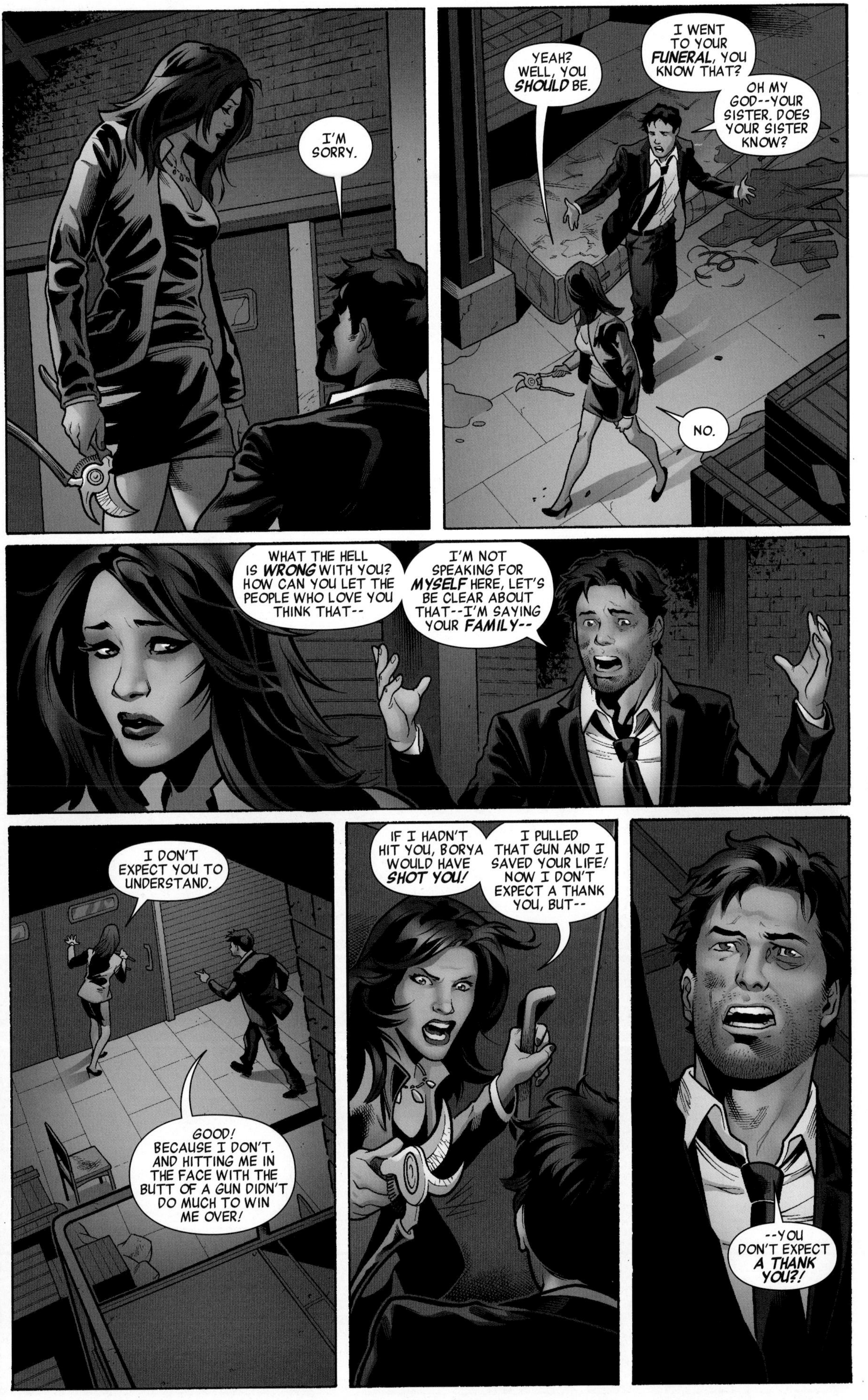
I'M SORRY.
YEAH? WELL, YOU *SHOULD* BE.
I WENT TO YOUR *FUNERAL*, YOU KNOW THAT?
OH MY GOD--YOUR SISTER. DOES YOUR SISTER KNOW?
NO.
WHAT THE HELL IS *WRONG* WITH YOU? HOW CAN YOU LET THE PEOPLE WHO LOVE YOU THINK THAT--
I'M NOT SPEAKING FOR *MYSELF* HERE, LET'S BE CLEAR ABOUT THAT--I'M SAYING YOUR *FAMILY--*
I DON'T EXPECT YOU TO UNDERSTAND.
GOOD! BECAUSE I DON'T. AND HITTING ME IN THE FACE WITH THE BUTT OF A GUN DIDN'T DO MUCH TO WIN ME OVER!
IF I HADN'T HIT YOU, BORYA WOULD HAVE *SHOT YOU!*
I PULLED THAT GUN AND I SAVED YOUR LIFE! NOW I DON'T EXPECT A THANK YOU, BUT--
--YOU DON'T EXPECT *A THANK YOU?!*

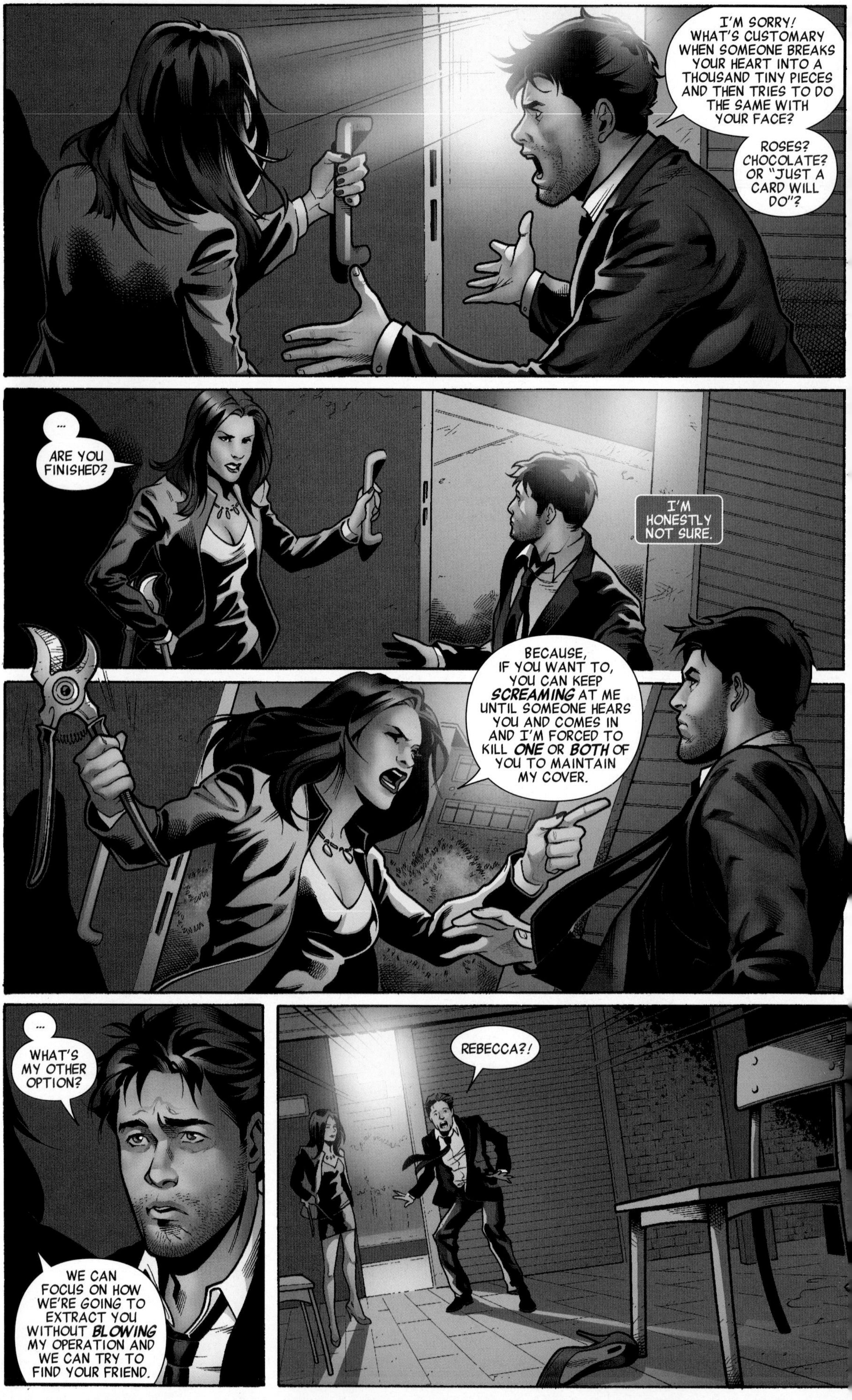
I'M SORRY! WHAT'S CUSTOMARY WHEN SOMEONE BREAKS YOUR HEART INTO A THOUSAND TINY PIECES AND THEN TRIES TO DO THE SAME WITH YOUR FACE?
ROSES? CHOCOLATE? OR "JUST A CARD WILL DO"?
...
ARE YOU FINISHED?
I'M HONESTLY NOT SURE.
BECAUSE, IF YOU WANT TO, YOU CAN KEEP SCREAMING AT ME UNTIL SOMEONE HEARS YOU AND COMES IN AND I'M FORCED TO KILL ONE OR BOTH OF YOU TO MAINTAIN MY COVER.
...
WHAT'S MY OTHER OPTION?
WE CAN FOCUS ON HOW WE'RE GOING TO EXTRACT YOU WITHOUT BLOWING MY OPERATION AND WE CAN TRY TO FIND YOUR FRIEND.
REBECCA?!

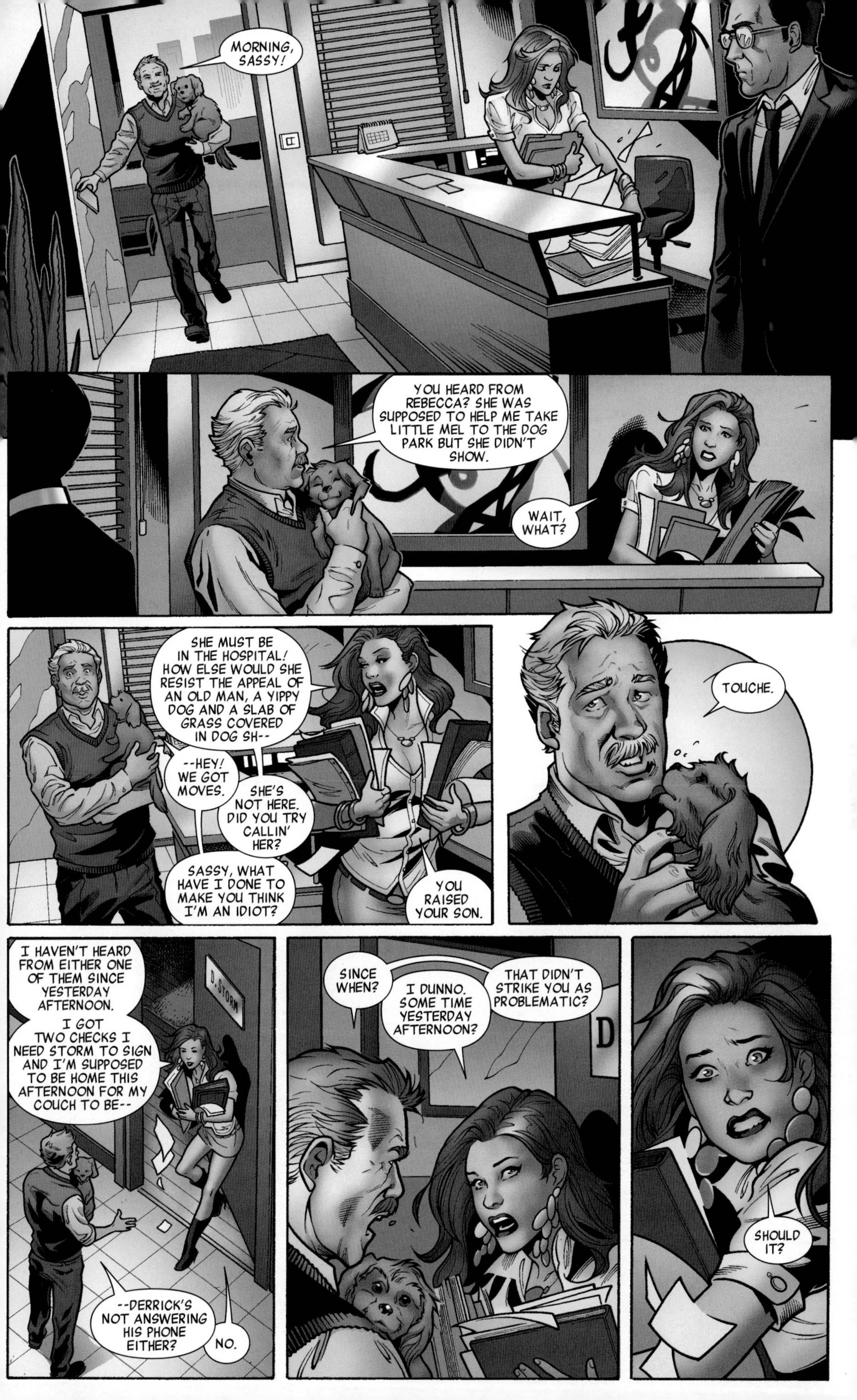
MORNING, SASSY!
YOU HEARD FROM REBECCA? SHE WAS SUPPOSED TO HELP ME TAKE LITTLE MEL TO THE DOG PARK BUT SHE DIDN'T SHOW.
WAIT, WHAT?
SHE MUST BE IN THE HOSPITAL! HOW ELSE WOULD SHE RESIST THE APPEAL OF AN OLD MAN, A YIPPY DOG AND A SLAB OF GRASS COVERED IN DOG SH--
--HEY! WE GOT MOVES.
SHE'S NOT HERE. DID YOU TRY CALLIN' HER?
SASSY, WHAT HAVE I DONE TO MAKE YOU THINK I'M AN IDIOT?
YOU RAISED YOUR SON.
TOUCHE.
I HAVEN'T HEARD FROM EITHER ONE OF THEM SINCE YESTERDAY AFTERNOON.
I GOT TWO CHECKS I NEED STORM TO SIGN AND I'M SUPPOSED TO BE HOME THIS AFTERNOON FOR MY COUCH TO BE--
D. STORM
--DERRICK'S NOT ANSWERING HIS PHONE EITHER?
NO.
SINCE WHEN?
I DUNNO. SOME TIME YESTERDAY AFTERNOON?
THAT DIDN'T STRIKE YOU AS PROBLEMATIC?
D
SHOULD IT?

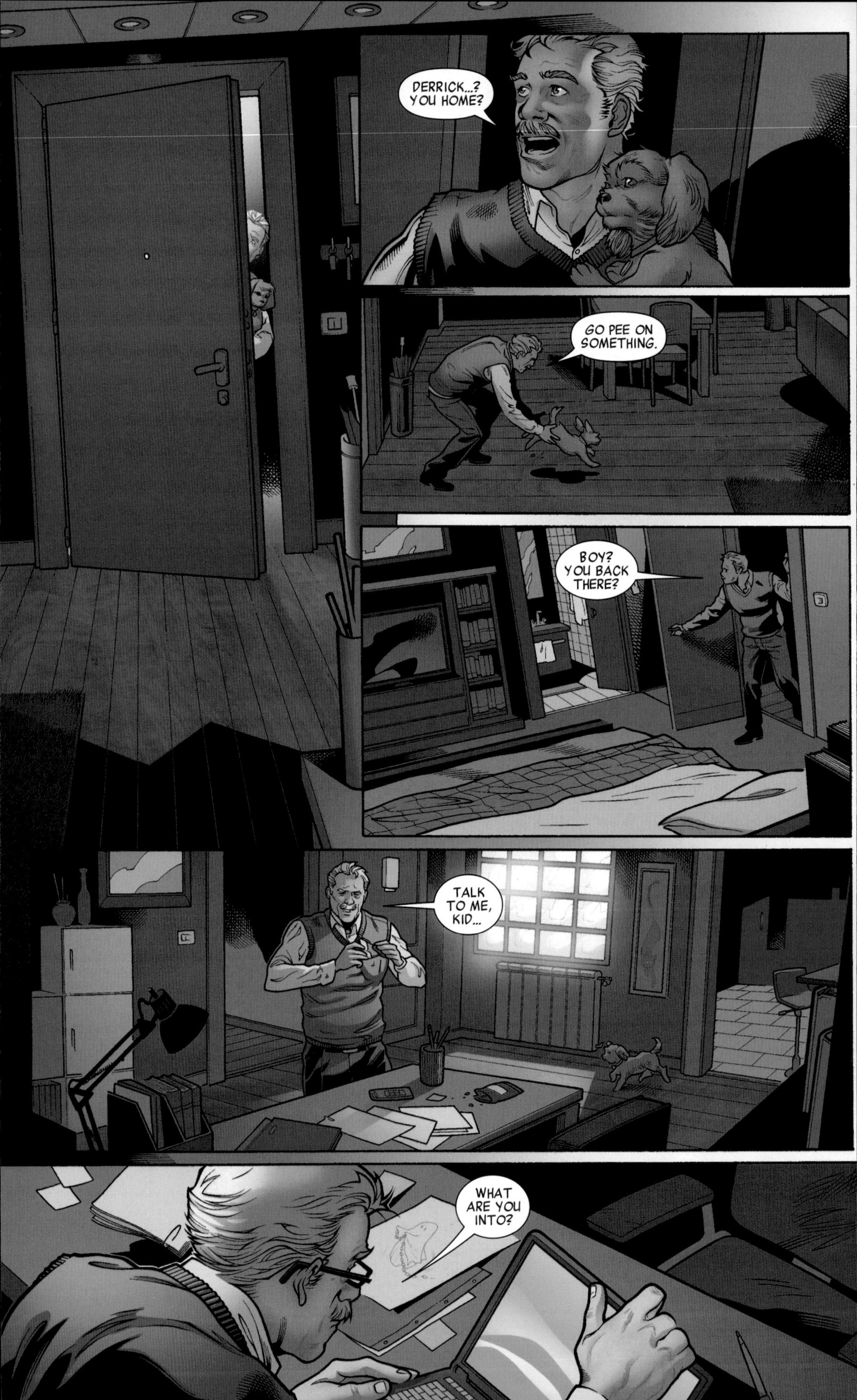
DERRICK...? YOU HOME?
GO PEE ON SOMETHING.
BOY? YOU BACK THERE?
TALK TO ME, KID...
WHAT ARE YOU INTO?

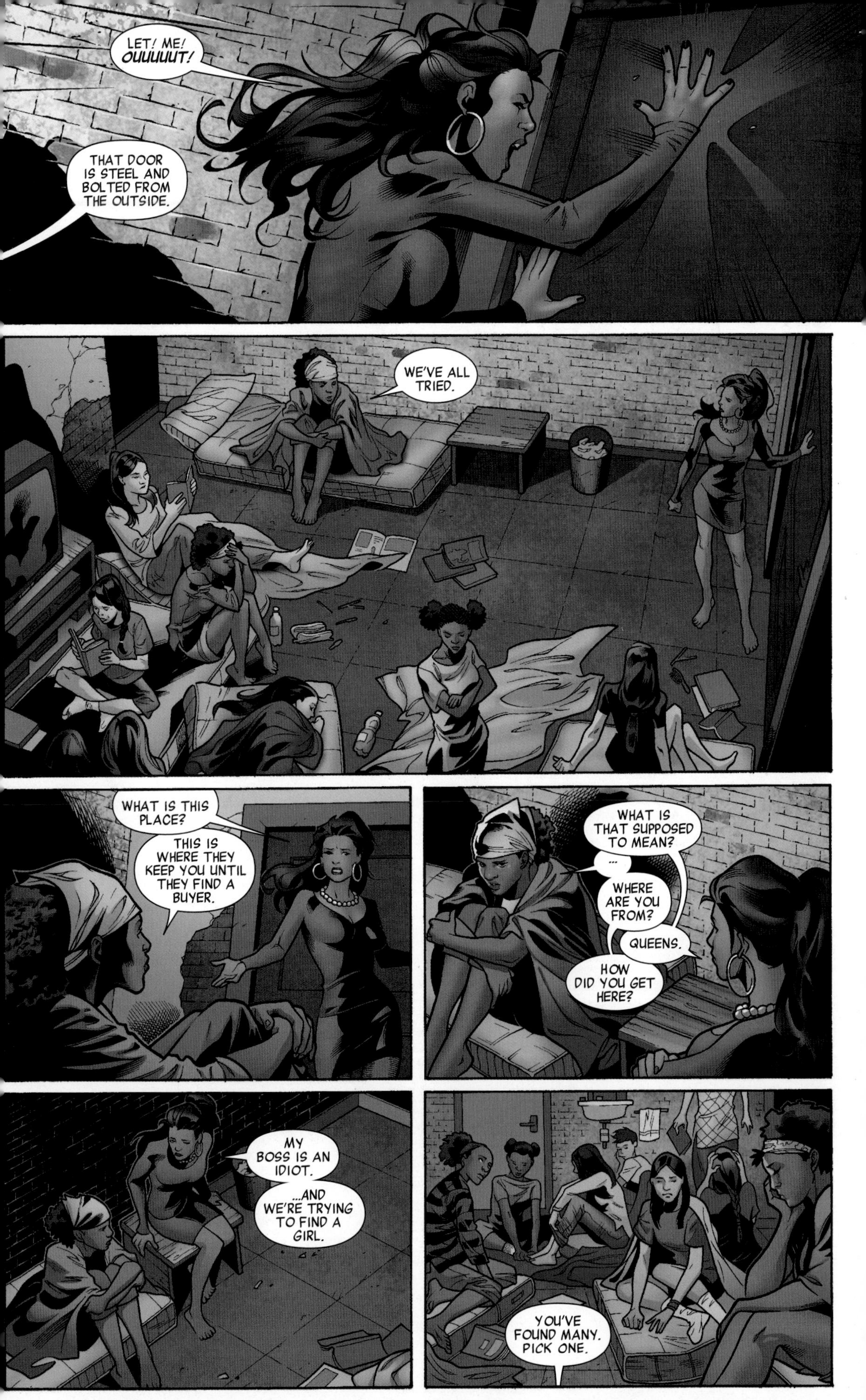
LET! ME! OUUUUUT!
THAT DOOR IS STEEL AND BOLTED FROM THE OUTSIDE.
WE'VE ALL TRIED.
WHAT IS THIS PLACE?
THIS IS WHERE THEY KEEP YOU UNTIL THEY FIND A BUYER.
WHAT IS THAT SUPPOSED TO MEAN?
...
WHERE ARE YOU FROM?
QUEENS.
HOW DID YOU GET HERE?
MY BOSS IS AN IDIOT.
...AND WE'RE TRYING TO FIND A GIRL.
YOU'VE FOUND MANY. PICK ONE.

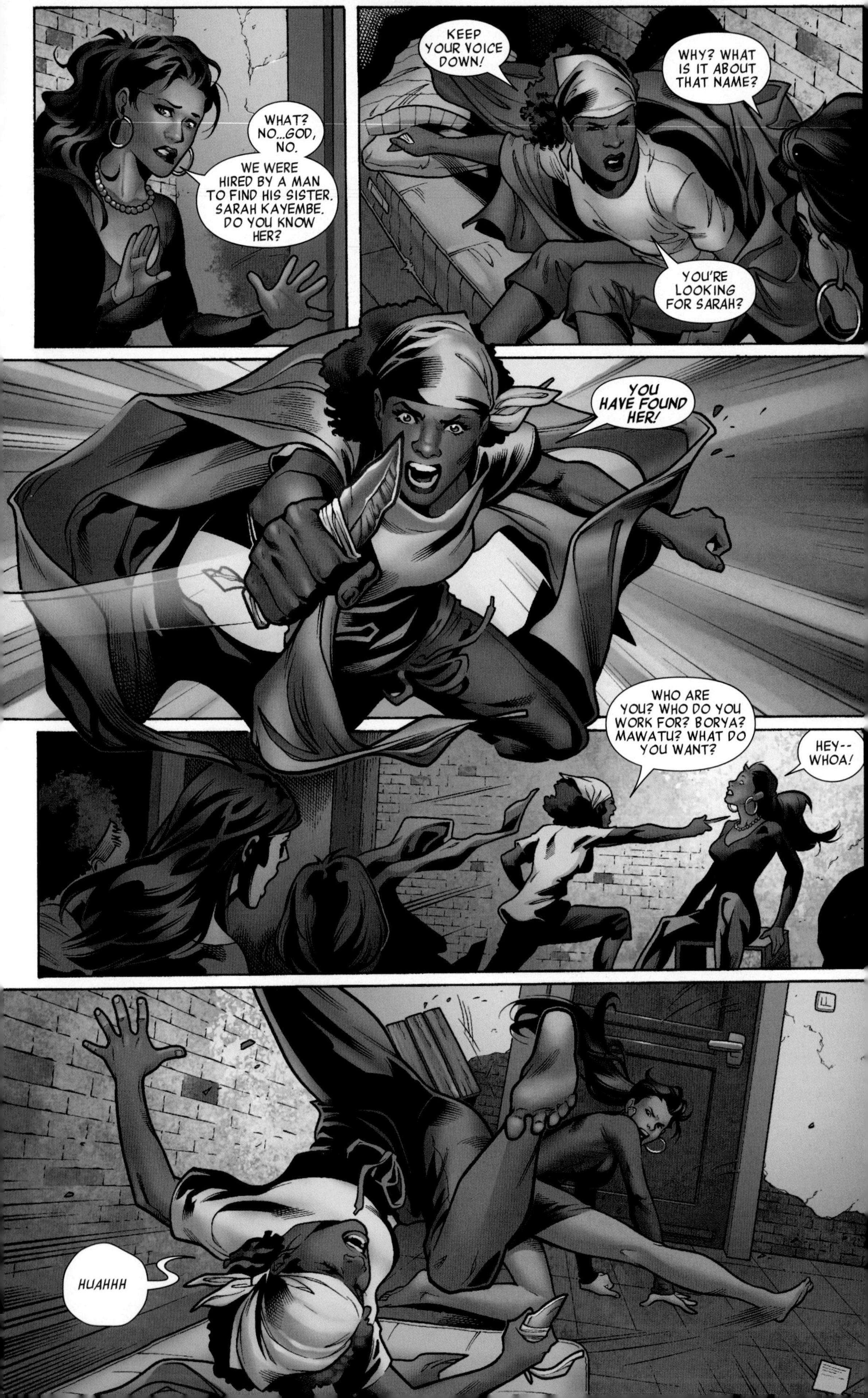
WHAT? NO...GOD, NO.
WE WERE HIRED BY A MAN TO FIND HIS SISTER. SARAH KAYEMBE. DO YOU KNOW HER?
KEEP YOUR VOICE DOWN!
WHY? WHAT IS IT ABOUT THAT NAME?
YOU'RE LOOKING FOR SARAH?
YOU HAVE FOUND HER!
WHO ARE YOU? WHO DO YOU WORK FOR? BORYA? MAWATU? WHAT DO YOU WANT?
HEY-- WHOA!
HUAHHH

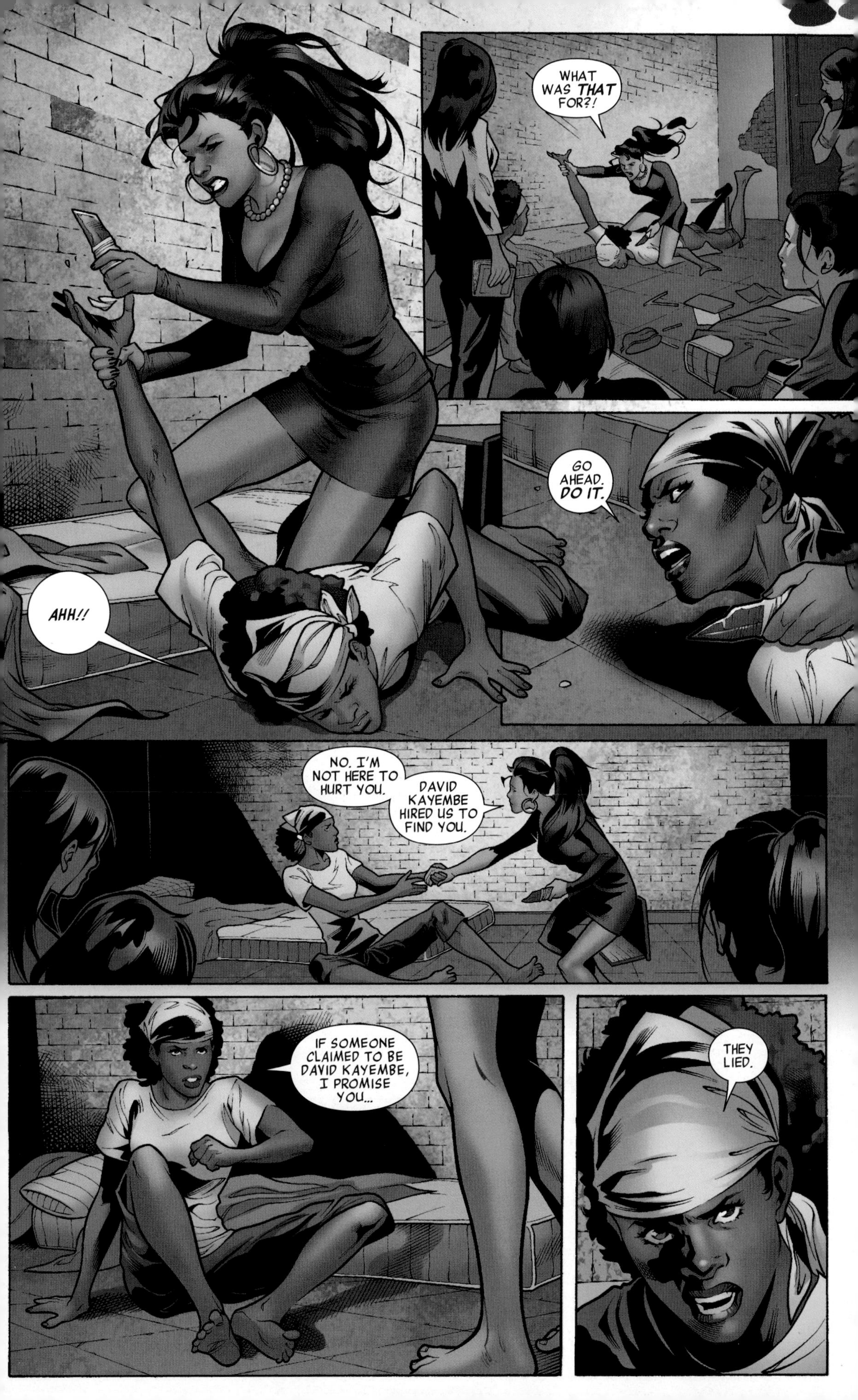
WHAT WAS THAT FOR?!
AHH!!
GO AHEAD. DO IT.
NO. I'M NOT HERE TO HURT YOU.
DAVID KAYEMBE HIRED US TO FIND YOU.
IF SOMEONE CLAIMED TO BE DAVID KAYEMBE, I PROMISE YOU...
THEY LIED.

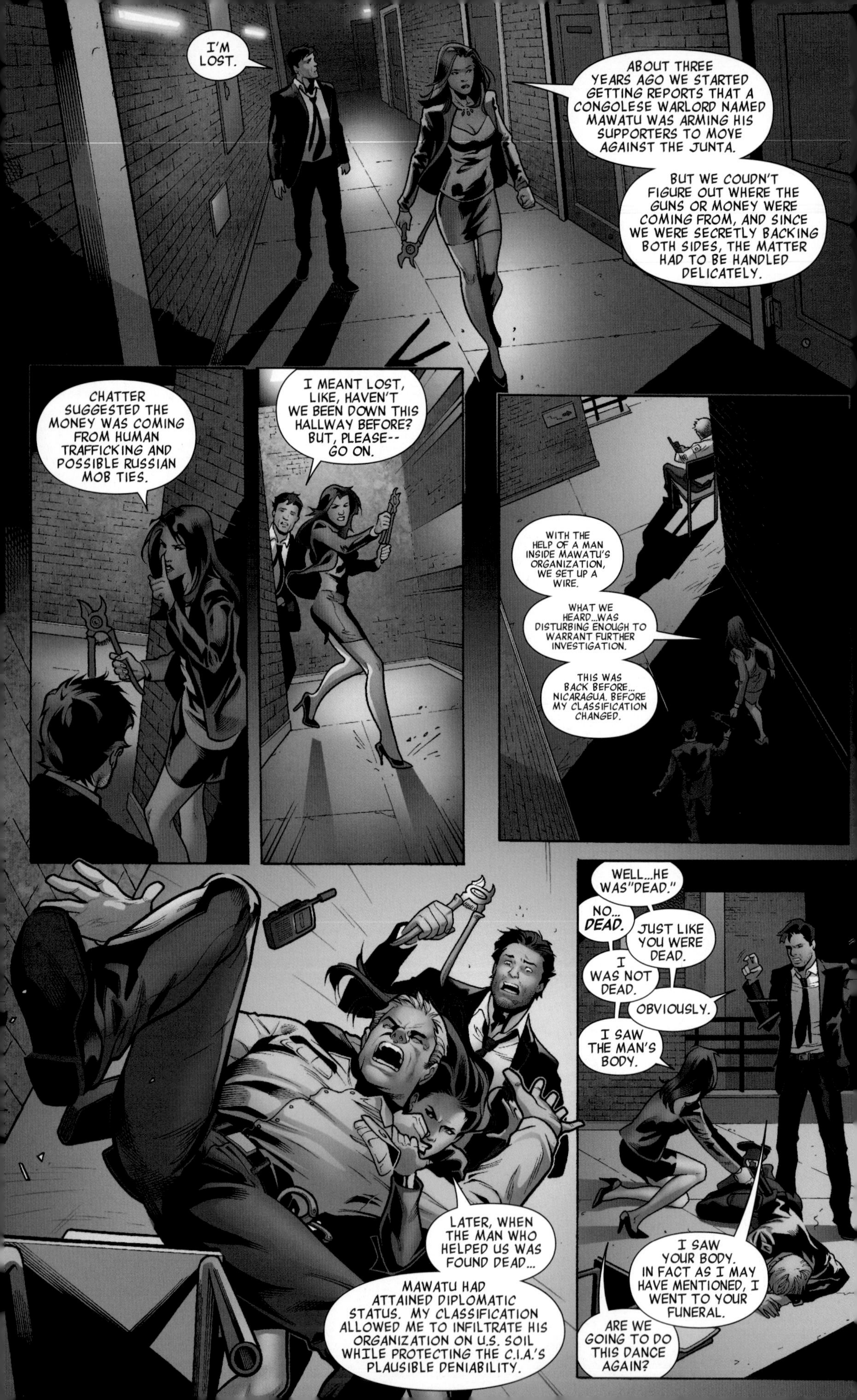
I'M LOST.
ABOUT THREE YEARS AGO WE STARTED GETTING REPORTS THAT A CONGOLESE WARLORD NAMED MAWATU WAS ARMING HIS SUPPORTERS TO MOVE AGAINST THE JUNTA.
BUT WE COUDN'T FIGURE OUT WHERE THE GUNS OR MONEY WERE COMING FROM, AND SINCE WE WERE SECRETLY BACKING BOTH SIDES, THE MATTER HAD TO BE HANDLED DELICATELY.
CHATTER SUGGESTED THE MONEY WAS COMING FROM HUMAN TRAFFICKING AND POSSIBLE RUSSIAN MOB TIES.
I MEANT LOST, LIKE, HAVEN'T WE BEEN DOWN THIS HALLWAY BEFORE? BUT, PLEASE-- GO ON.
WITH THE HELP OF A MAN INSIDE MAWATU'S ORGANIZATION, WE SET UP A WIRE.
WHAT WE HEARD...WAS DISTURBING ENOUGH TO WARRANT FURTHER INVESTIGATION.
THIS WAS BACK BEFORE... NICARAGUA. BEFORE MY CLASSIFICATION CHANGED.
LATER, WHEN THE MAN WHO HELPED US WAS FOUND DEAD...
MAWATU HAD ATTAINED DIPLOMATIC STATUS. MY CLASSIFICATION ALLOWED ME TO INFILTRATE HIS ORGANIZATION ON U.S. SOIL WHILE PROTECTING THE C.I.A.'S PLAUSIBLE DENIABILITY.
WELL...HE WAS "DEAD."
NO... *DEAD.*
JUST LIKE YOU WERE DEAD.
I WAS NOT DEAD.
OBVIOUSLY.
I SAW THE MAN'S BODY.
I SAW YOUR BODY. IN FACT AS I MAY HAVE MENTIONED, I WENT TO YOUR FUNERAL.
ARE WE GOING TO DO THIS DANCE AGAIN?

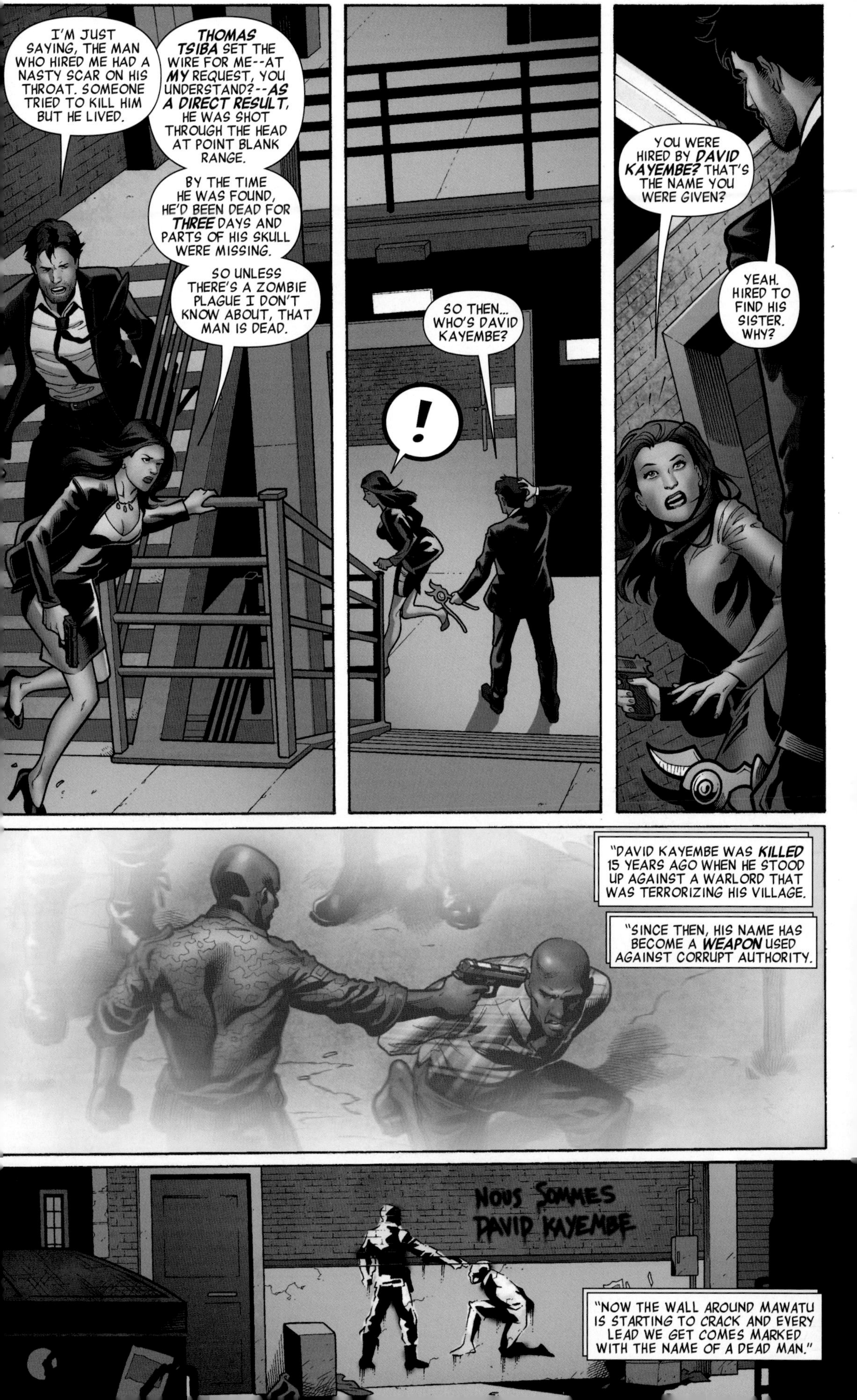
I'M JUST SAYING, THE MAN WHO HIRED ME HAD A NASTY SCAR ON HIS THROAT. SOMEONE TRIED TO KILL HIM BUT HE LIVED.
THOMAS TSIBA SET THE WIRE FOR ME--AT MY REQUEST, YOU UNDERSTAND?--AS A DIRECT RESULT, HE WAS SHOT THROUGH THE HEAD AT POINT BLANK RANGE.
BY THE TIME HE WAS FOUND, HE'D BEEN DEAD FOR THREE DAYS AND PARTS OF HIS SKULL WERE MISSING.
SO UNLESS THERE'S A ZOMBIE PLAGUE I DON'T KNOW ABOUT, THAT MAN IS DEAD.
!
SO THEN... WHO'S DAVID KAYEMBE?
YOU WERE HIRED BY DAVID KAYEMBE? THAT'S THE NAME YOU WERE GIVEN?
YEAH. HIRED TO FIND HIS SISTER. WHY?
"DAVID KAYEMBE WAS KILLED 15 YEARS AGO WHEN HE STOOD UP AGAINST A WARLORD THAT WAS TERRORIZING HIS VILLAGE.
"SINCE THEN, HIS NAME HAS BECOME A WEAPON USED AGAINST CORRUPT AUTHORITY.
NOUS SOMMES DAVID KAYEMBE
"NOW THE WALL AROUND MAWATU IS STARTING TO CRACK AND EVERY LEAD WE GET COMES MARKED WITH THE NAME OF A DEAD MAN."

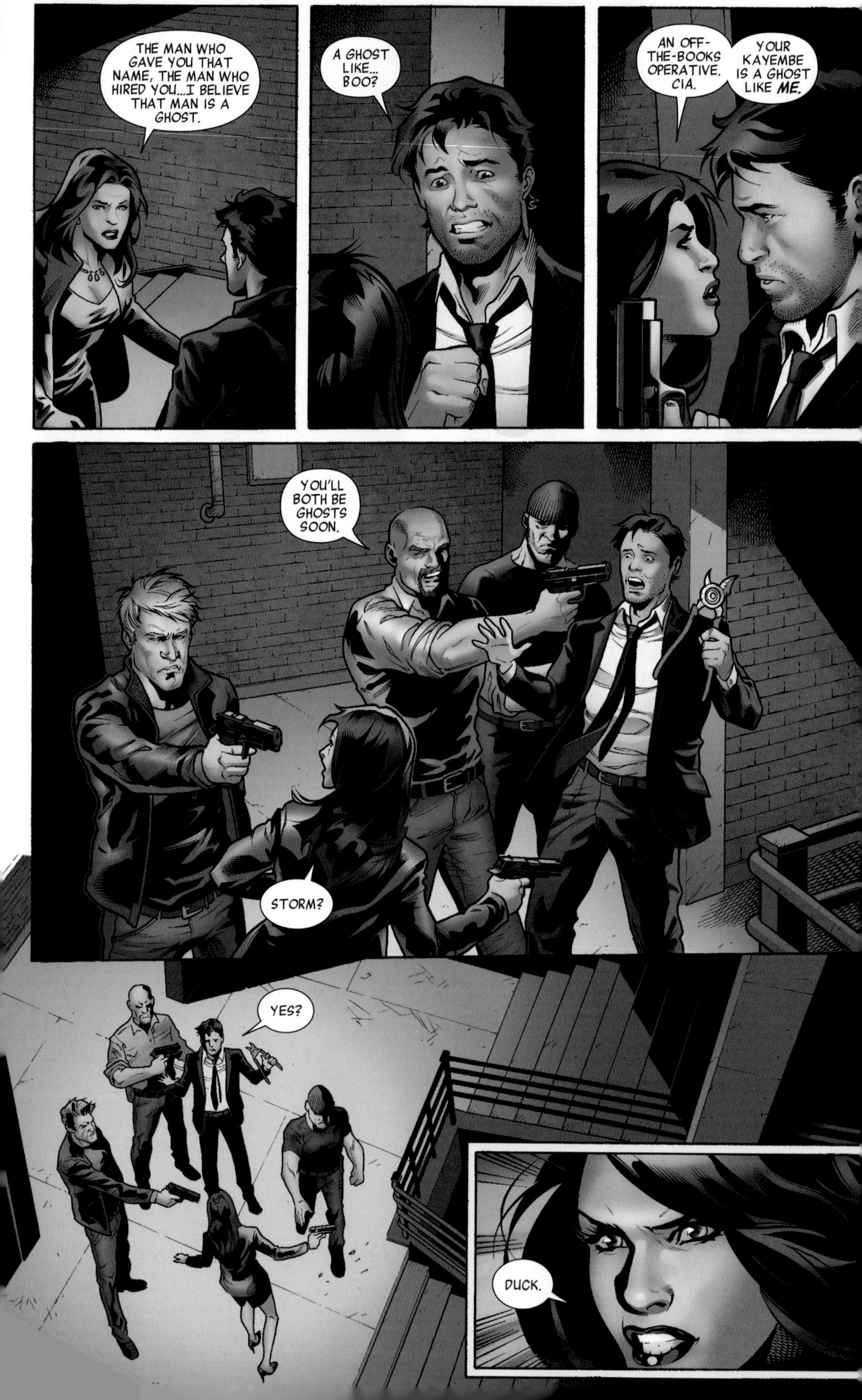
THE MAN WHO GAVE YOU THAT NAME, THE MAN WHO HIRED YOU...I BELIEVE THAT MAN IS A GHOST.
A GHOST LIKE... BOO?
AN OFF-THE-BOOKS OPERATIVE. CIA.
YOUR KAYEMBE IS A GHOST LIKE ME.
YOU'LL BOTH BE GHOSTS SOON.
STORM?
YES?
DUCK.

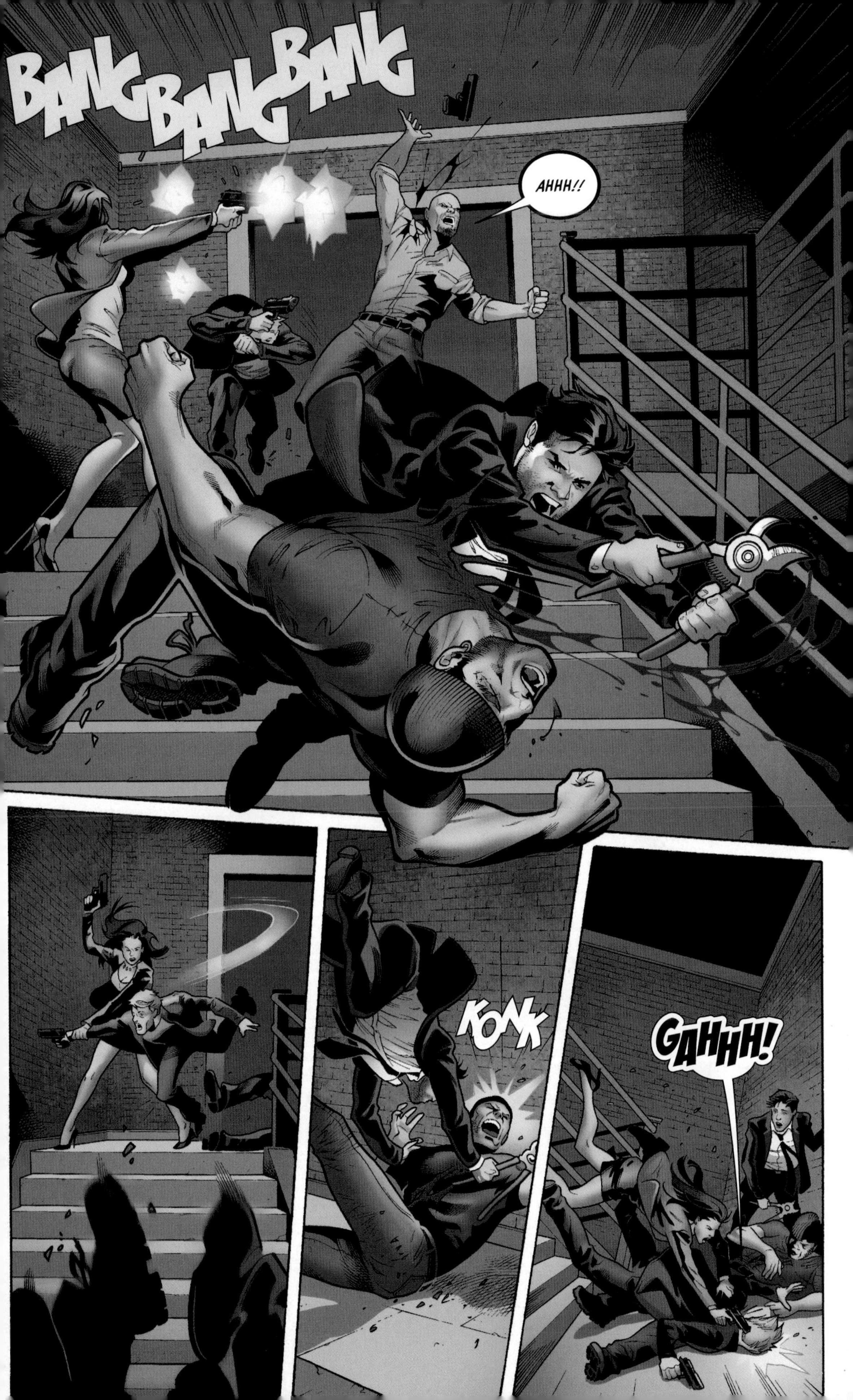
BANG BANG BANG
AHHH!!
KONK
GAHHH!

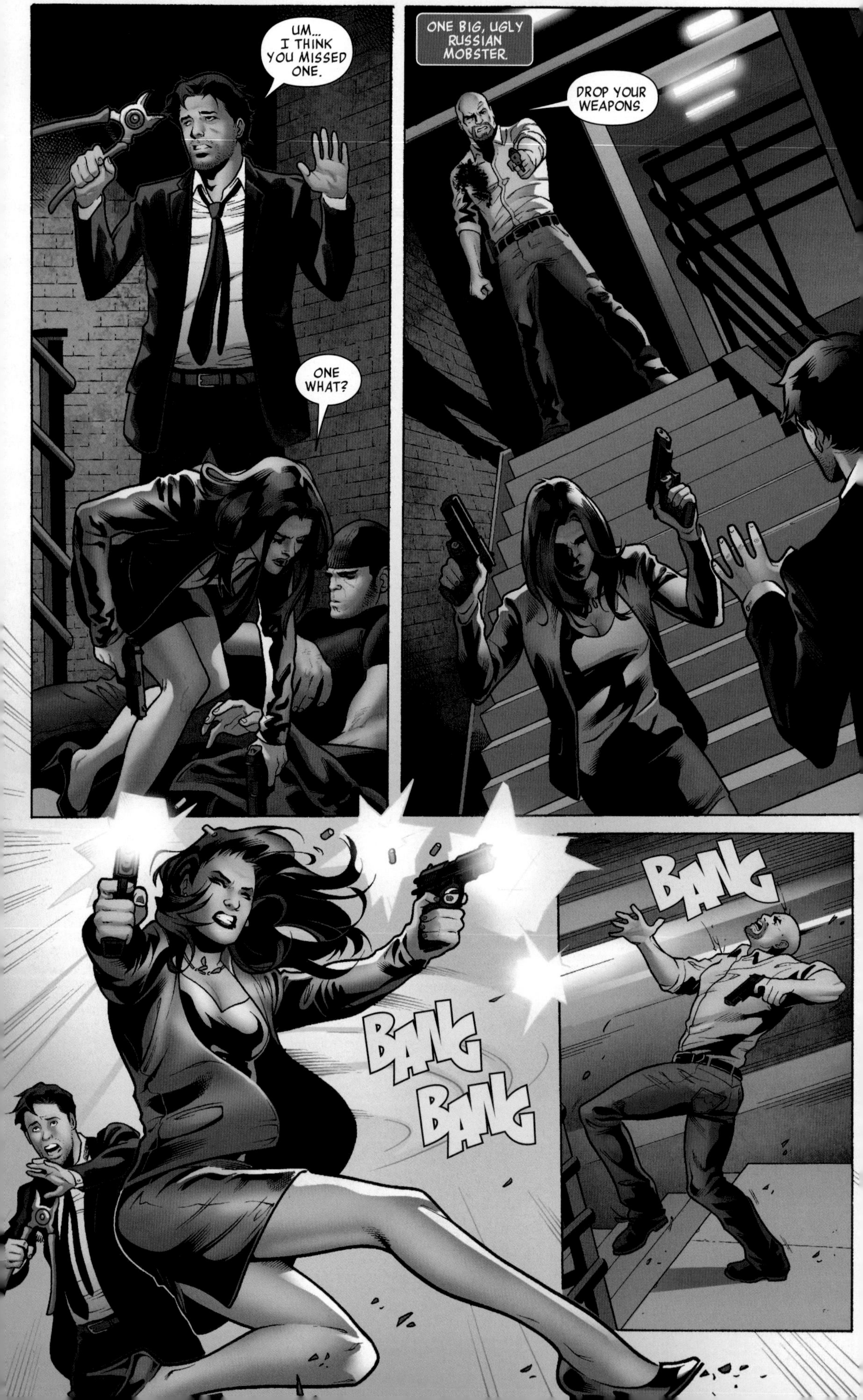
UM... I THINK YOU MISSED ONE.
ONE WHAT?
ONE BIG, UGLY RUSSIAN MOBSTER.
DROP YOUR WEAPONS.
BANG
BANG
BANG

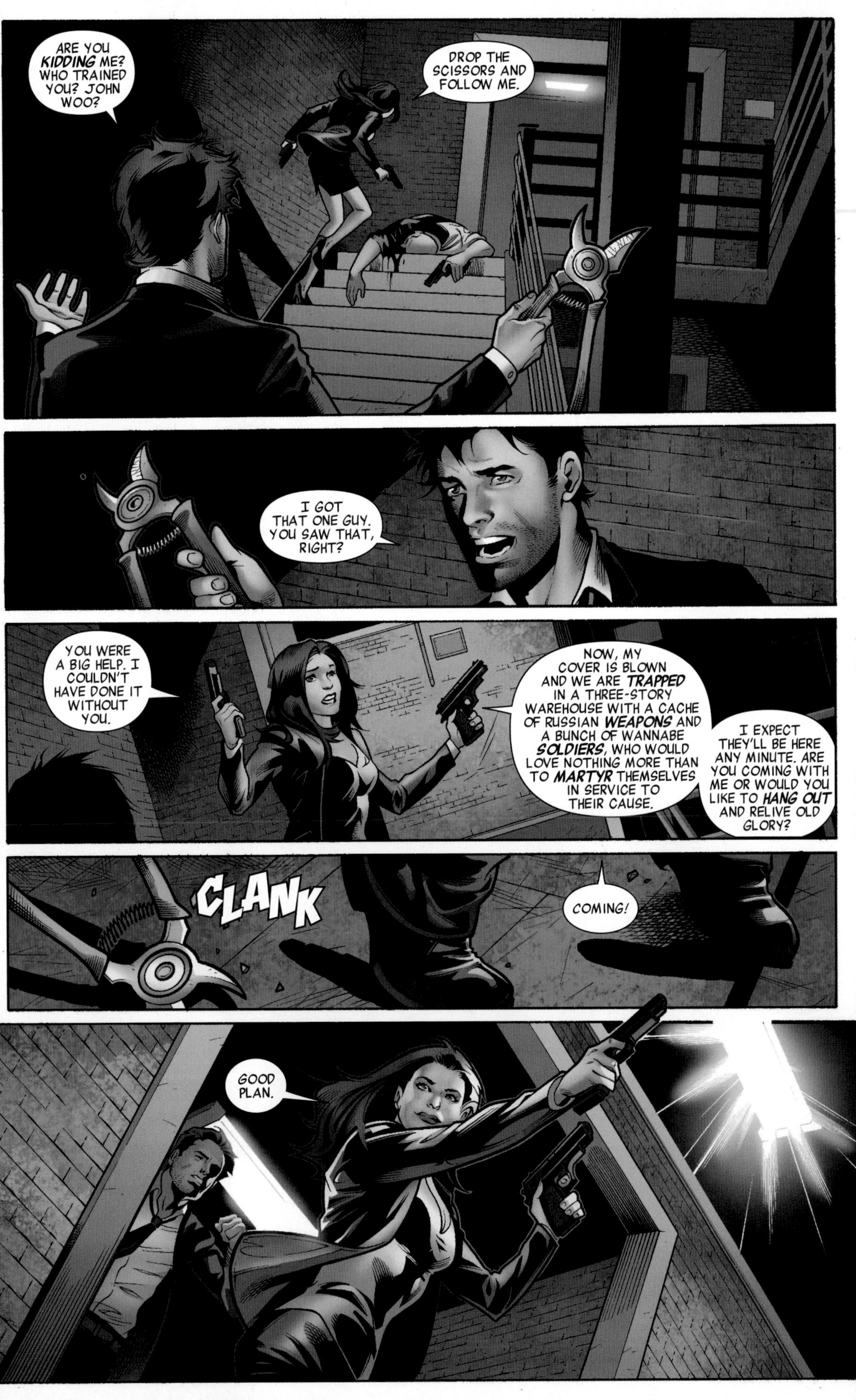
ARE YOU KIDDING ME? WHO TRAINED YOU? JOHN WOO?
DROP THE SCISSORS AND FOLLOW ME.
I GOT THAT ONE GUY. YOU SAW THAT, RIGHT?
YOU WERE A BIG HELP. I COULDN'T HAVE DONE IT WITHOUT YOU.
NOW, MY COVER IS BLOWN AND WE ARE TRAPPED IN A THREE-STORY WAREHOUSE WITH A CACHE OF RUSSIAN WEAPONS AND A BUNCH OF WANNABE SOLDIERS, WHO WOULD LOVE NOTHING MORE THAN TO MARTYR THEMSELVES IN SERVICE TO THEIR CAUSE.
I EXPECT THEY'LL BE HERE ANY MINUTE. ARE YOU COMING WITH ME OR WOULD YOU LIKE TO HANG OUT AND RELIVE OLD GLORY?
CLANK
COMING!
GOOD PLAN.

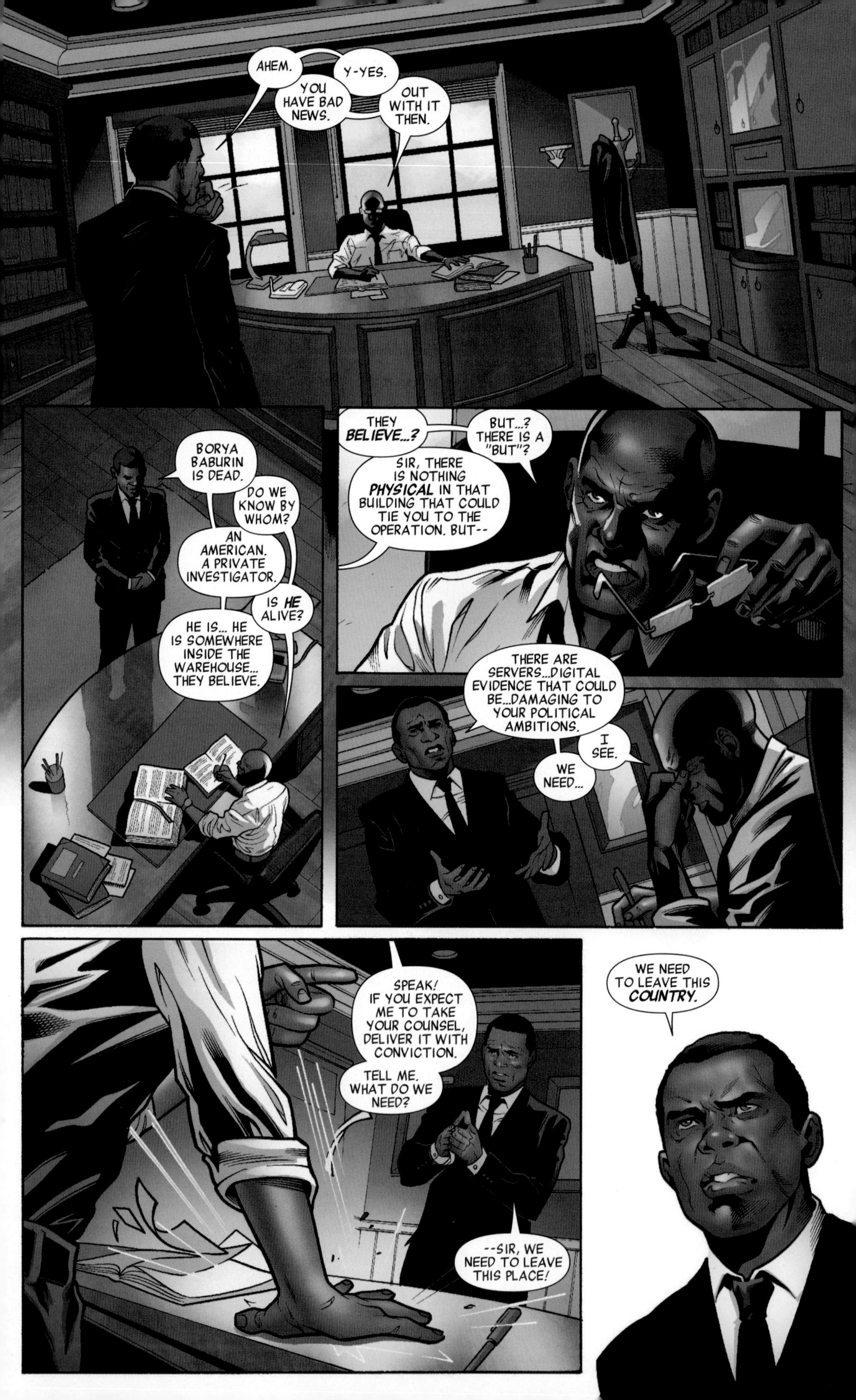
AHEM.
Y-YES.
YOU HAVE BAD NEWS.
OUT WITH IT THEN.
BORYA BABURIN IS DEAD.
DO WE KNOW BY WHOM?
AN AMERICAN. A PRIVATE INVESTIGATOR.
IS HE ALIVE?
HE IS... HE IS SOMEWHERE INSIDE THE WAREHOUSE... THEY BELIEVE.
THEY BELIEVE...?
SIR, THERE IS NOTHING PHYSICAL IN THAT BUILDING THAT COULD TIE YOU TO THE OPERATION. BUT--
BUT...? THERE IS A "BUT"?
THERE ARE SERVERS...DIGITAL EVIDENCE THAT COULD BE...DAMAGING TO YOUR POLITICAL AMBITIONS.
I SEE.
WE NEED...
SPEAK! IF YOU EXPECT ME TO TAKE YOUR COUNSEL, DELIVER IT WITH CONVICTION.
TELL ME. WHAT DO WE NEED?
--SIR, WE NEED TO LEAVE THIS PLACE!
WE NEED TO LEAVE THIS COUNTRY.

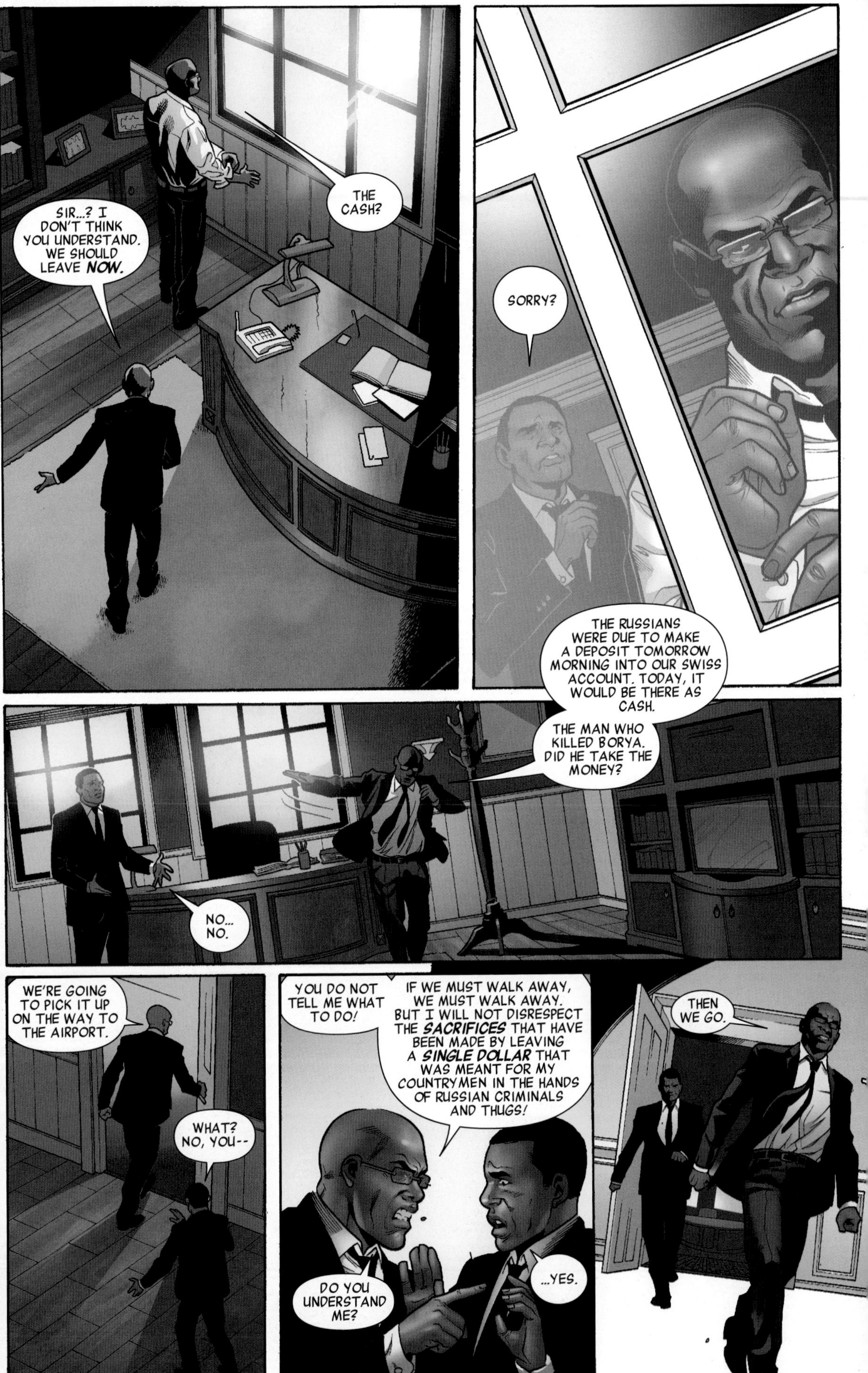
THE CASH?
SIR...? I DON'T THINK YOU UNDERSTAND. WE SHOULD LEAVE **NOW.**
SORRY?
THE RUSSIANS WERE DUE TO MAKE A DEPOSIT TOMORROW MORNING INTO OUR SWISS ACCOUNT. TODAY, IT WOULD BE THERE AS CASH.
THE MAN WHO KILLED BORYA. DID HE TAKE THE MONEY?
NO... NO.
WE'RE GOING TO PICK IT UP ON THE WAY TO THE AIRPORT.
WHAT? NO, YOU--
YOU DO NOT TELL ME WHAT TO DO!
IF WE MUST WALK AWAY, WE MUST WALK AWAY. BUT I WILL NOT DISRESPECT THE **SACRIFICES** THAT HAVE BEEN MADE BY LEAVING A **SINGLE DOLLAR** THAT WAS MEANT FOR MY COUNTRYMEN IN THE HANDS OF RUSSIAN CRIMINALS AND THUGS!
DO YOU UNDERSTAND ME?
...YES.
THEN WE GO.

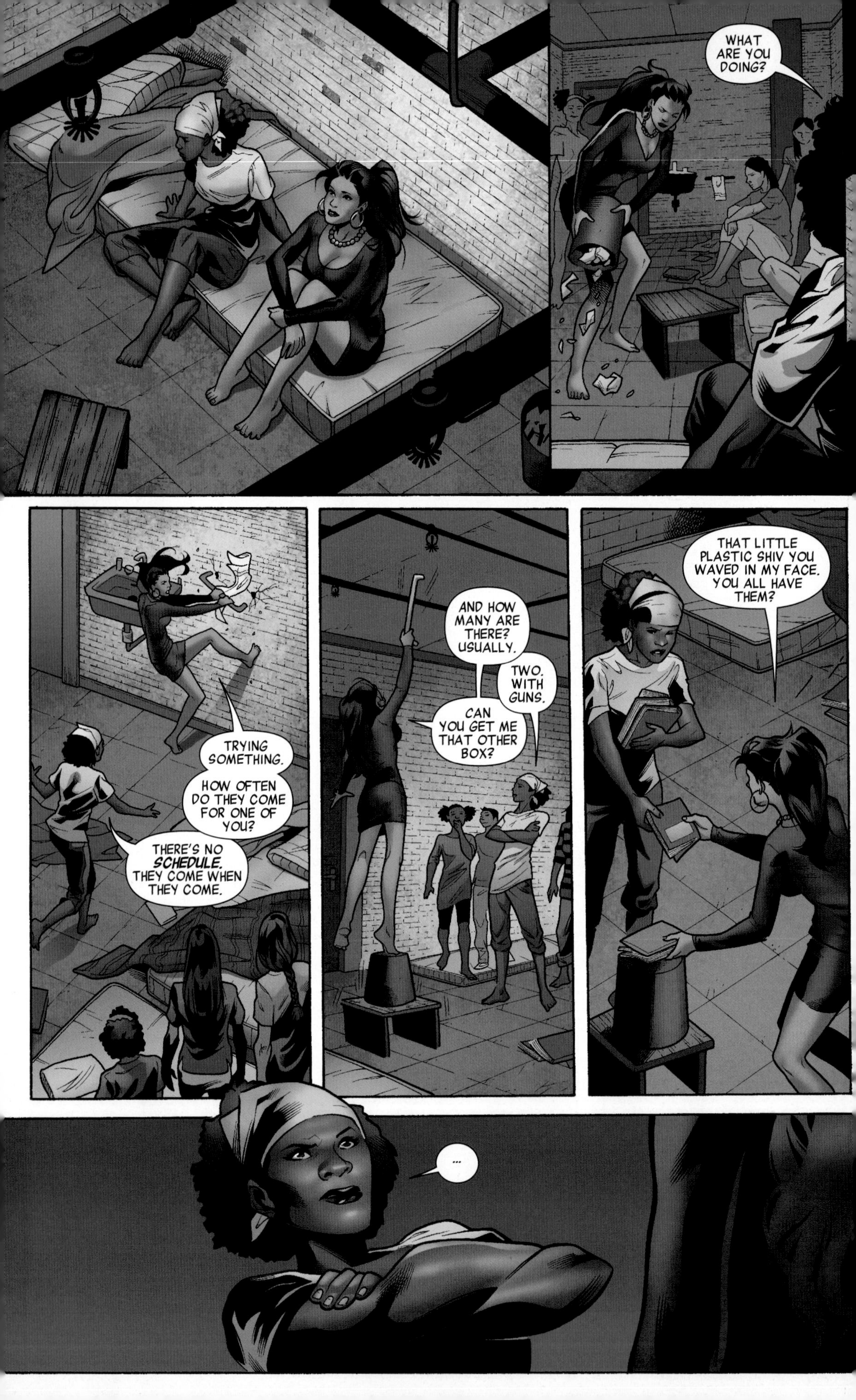
WHAT ARE YOU DOING?
TRYING SOMETHING.
HOW OFTEN DO THEY COME FOR ONE OF YOU?
THERE'S NO ***SCHEDULE.*** THEY COME WHEN THEY COME.
AND HOW MANY ARE THERE? USUALLY.
TWO. WITH GUNS.
CAN YOU GET ME THAT OTHER BOX?
THAT LITTLE PLASTIC SHIV YOU WAVED IN MY FACE. YOU ALL HAVE THEM?
...

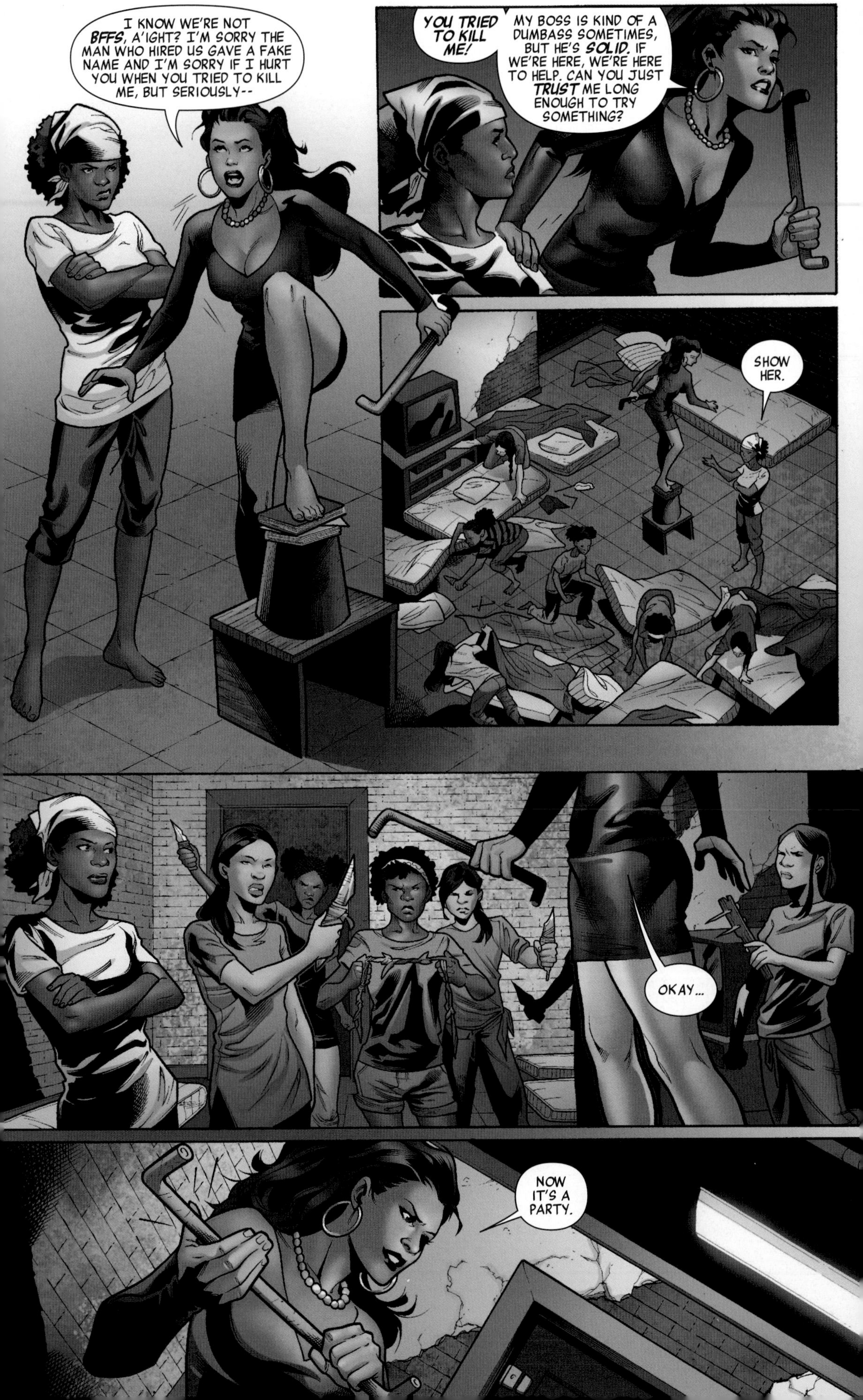
I KNOW WE'RE NOT BFFS, A'IGHT? I'M SORRY THE MAN WHO HIRED US GAVE A FAKE NAME AND I'M SORRY IF I HURT YOU WHEN YOU TRIED TO KILL ME, BUT SERIOUSLY--
YOU TRIED TO KILL ME!
MY BOSS IS KIND OF A DUMBASS SOMETIMES, BUT HE'S SOLID. IF WE'RE HERE, WE'RE HERE TO HELP. CAN YOU JUST TRUST ME LONG ENOUGH TO TRY SOMETHING?
SHOW HER.
OKAY...
NOW IT'S A PARTY.

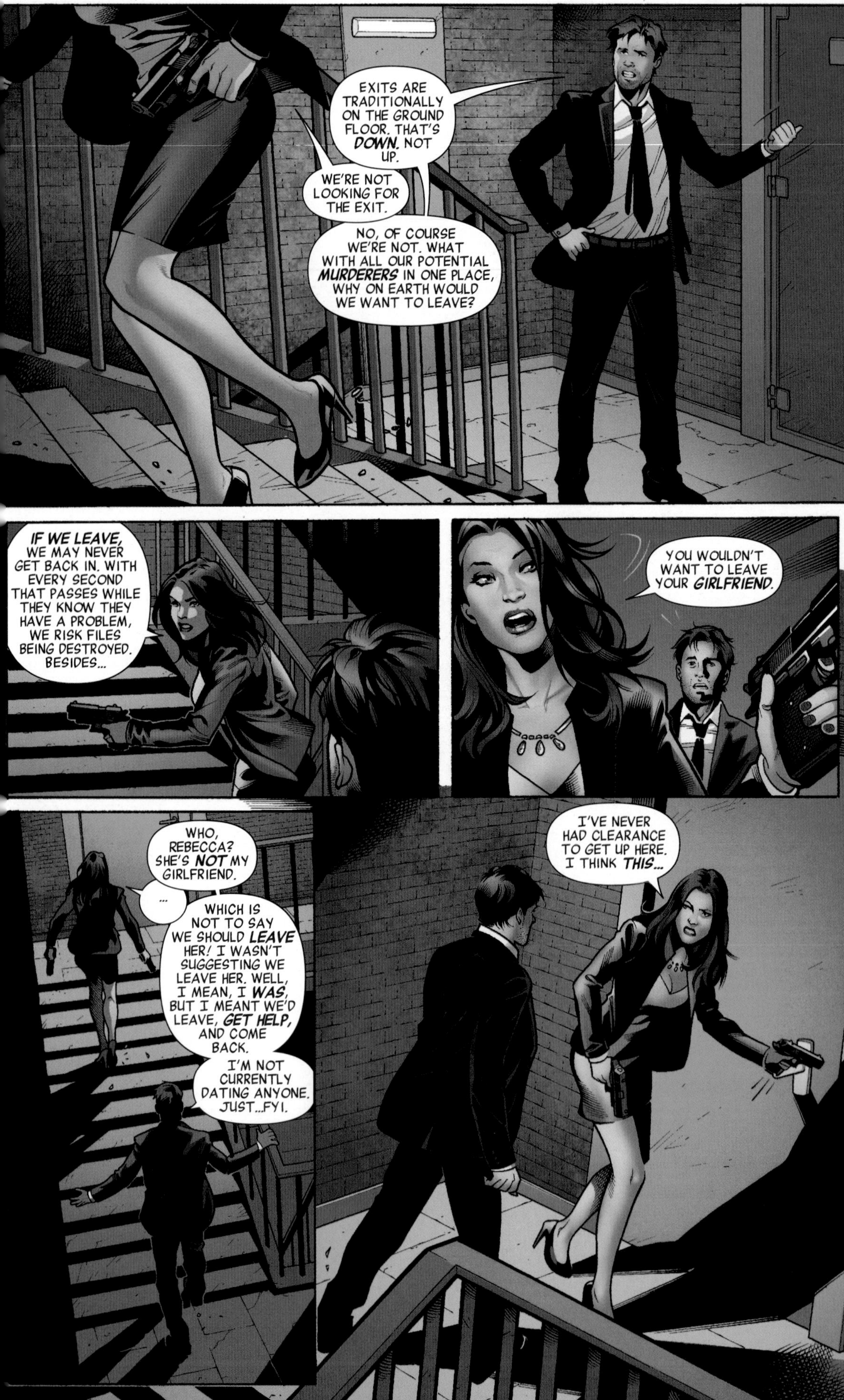
EXITS ARE TRADITIONALLY ON THE GROUND FLOOR. THAT'S **DOWN.** NOT UP.
WE'RE NOT LOOKING FOR THE EXIT.
NO, OF COURSE WE'RE NOT. WHAT WITH ALL OUR POTENTIAL **MURDERERS** IN ONE PLACE, WHY ON EARTH WOULD WE WANT TO LEAVE?
IF WE LEAVE, WE MAY NEVER GET BACK IN. WITH EVERY SECOND THAT PASSES WHILE THEY KNOW THEY HAVE A PROBLEM, WE RISK FILES BEING DESTROYED. BESIDES...
YOU WOULDN'T WANT TO LEAVE YOUR **GIRLFRIEND.**
WHO, REBECCA? SHE'S **NOT** MY GIRLFRIEND.
...
WHICH IS NOT TO SAY WE SHOULD **LEAVE** HER! I WASN'T SUGGESTING WE LEAVE HER. WELL, I MEAN, I **WAS,** BUT I MEANT WE'D LEAVE, **GET HELP,** AND COME BACK.
I'M NOT CURRENTLY DATING ANYONE. JUST...FYI.
I'VE NEVER HAD CLEARANCE TO GET UP HERE. I THINK **THIS...**

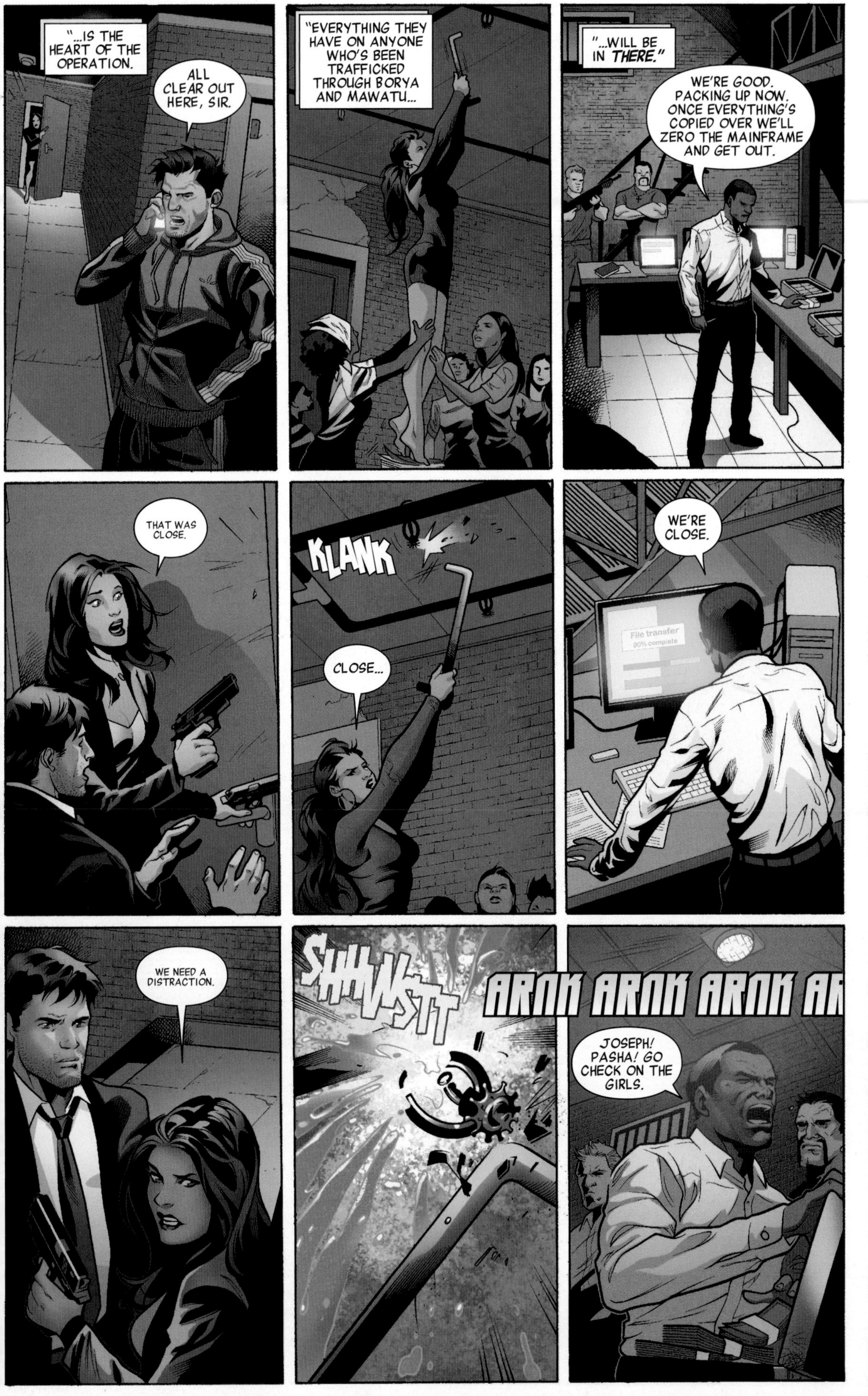
"...IS THE HEART OF THE OPERATION.
ALL CLEAR OUT HERE, SIR.
"EVERYTHING THEY HAVE ON ANYONE WHO'S BEEN TRAFFICKED THROUGH BORYA AND MAWATU...
"...WILL BE IN THERE."
WE'RE GOOD. PACKING UP NOW. ONCE EVERYTHING'S COPIED OVER WE'LL ZERO THE MAINFRAME AND GET OUT.
THAT WAS CLOSE.
KLANK
CLOSE...
WE'RE CLOSE.
File transfer
90% complete
WE NEED A DISTRACTION.
SHHVSTT
ARNK ARNK ARNK AR
JOSEPH! PASHA! GO CHECK ON THE GIRLS.

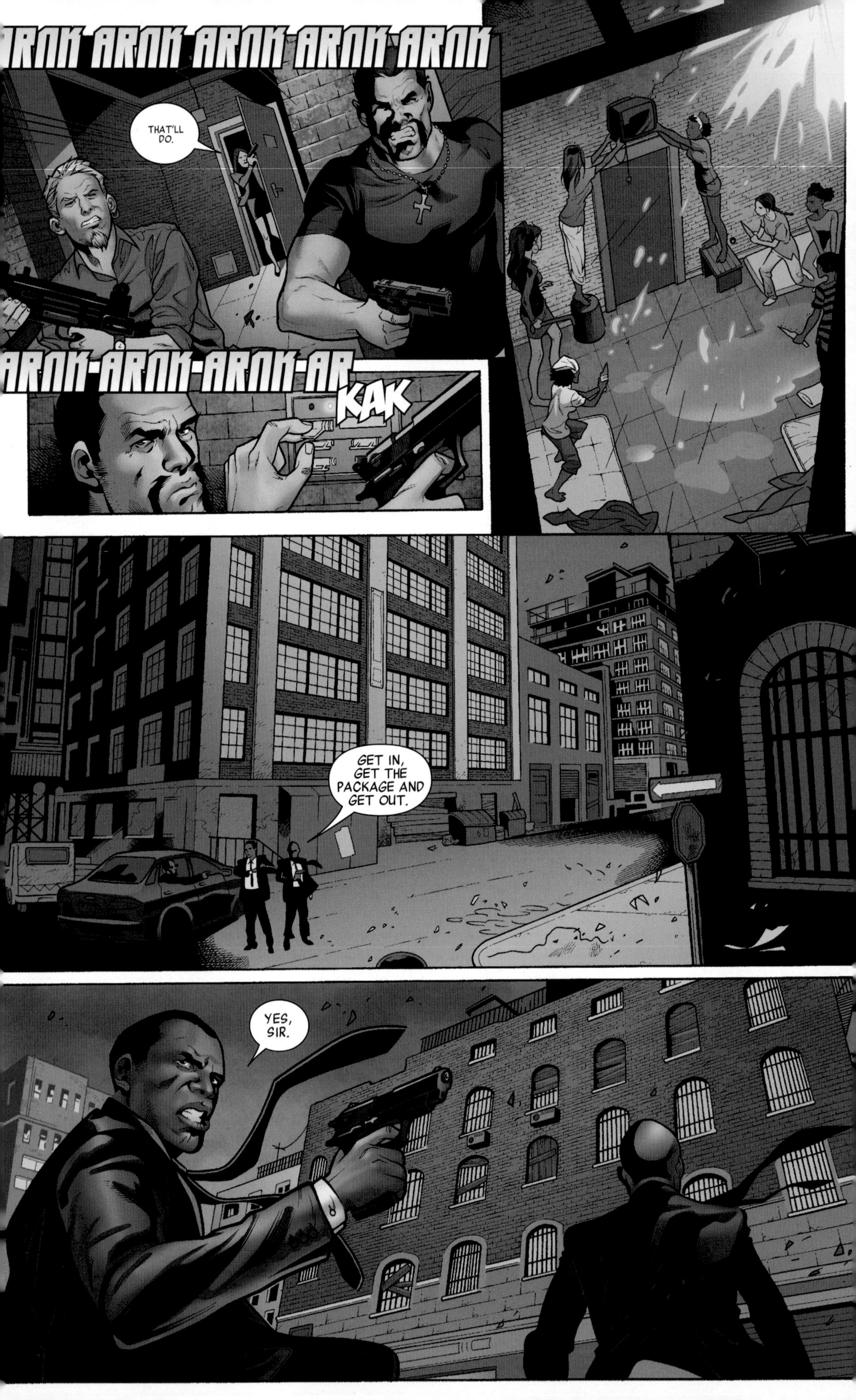

ARNK ARNK ARNK ARNK ARNK
THAT'LL DO.
ARNK-ARNK-ARNK-AR
KAK
GET IN, GET THE PACKAGE AND GET OUT.
YES, SIR.

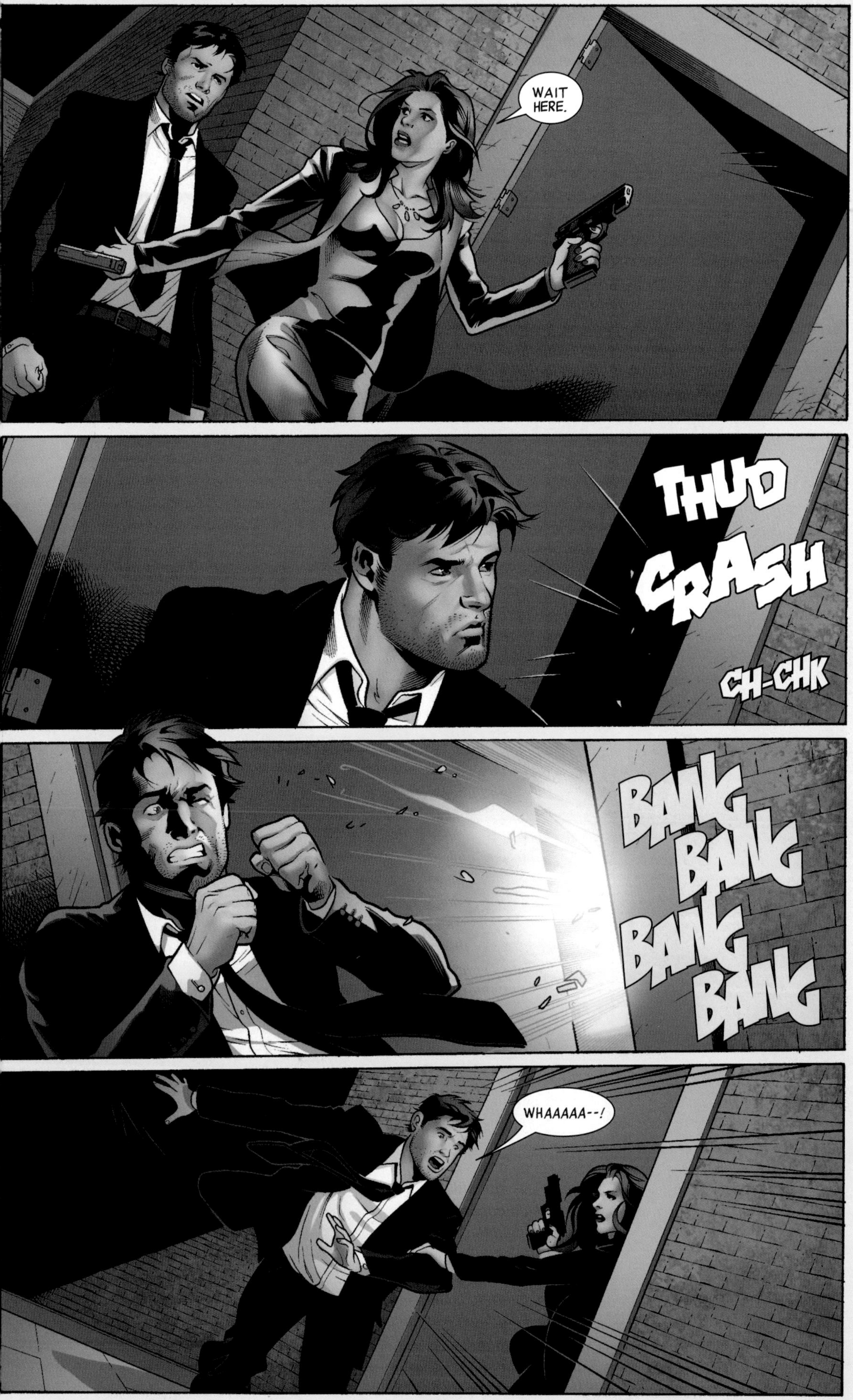
WAIT HERE.
THUD
CRASH
CH-CHK
BANG
BANG
BANG
BANG
WHAAAAA--!

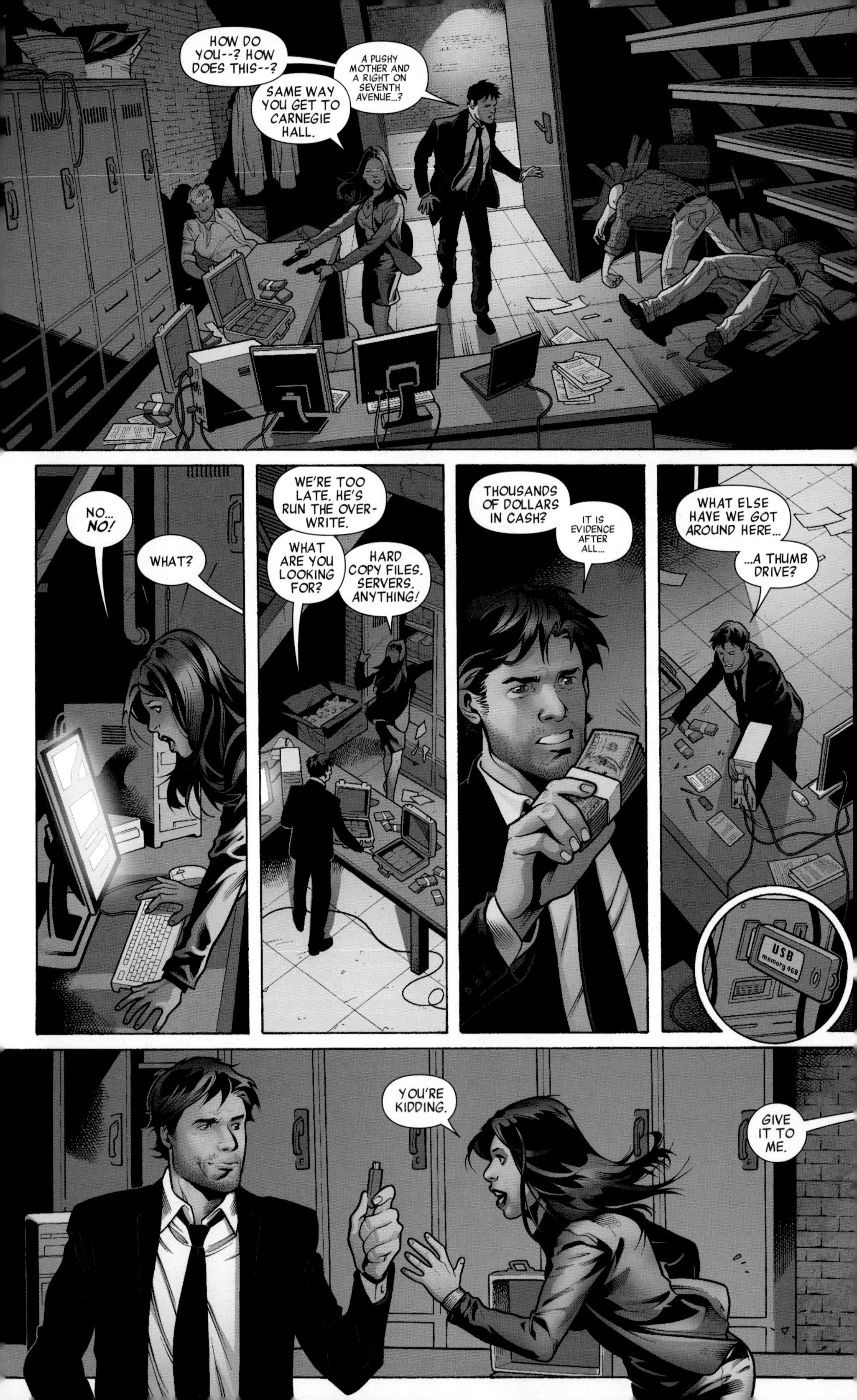
HOW DO YOU--? HOW DOES THIS--?
A PUSHY MOTHER AND A RIGHT ON SEVENTH AVENUE...?
SAME WAY YOU GET TO CARNEGIE HALL.
NO... NO!
WHAT?
WE'RE TOO LATE. HE'S RUN THE OVER-WRITE.
WHAT ARE YOU LOOKING FOR?
HARD COPY FILES. SERVERS. ANYTHING!
THOUSANDS OF DOLLARS IN CASH?
IT IS EVIDENCE AFTER ALL...
WHAT ELSE HAVE WE GOT AROUND HERE...
...A THUMB DRIVE?
USB
memory 4GB
YOU'RE KIDDING.
GIVE IT TO ME.

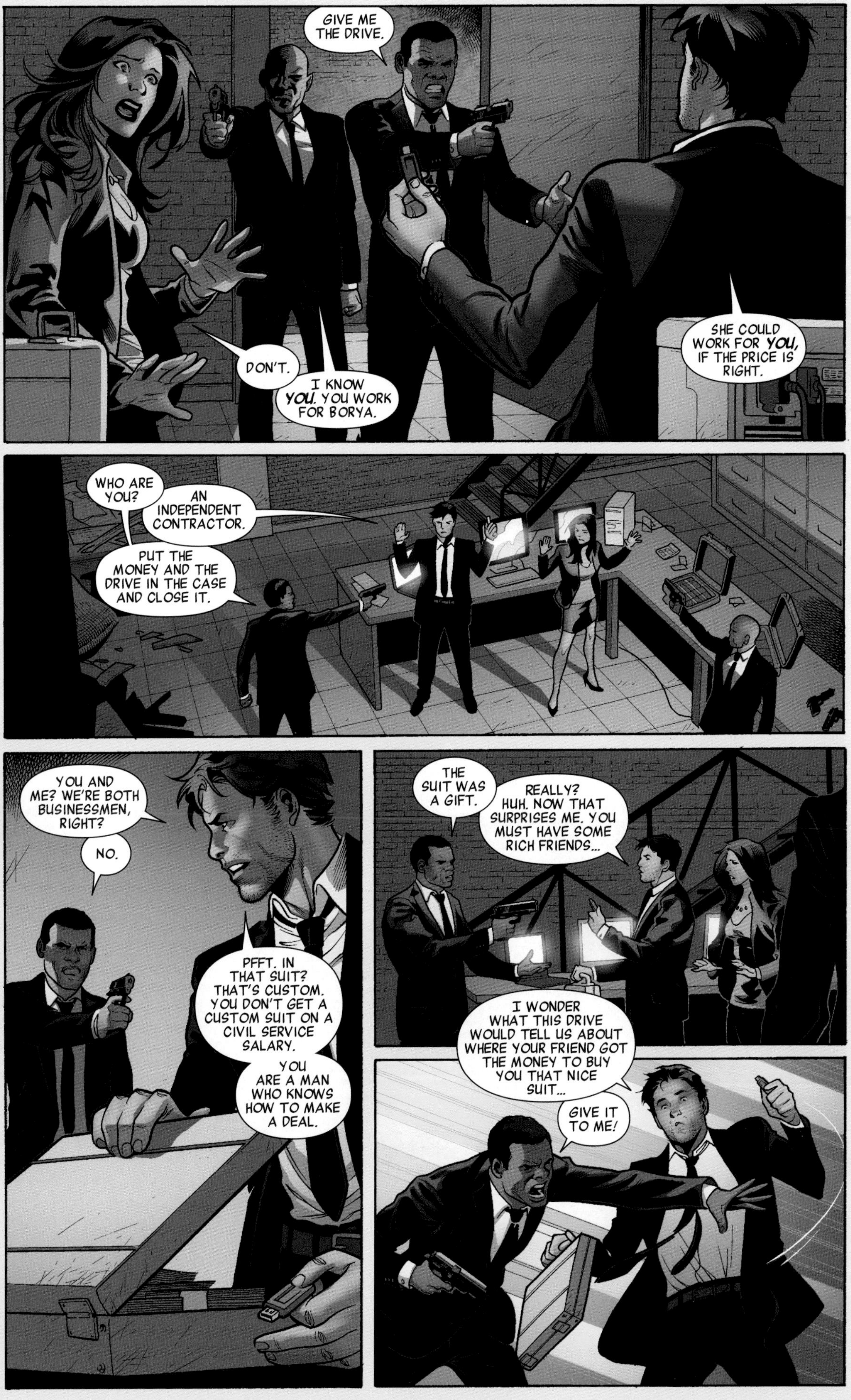
GIVE ME THE DRIVE.
DON'T.
I KNOW *YOU*. YOU WORK FOR BORYA.
SHE COULD WORK FOR *YOU*, IF THE PRICE IS RIGHT.
WHO ARE YOU?
AN INDEPENDENT CONTRACTOR.
PUT THE MONEY AND THE DRIVE IN THE CASE AND CLOSE IT.
YOU AND ME? WE'RE BOTH BUSINESSMEN, RIGHT?
NO.
PFFT. IN THAT SUIT? THAT'S CUSTOM. YOU DON'T GET A CUSTOM SUIT ON A CIVIL SERVICE SALARY.
YOU ARE A MAN WHO KNOWS HOW TO MAKE A DEAL.
THE SUIT WAS A GIFT.
REALLY? HUH. NOW THAT SURPRISES ME. YOU MUST HAVE SOME RICH FRIENDS...
I WONDER WHAT THIS DRIVE WOULD TELL US ABOUT WHERE YOUR FRIEND GOT THE MONEY TO BUY YOU THAT NICE SUIT...
GIVE IT TO ME!

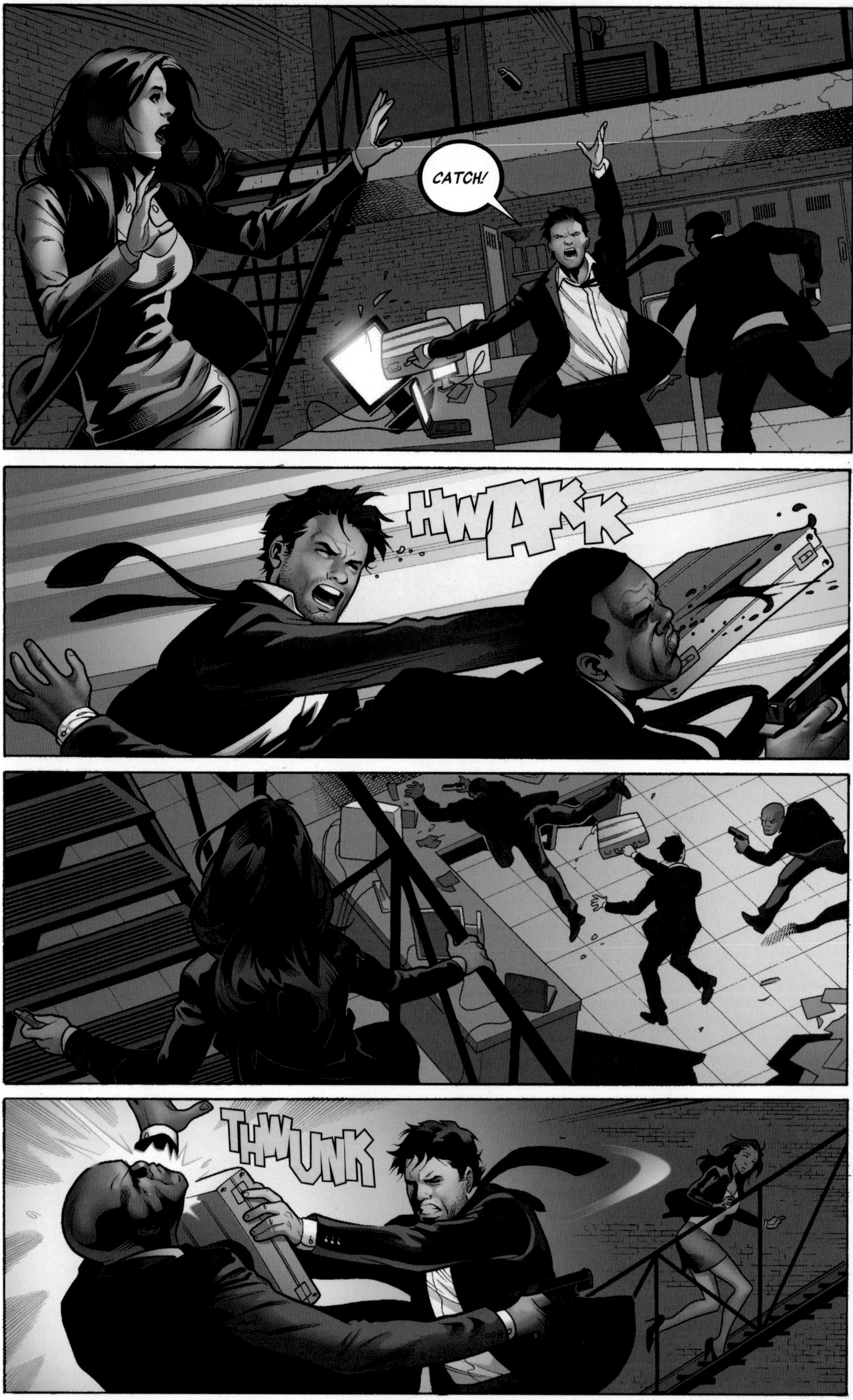
CATCH!
HWAKK
THWUNK

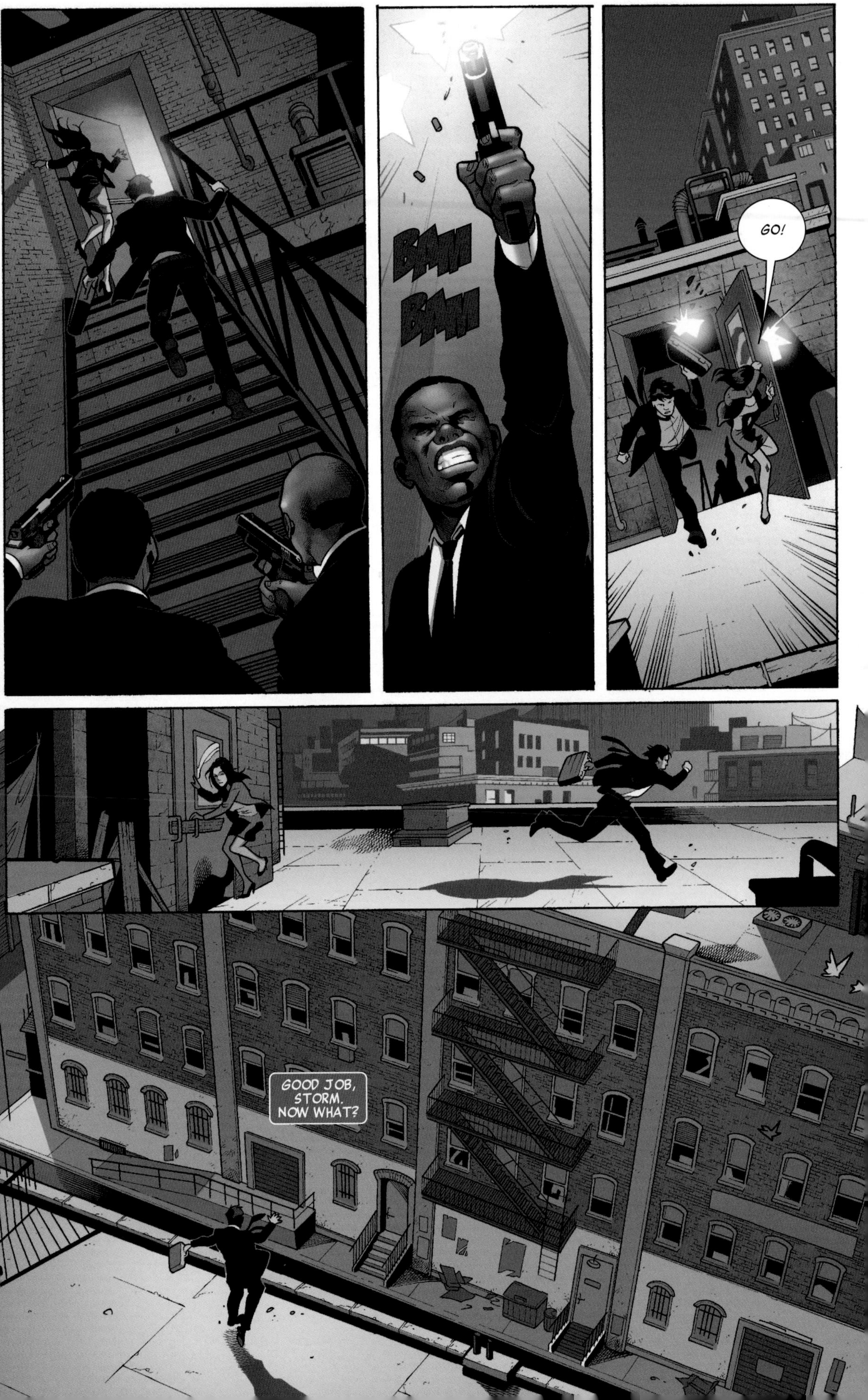
BAM
BAM
GO!
GOOD JOB, STORM. NOW WHAT?

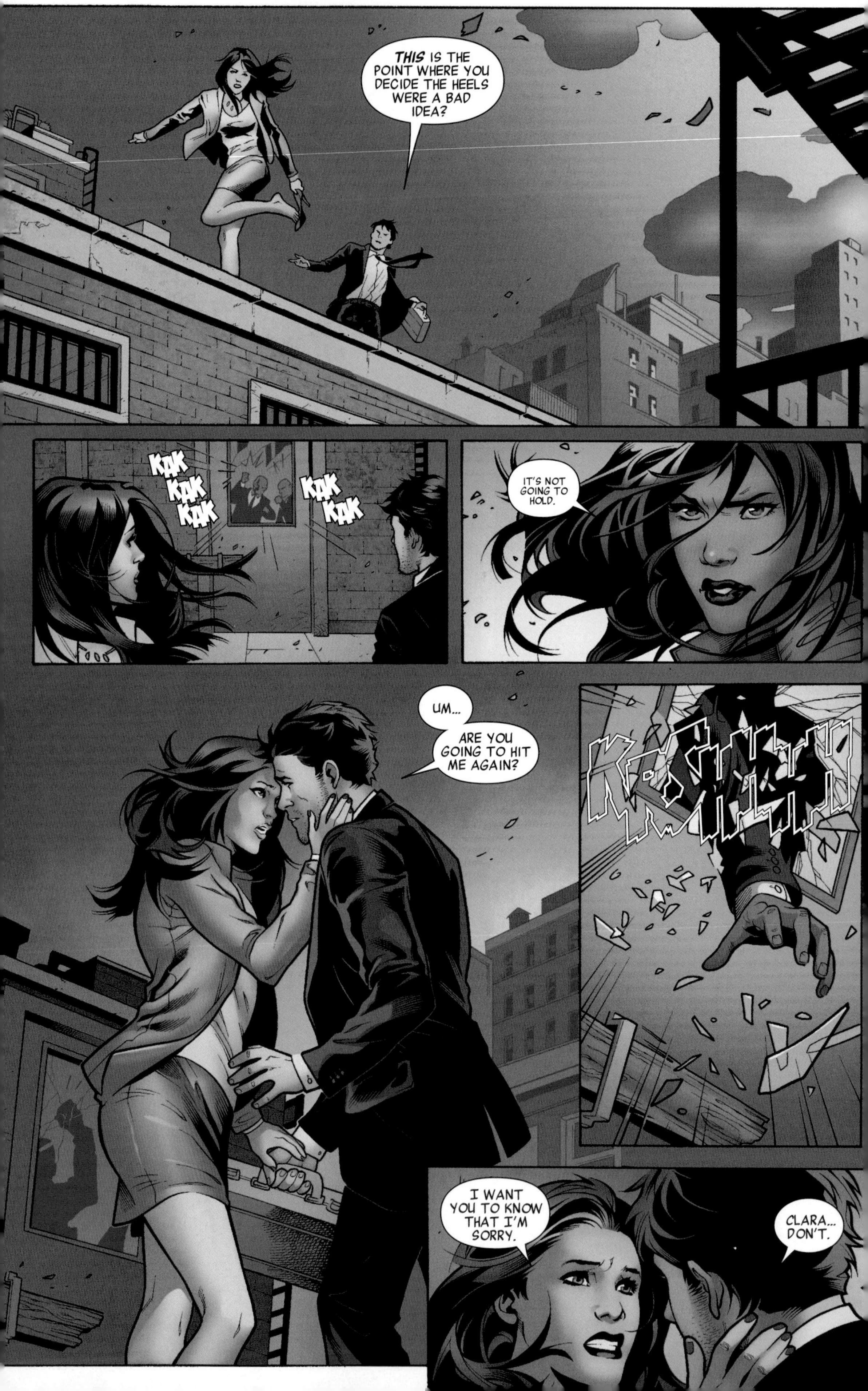
THIS IS THE POINT WHERE YOU DECIDE THE HEELS WERE A BAD IDEA?
KAK KAK KAK
KAK KAK
IT'S NOT GOING TO HOLD.
UM...
ARE YOU GOING TO HIT ME AGAIN?
I WANT YOU TO KNOW THAT I'M SORRY.
CLARA... DON'T.

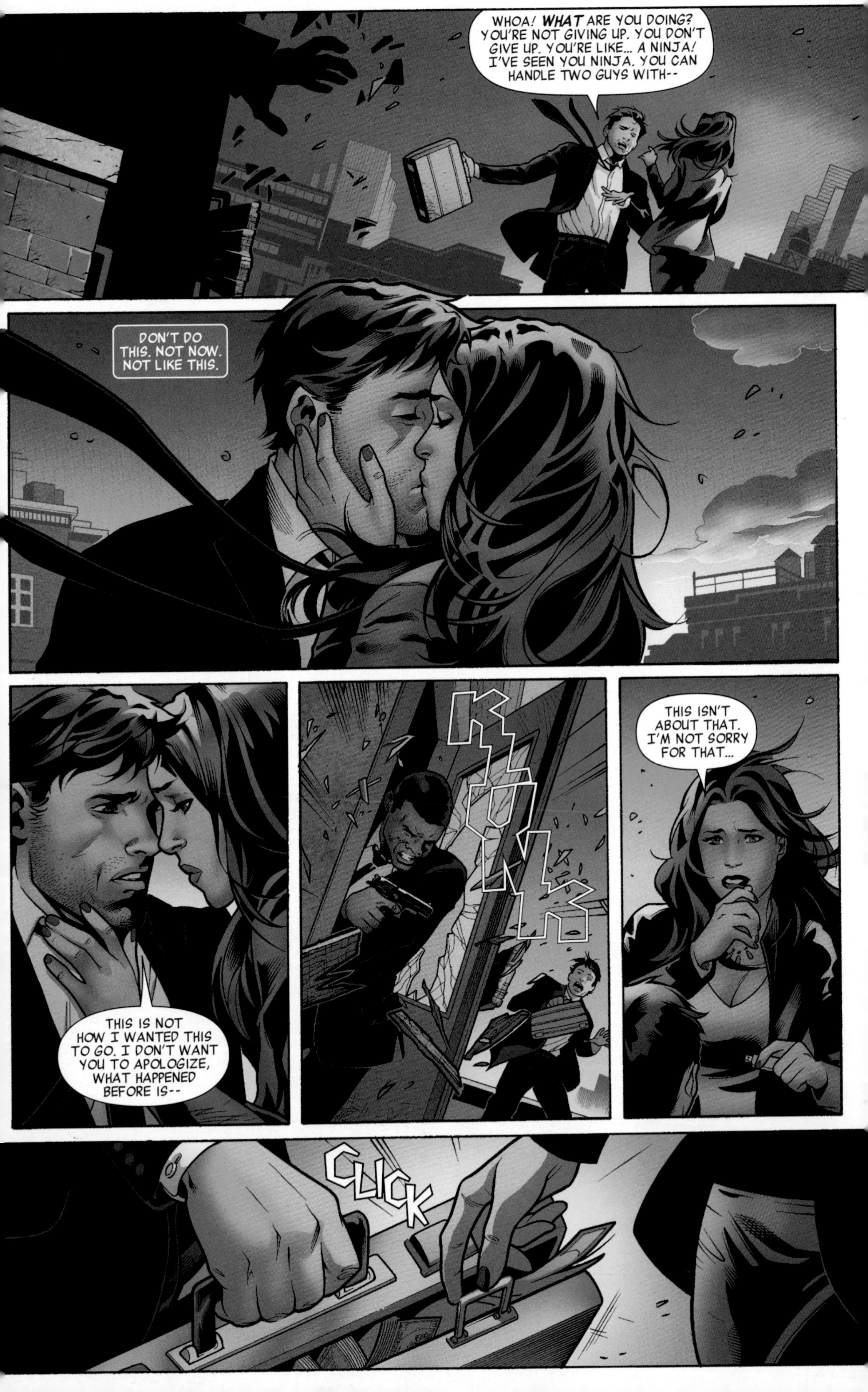

WHOA! WHAT ARE YOU DOING? YOU'RE NOT GIVING UP. YOU DON'T GIVE UP. YOU'RE LIKE... A NINJA! I'VE SEEN YOU NINJA. YOU CAN HANDLE TWO GUYS WITH--
DON'T DO THIS. NOT NOW. NOT LIKE THIS.
THIS IS NOT HOW I WANTED THIS TO GO. I DON'T WANT YOU TO APOLOGIZE, WHAT HAPPENED BEFORE IS--
KLUNK
THIS ISN'T ABOUT THAT. I'M NOT SORRY FOR THAT...
CLICK

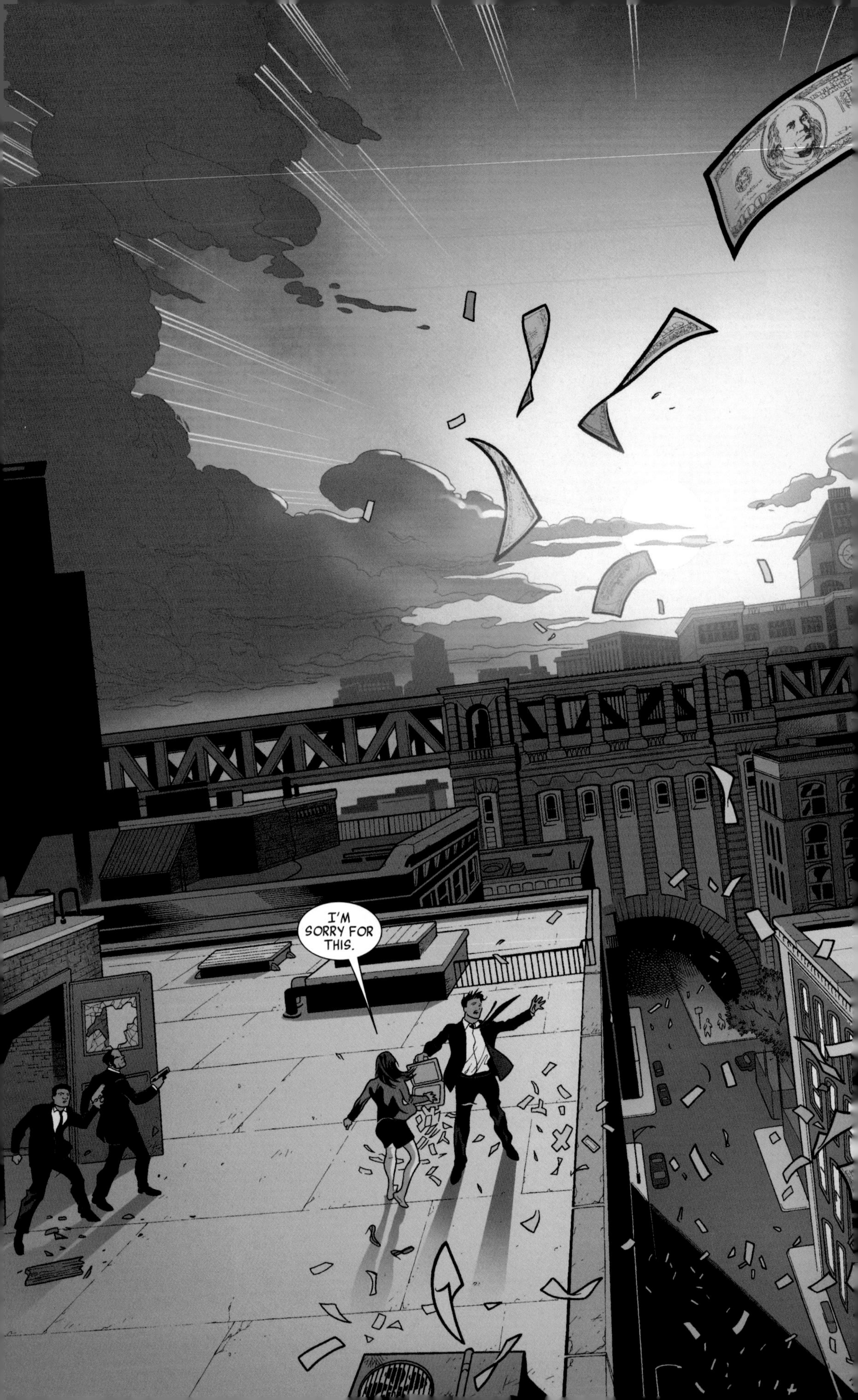
I'M SORRY FOR THIS.

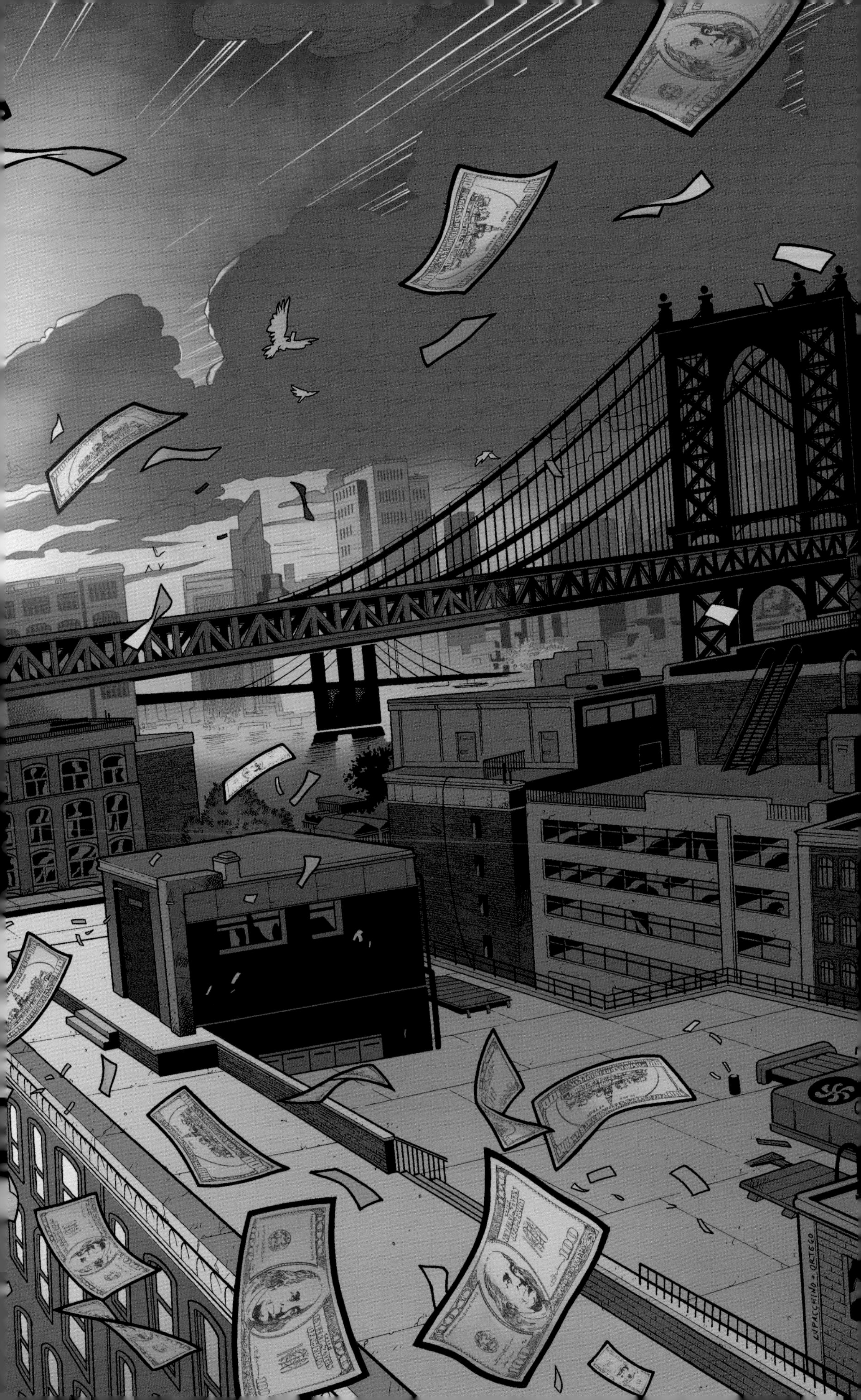
LUPACCHINO + ORTEGO

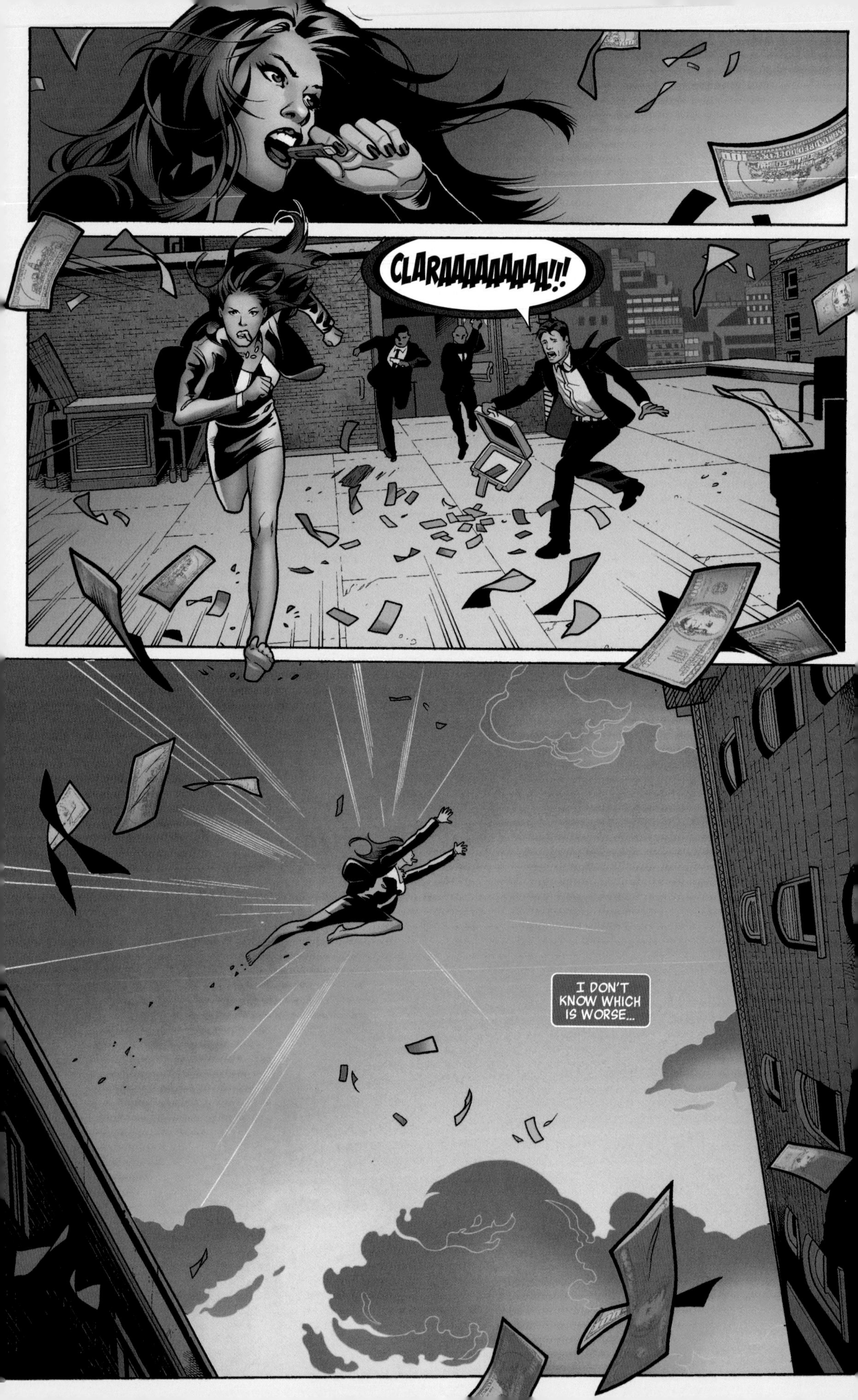
CLARAAAAAAAA!!!
I DON'T KNOW WHICH IS WORSE...

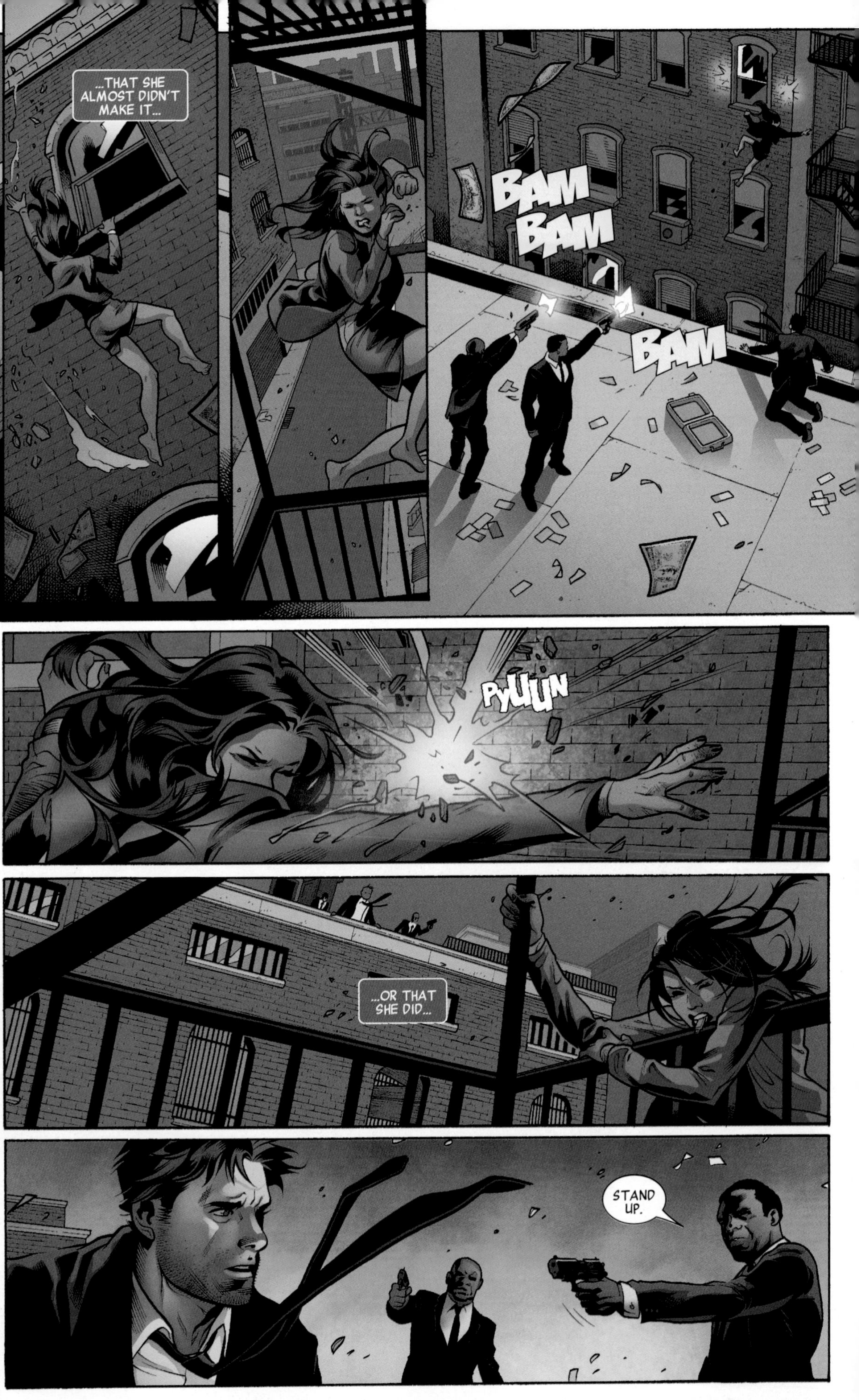
...THAT SHE ALMOST DIDN'T MAKE IT...
BAM
BAM
BAM
PYUUN
...OR THAT SHE DID...
STAND UP.

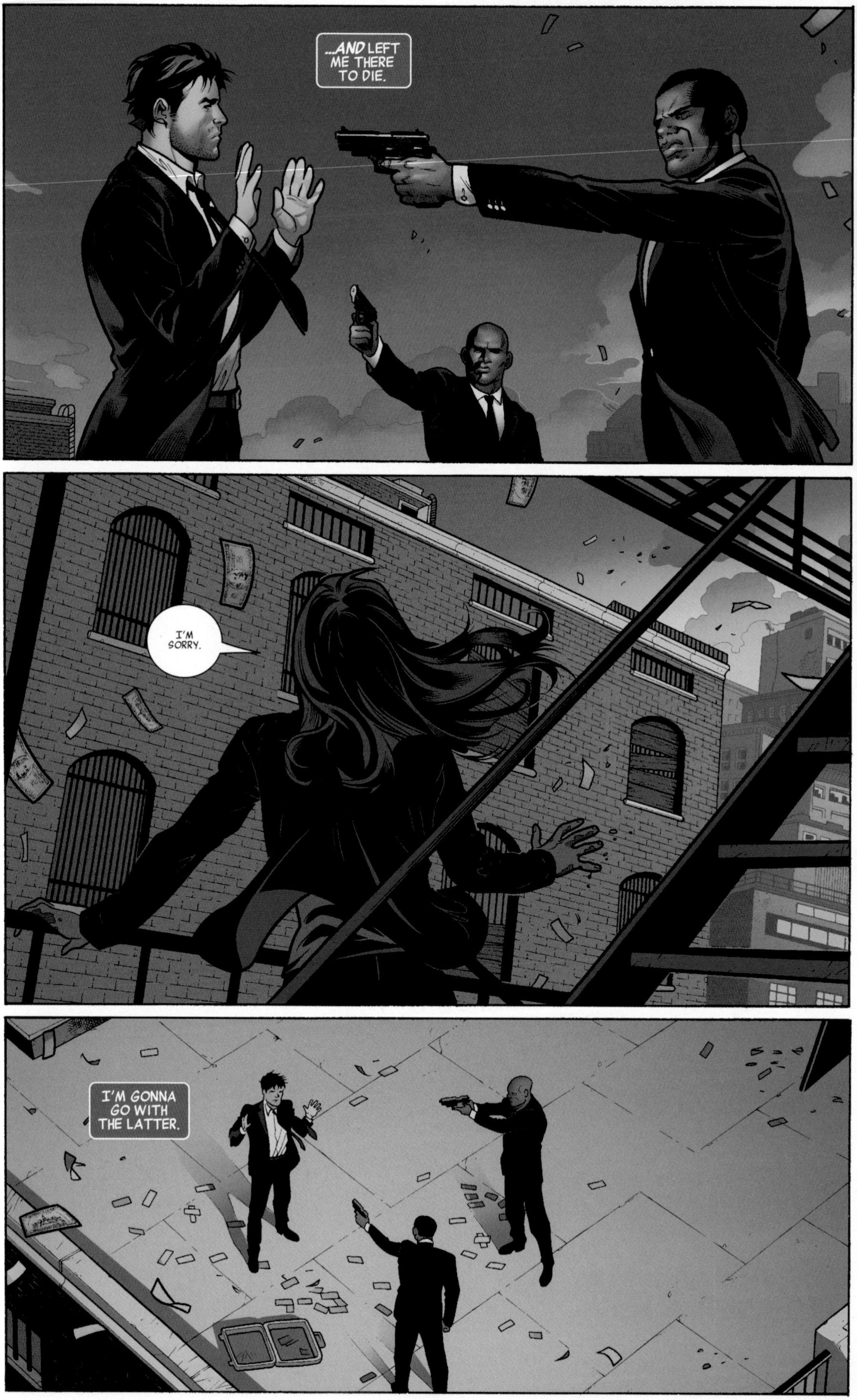
...AND LEFT ME THERE TO DIE.
I'M SORRY.
I'M GONNA GO WITH THE LATTER.

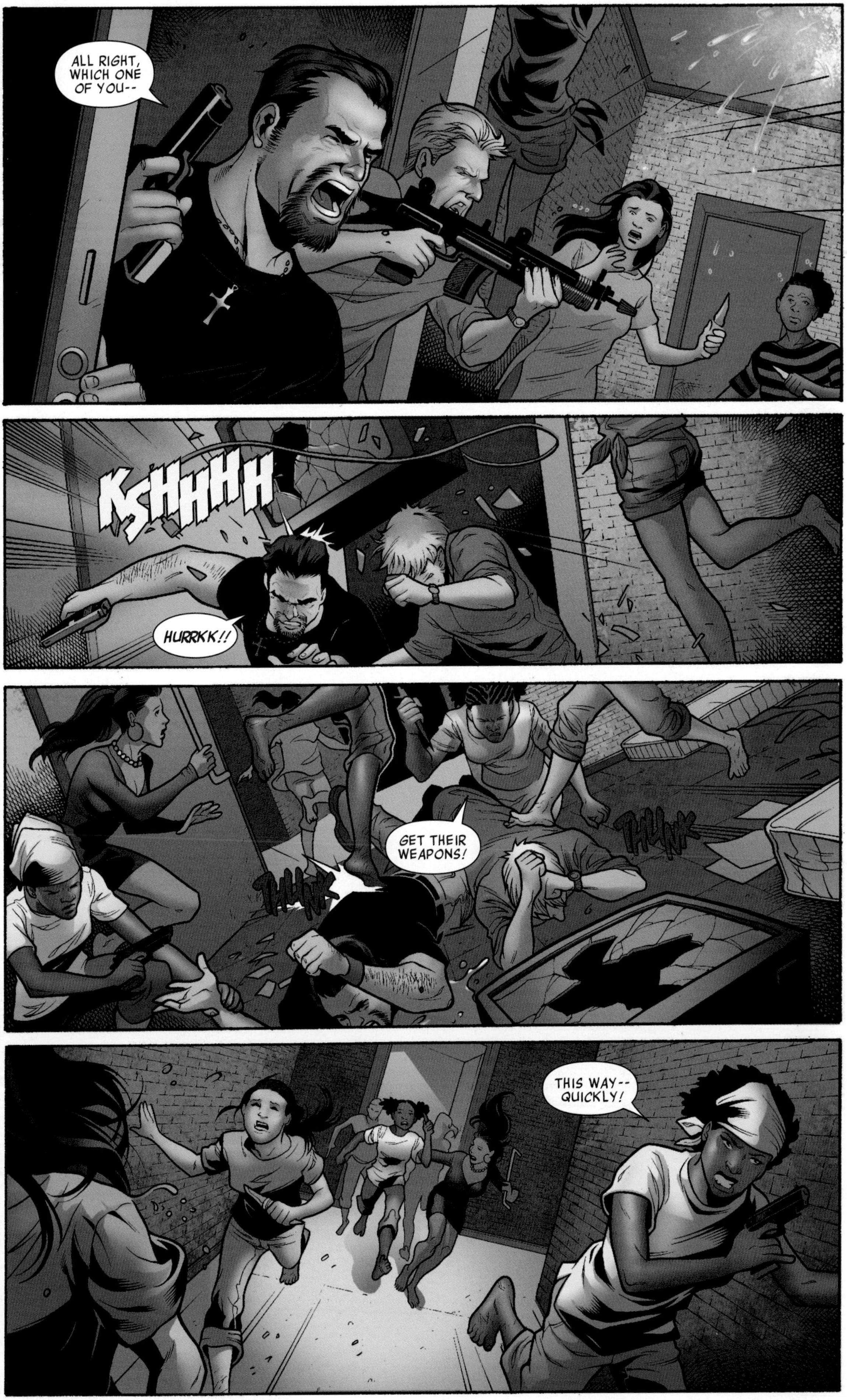
ALL RIGHT, WHICH ONE OF YOU--
KSHHHH
HURRKK!!
GET THEIR WEAPONS!
THUNK
THUNK
THIS WAY-- QUICKLY!

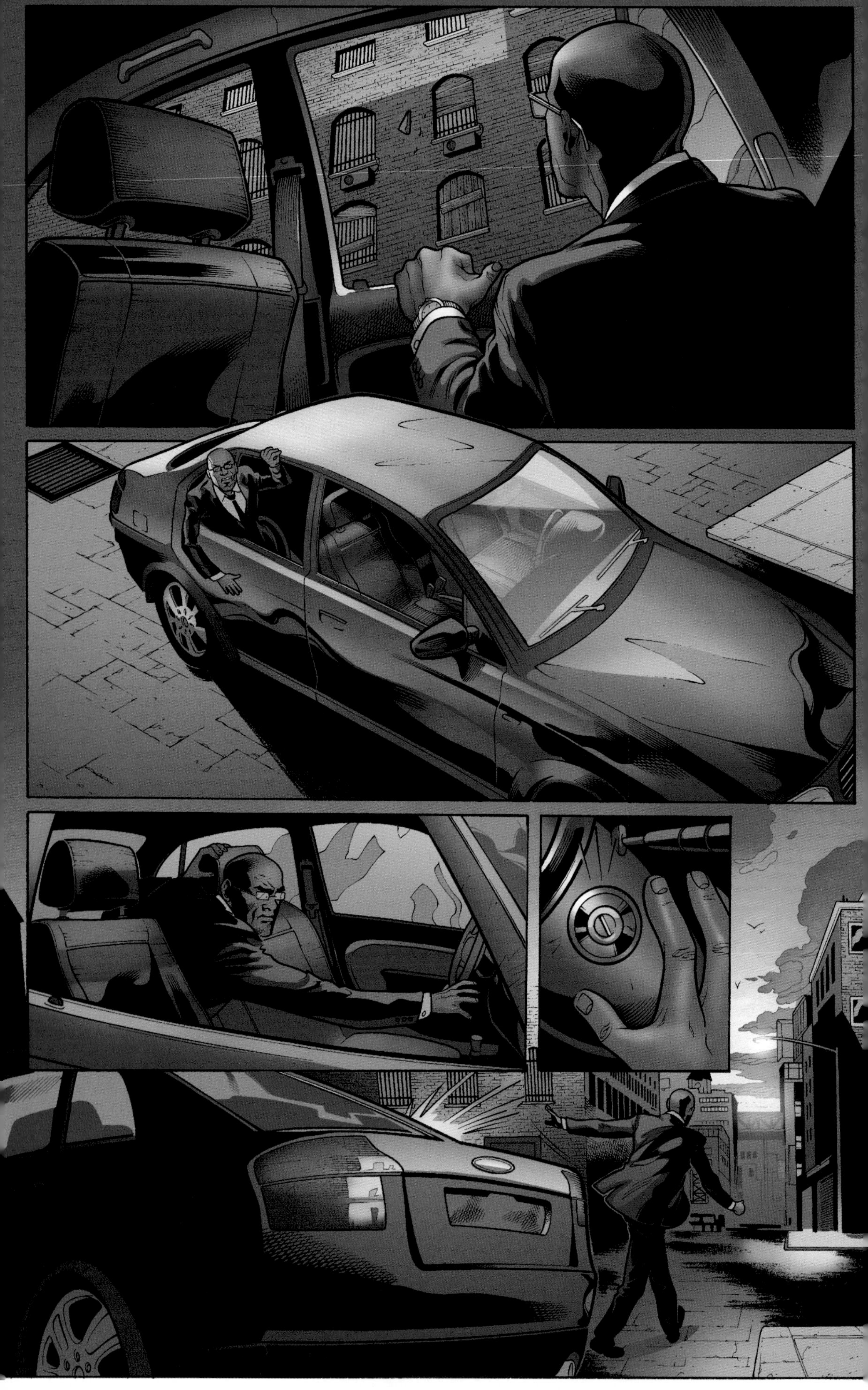

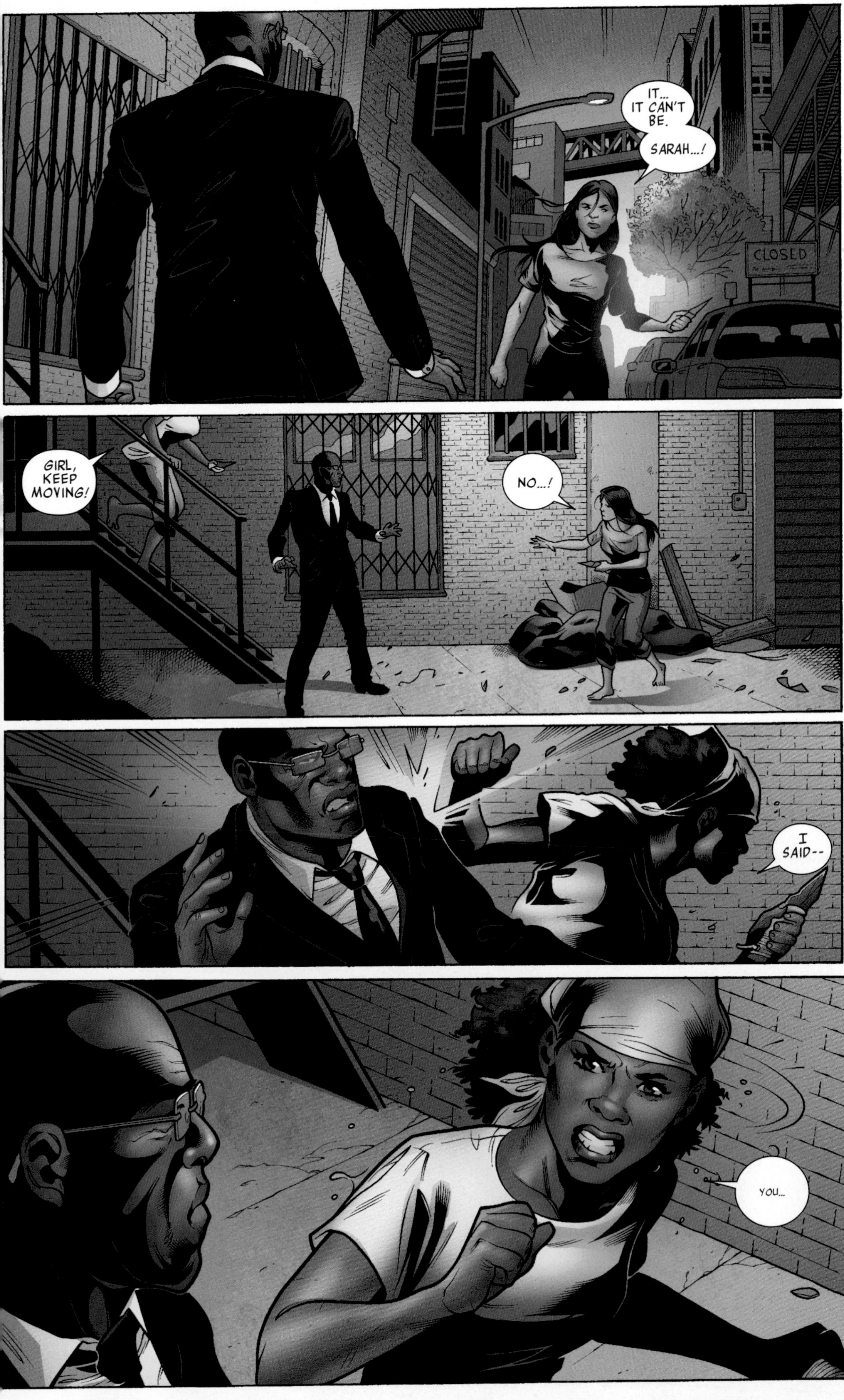
IT... IT CAN'T BE.
SARAH...!
CLOSED
GIRL, KEEP MOVING!
NO...!
I SAID--
YOU...

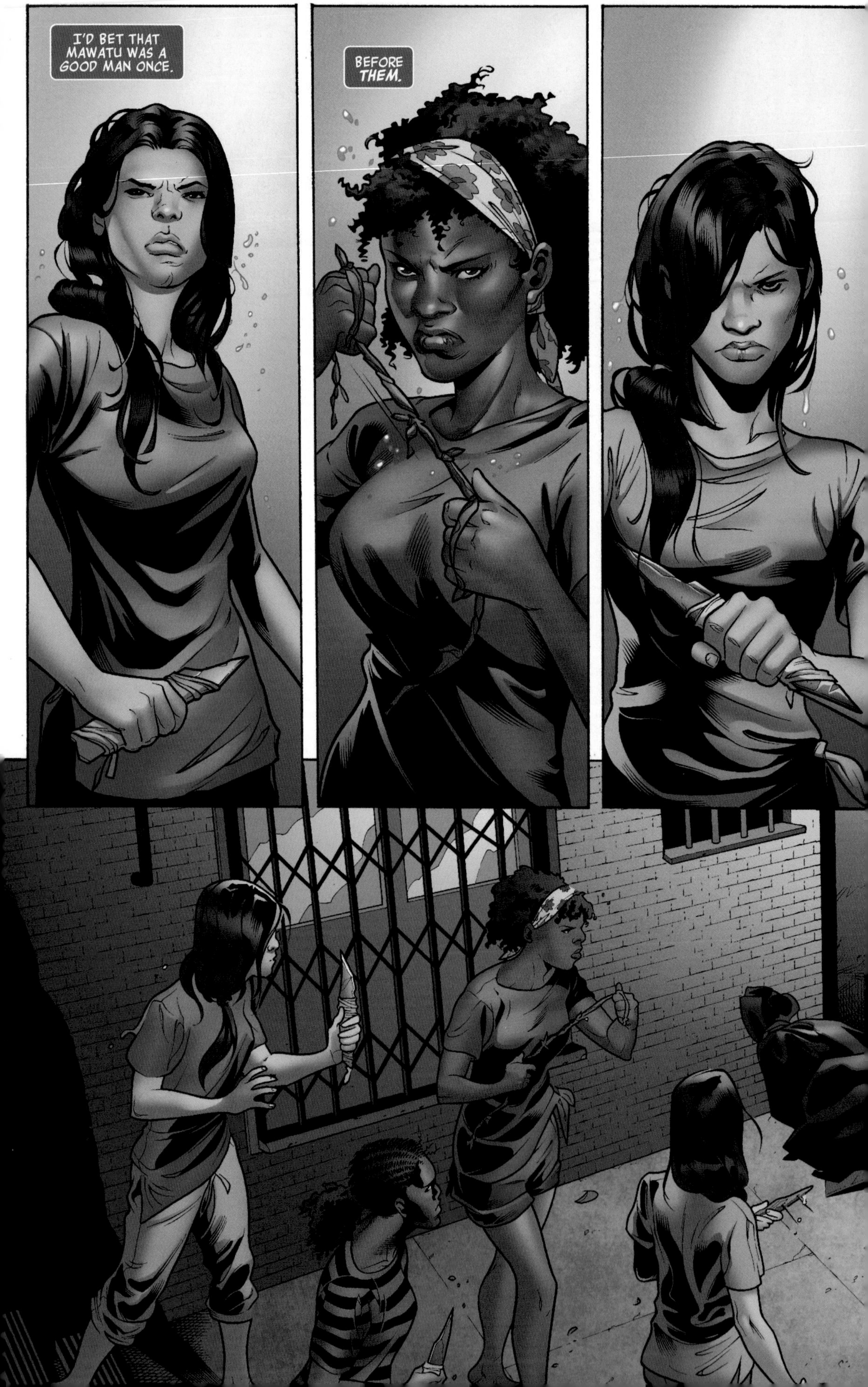
I'D BET THAT MAWATU WAS A GOOD MAN ONCE.
BEFORE *THEM*.

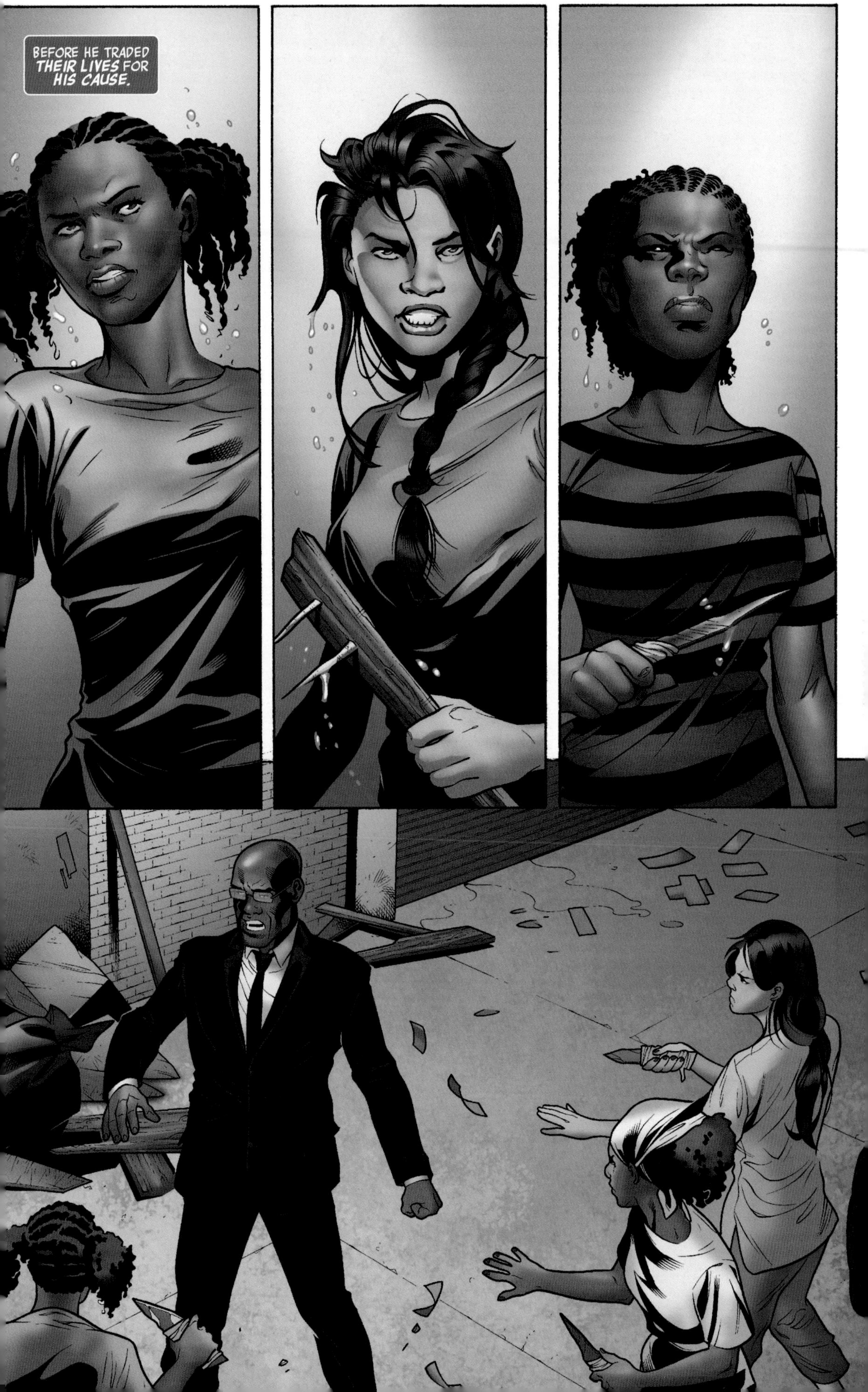
BEFORE HE TRADED THEIR LIVES FOR HIS CAUSE.

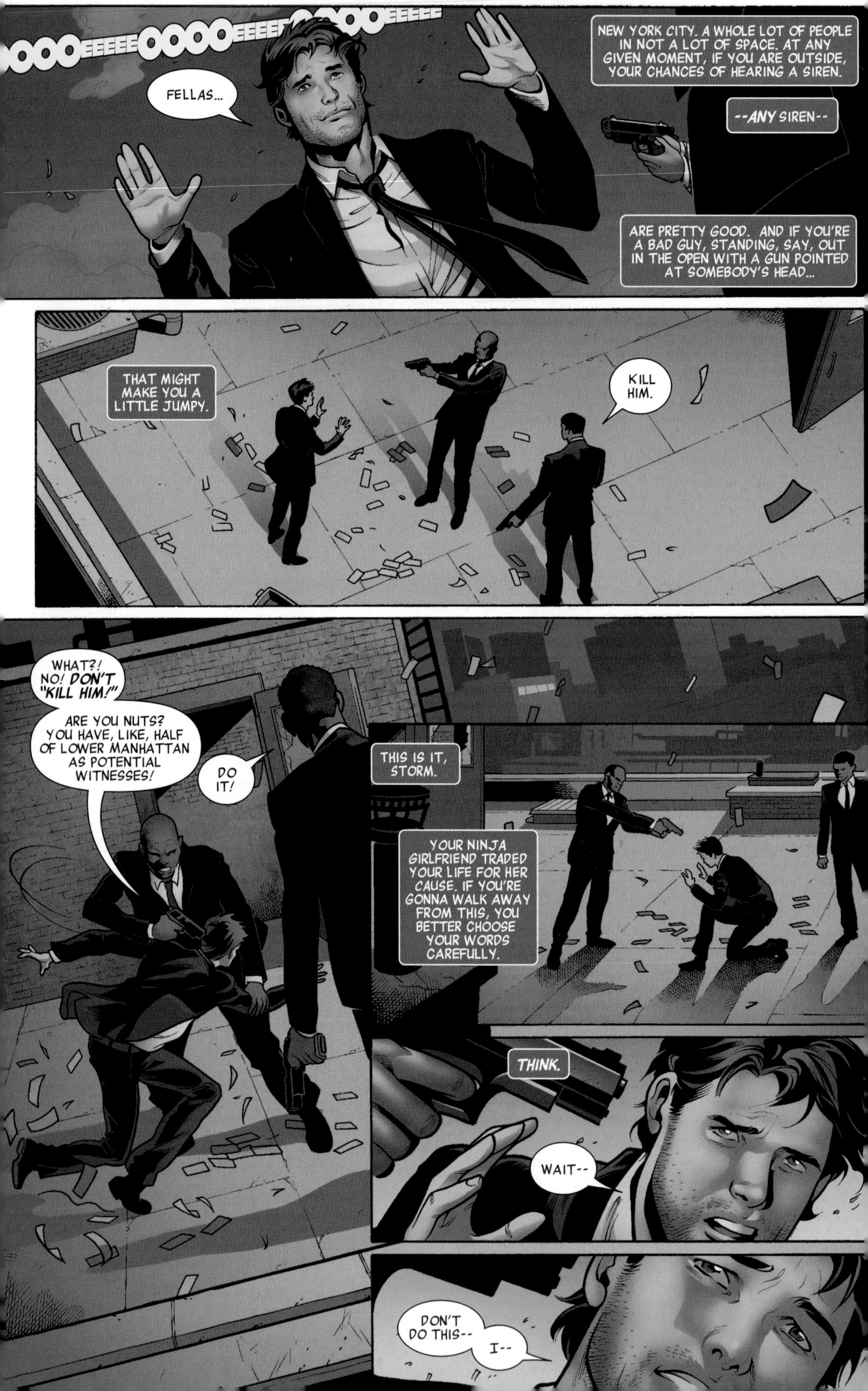
OOOOEEEEEOOOOEEEEOOOOEEEEE
FELLAS...
NEW YORK CITY. A WHOLE LOT OF PEOPLE IN NOT A LOT OF SPACE. AT ANY GIVEN MOMENT, IF YOU ARE OUTSIDE, YOUR CHANCES OF HEARING A SIREN.
--ANY SIREN--
ARE PRETTY GOOD. AND IF YOU'RE A BAD GUY, STANDING, SAY, OUT IN THE OPEN WITH A GUN POINTED AT SOMEBODY'S HEAD...
THAT MIGHT MAKE YOU A LITTLE JUMPY.
KILL HIM.
WHAT?! NO! DON'T "KILL HIM!"
ARE YOU NUTS? YOU HAVE, LIKE, HALF OF LOWER MANHATTAN AS POTENTIAL WITNESSES!
DO IT!
THIS IS IT, STORM.
YOUR NINJA GIRLFRIEND TRADED YOUR LIFE FOR HER CAUSE. IF YOU'RE GONNA WALK AWAY FROM THIS, YOU BETTER CHOOSE YOUR WORDS CAREFULLY.
THINK.
WAIT--
DON'T DO THIS--
I--

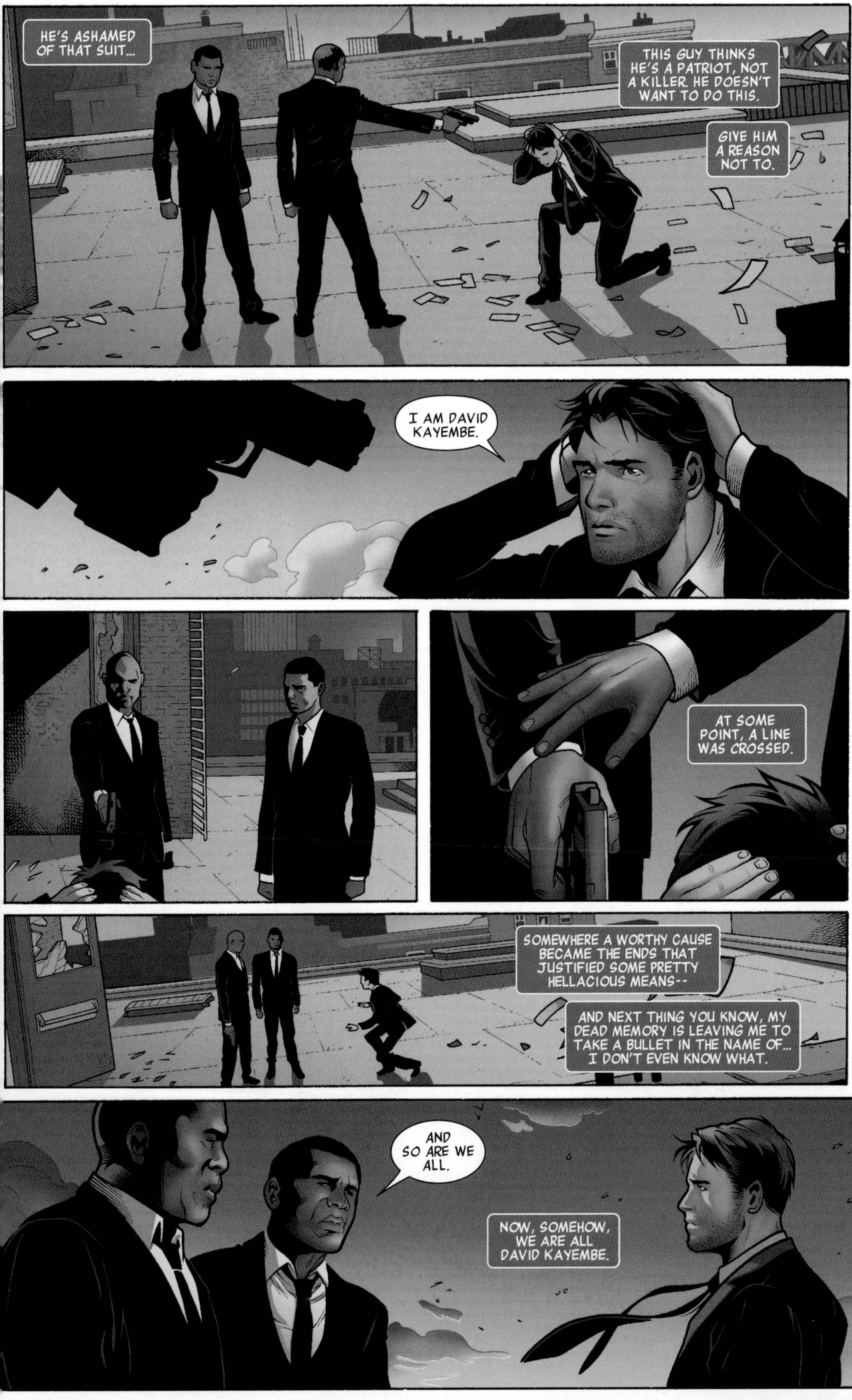
HE'S ASHAMED OF THAT SUIT...
THIS GUY THINKS HE'S A PATRIOT, NOT A KILLER. HE DOESN'T WANT TO DO THIS.
GIVE HIM A REASON NOT TO.
I AM DAVID KAYEMBE.
AT SOME POINT, A LINE WAS CROSSED.
SOMEWHERE A WORTHY CAUSE BECAME THE ENDS THAT JUSTIFIED SOME PRETTY HELLACIOUS MEANS--
AND NEXT THING YOU KNOW, MY DEAD MEMORY IS LEAVING ME TO TAKE A BULLET IN THE NAME OF... I DON'T EVEN KNOW WHAT.
AND SO ARE WE ALL.
NOW, SOMEHOW, WE ARE ALL DAVID KAYEMBE.

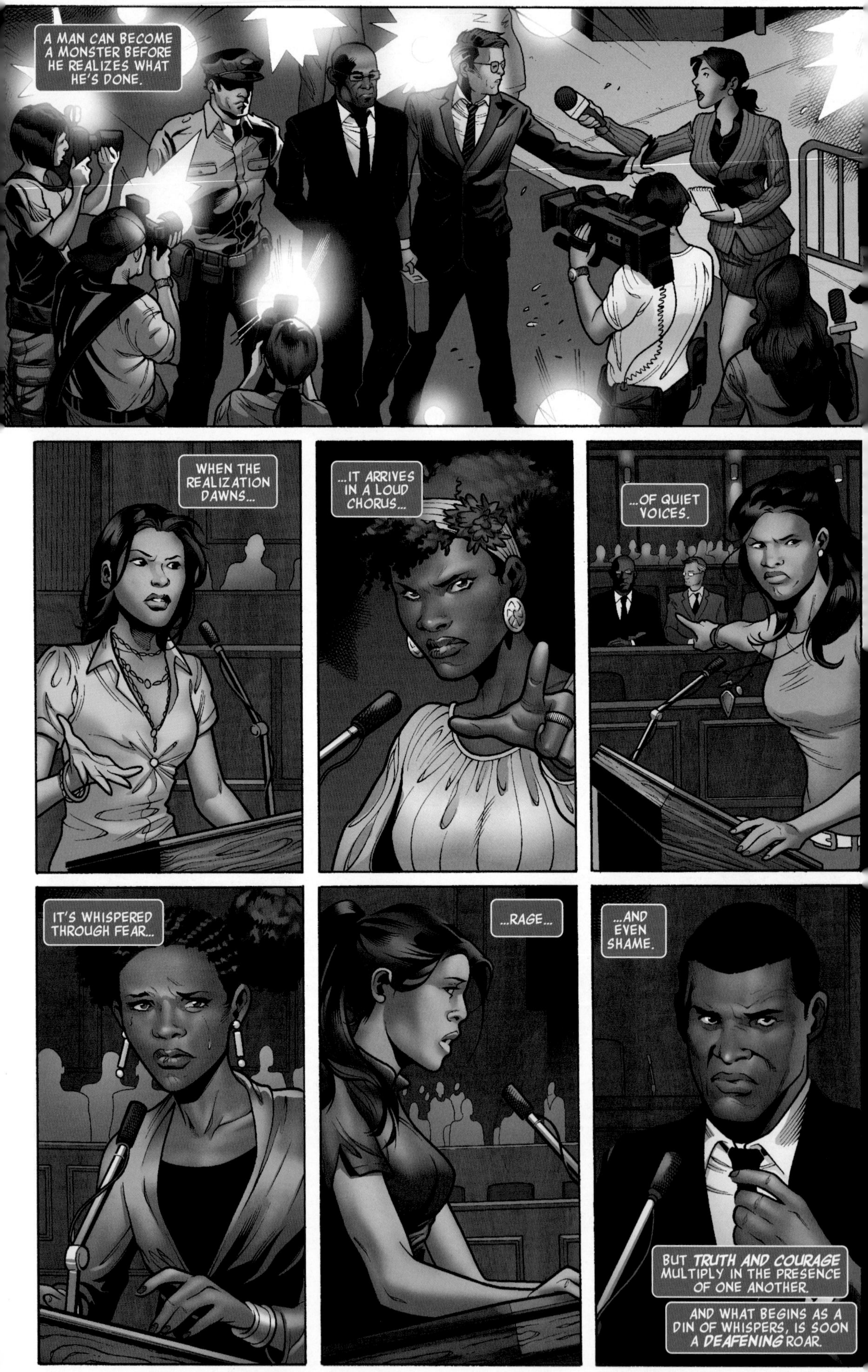
A MAN CAN BECOME A MONSTER BEFORE HE REALIZES WHAT HE'S DONE.
WHEN THE REALIZATION DAWNS...
...IT ARRIVES IN A LOUD CHORUS...
...OF QUIET VOICES.
IT'S WHISPERED THROUGH FEAR...
...RAGE...
...AND EVEN SHAME.
BUT TRUTH AND COURAGE MULTIPLY IN THE PRESENCE OF ONE ANOTHER.
AND WHAT BEGINS AS A DIN OF WHISPERS, IS SOON A DEAFENING ROAR.

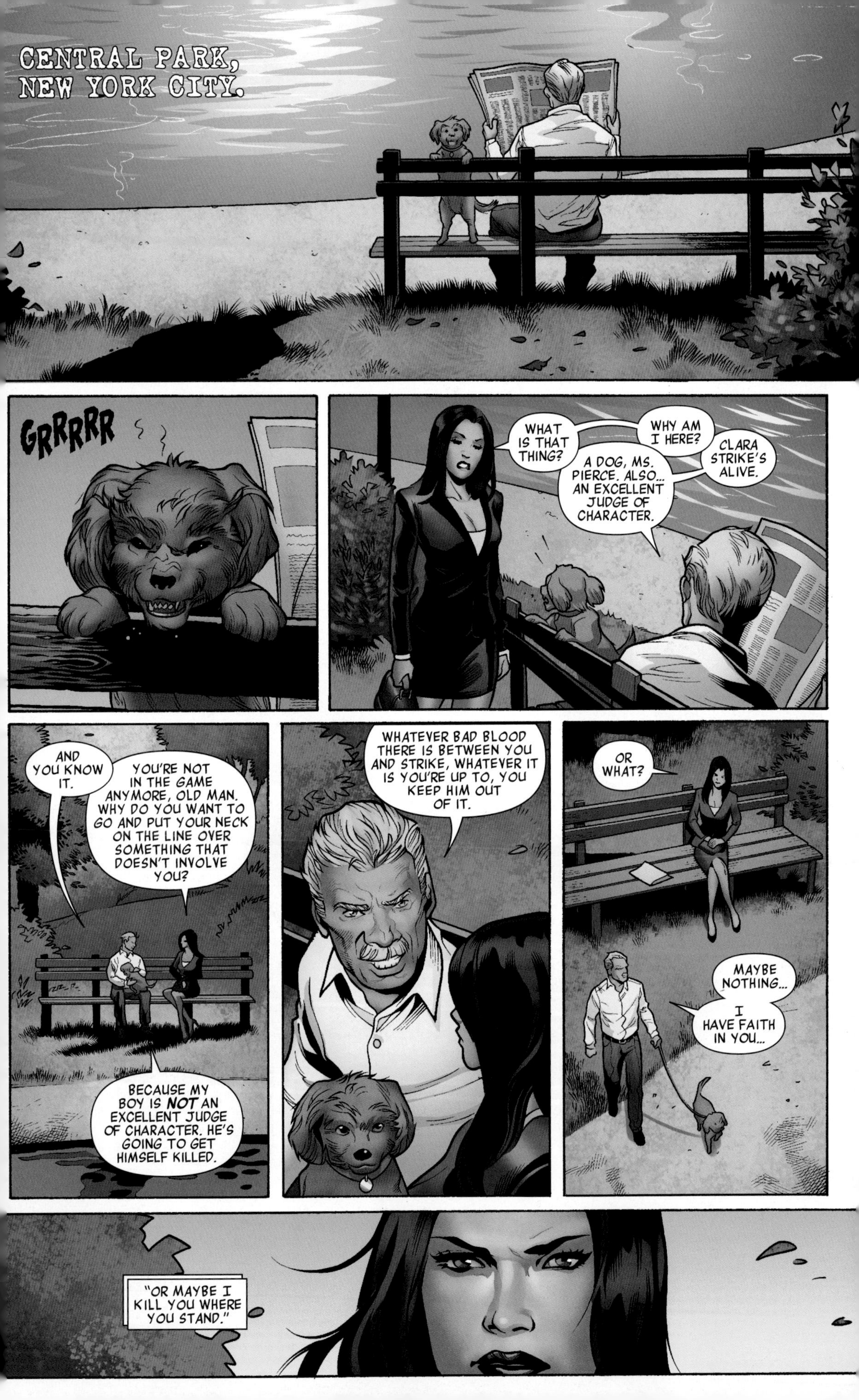
CENTRAL PARK, NEW YORK CITY.
GRRRRR
WHAT IS THAT THING?
WHY AM I HERE?
A DOG, MS. PIERCE. ALSO... AN EXCELLENT JUDGE OF CHARACTER.
CLARA STRIKE'S ALIVE.
YOU'RE NOT IN THE GAME ANYMORE, OLD MAN. WHY DO YOU WANT TO GO AND PUT YOUR NECK ON THE LINE OVER SOMETHING THAT DOESN'T INVOLVE YOU?
AND YOU KNOW IT.
BECAUSE MY BOY IS NOT AN EXCELLENT JUDGE OF CHARACTER. HE'S GOING TO GET HIMSELF KILLED.
WHATEVER BAD BLOOD THERE IS BETWEEN YOU AND STRIKE, WHATEVER IT IS YOU'RE UP TO, YOU KEEP HIM OUT OF IT.
OR WHAT?
MAYBE NOTHING...
I HAVE FAITH IN YOU...
"OR MAYBE I KILL YOU WHERE YOU STAND."

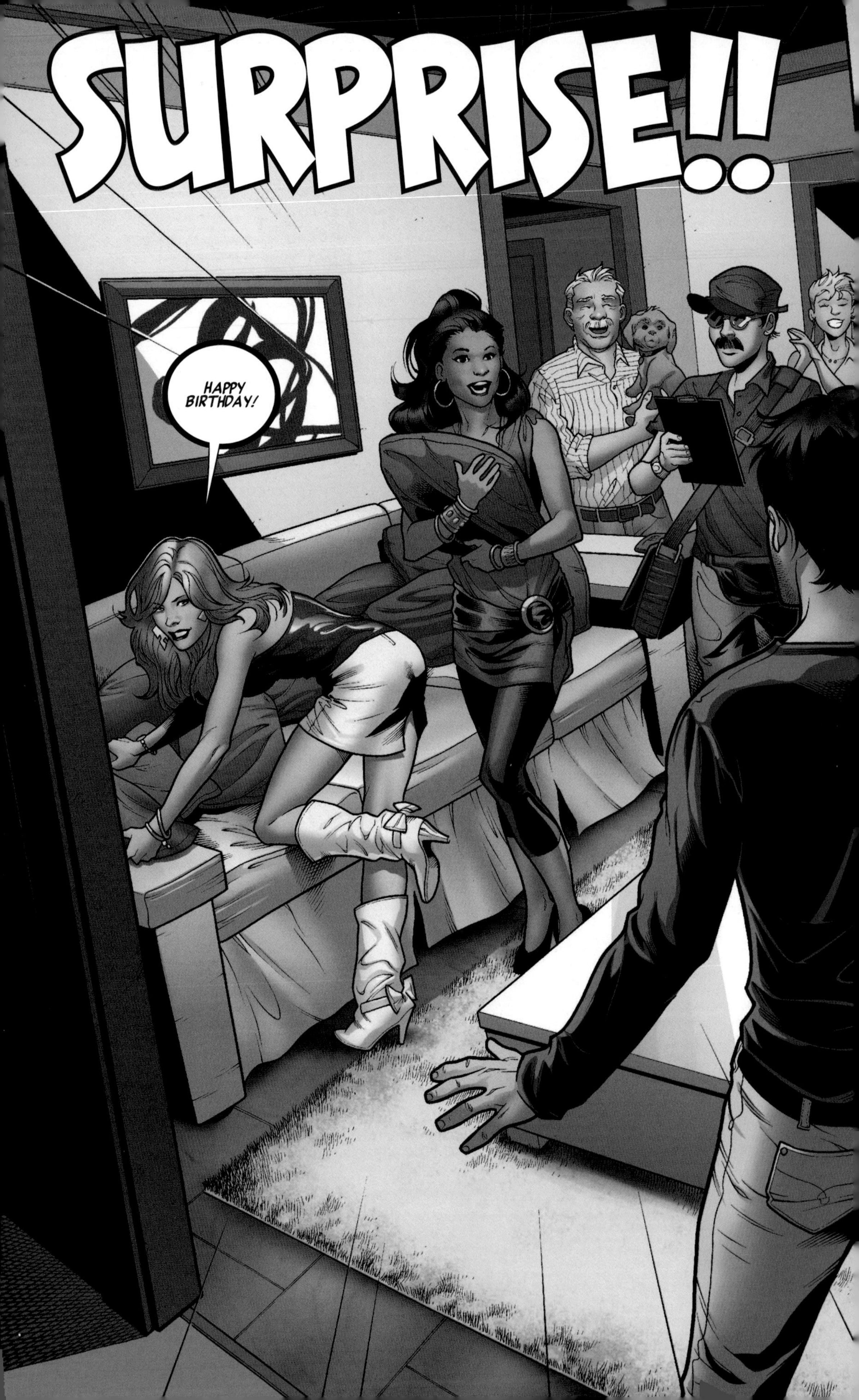
SURPRISE!!
HAPPY BIRTHDAY!

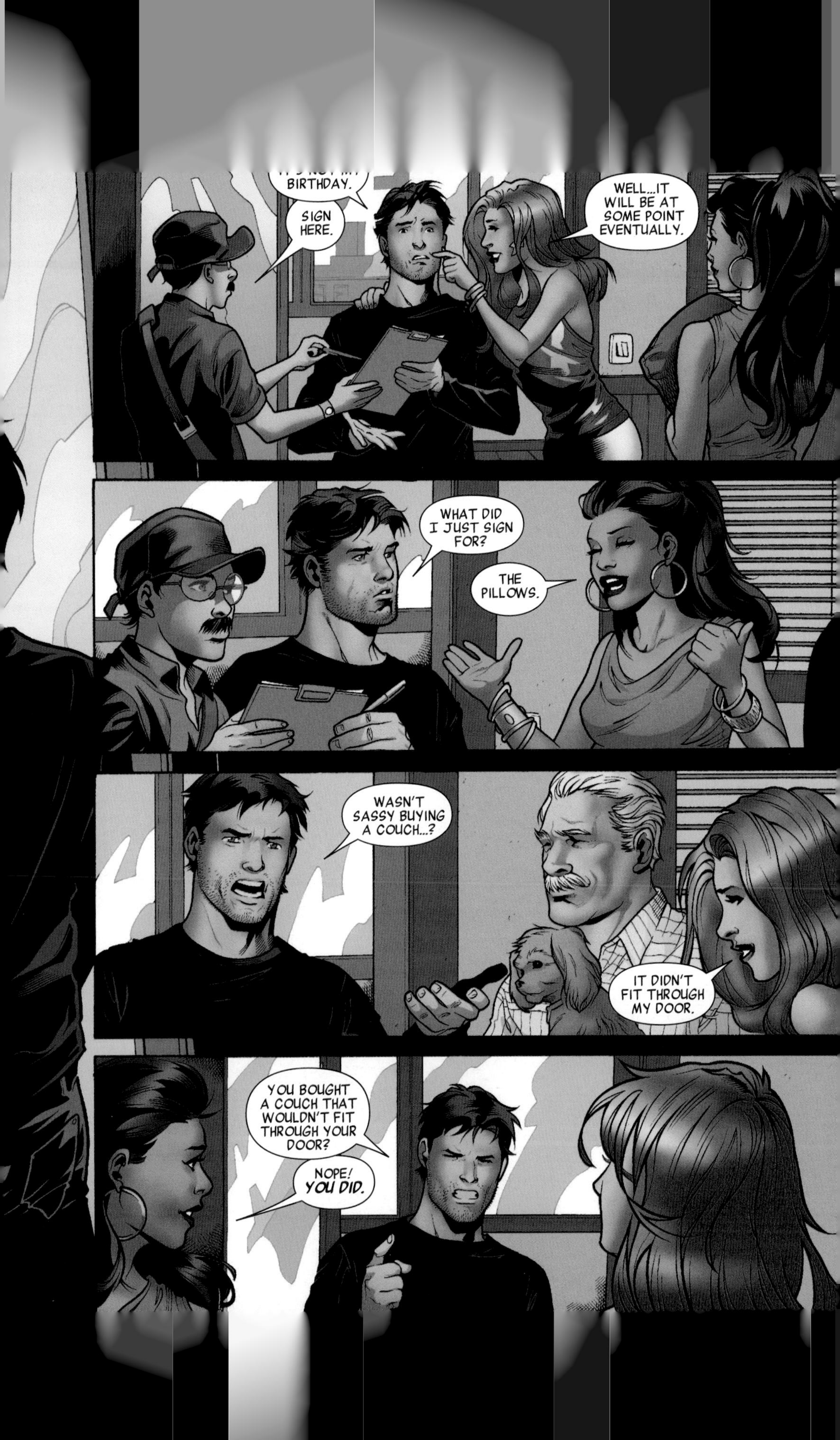

BIRTHDAY.
SIGN HERE.
WELL...IT WILL BE AT SOME POINT EVENTUALLY.
WHAT DID I JUST SIGN FOR?
THE PILLOWS.
WASN'T SASSY BUYING A COUCH...?
IT DIDN'T FIT THROUGH MY DOOR.
YOU BOUGHT A COUCH THAT WOULDN'T FIT THROUGH YOUR DOOR?
NOPE! YOU DID.

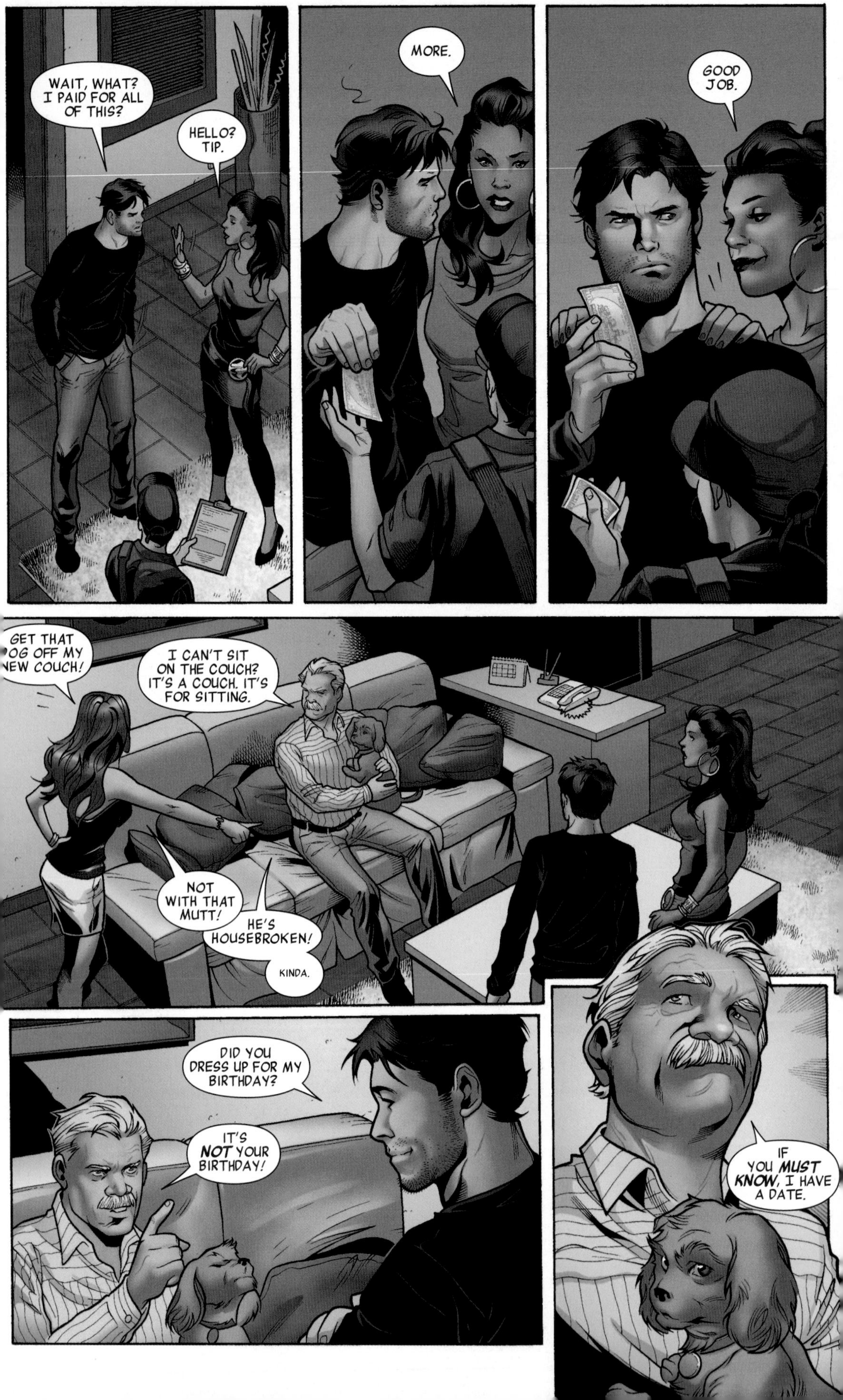
WAIT, WHAT? I PAID FOR ALL OF THIS?
HELLO? TIP.
MORE.
GOOD JOB.
GET THAT OG OFF MY NEW COUCH!
I CAN'T SIT ON THE COUCH? IT'S A COUCH. IT'S FOR SITTING.
NOT WITH THAT MUTT!
HE'S HOUSEBROKEN!
KINDA.
DID YOU DRESS UP FOR MY BIRTHDAY?
IT'S NOT YOUR BIRTHDAY!
IF YOU MUST KNOW, I HAVE A DATE.

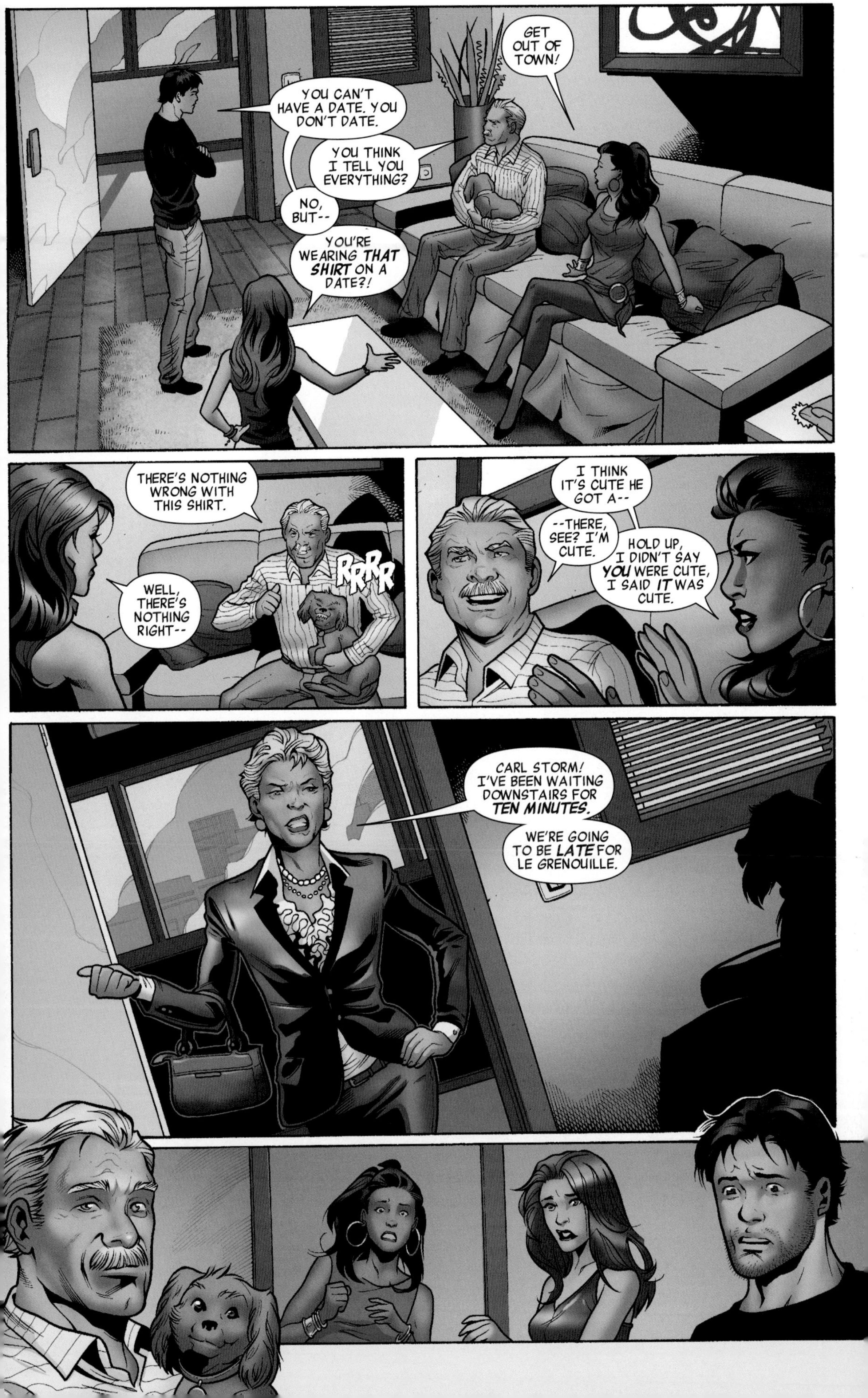

GET OUT OF TOWN!
YOU CAN'T HAVE A DATE. YOU DON'T DATE.
YOU THINK I TELL YOU EVERYTHING?
NO, BUT--
YOU'RE WEARING THAT SHIRT ON A DATE?!
THERE'S NOTHING WRONG WITH THIS SHIRT.
WELL, THERE'S NOTHING RIGHT--
RRRR
I THINK IT'S CUTE HE GOT A--
--THERE, SEE? I'M CUTE.
HOLD UP, I DIDN'T SAY YOU WERE CUTE, I SAID IT WAS CUTE.
CARL STORM! I'VE BEEN WAITING DOWNSTAIRS FOR TEN MINUTES.
WE'RE GOING TO BE LATE FOR LE GRENOUILLE.

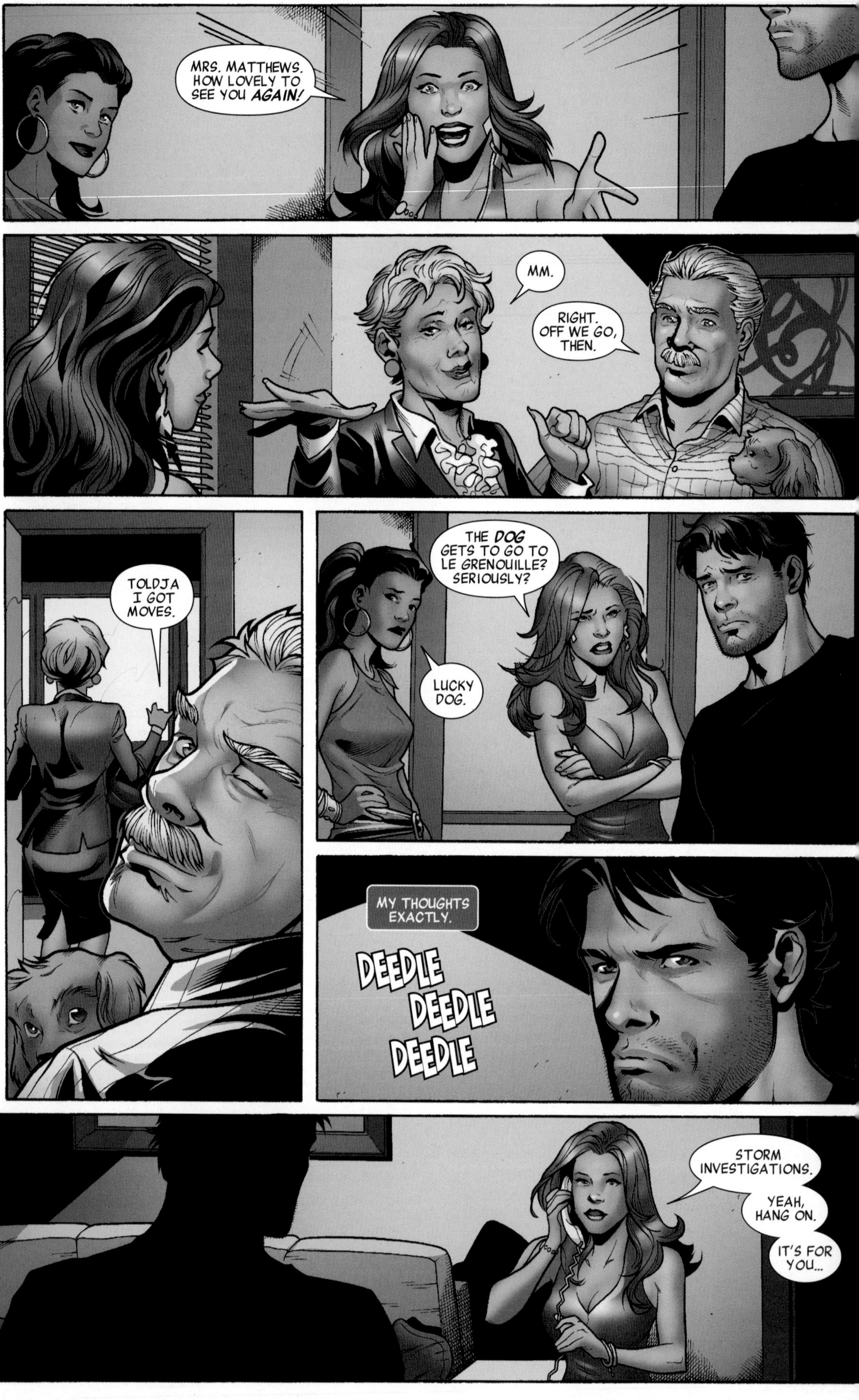
MRS. MATTHEWS. HOW LOVELY TO SEE YOU AGAIN!
MM.
RIGHT. OFF WE GO, THEN.
TOLDJA I GOT MOVES.
THE DOG GETS TO GO TO LE GRENOUILLE? SERIOUSLY?
LUCKY DOG.
MY THOUGHTS EXACTLY.
DEEDLE DEEDLE DEEDLE
STORM INVESTIGATIONS.
YEAH, HANG ON.
IT'S FOR YOU...

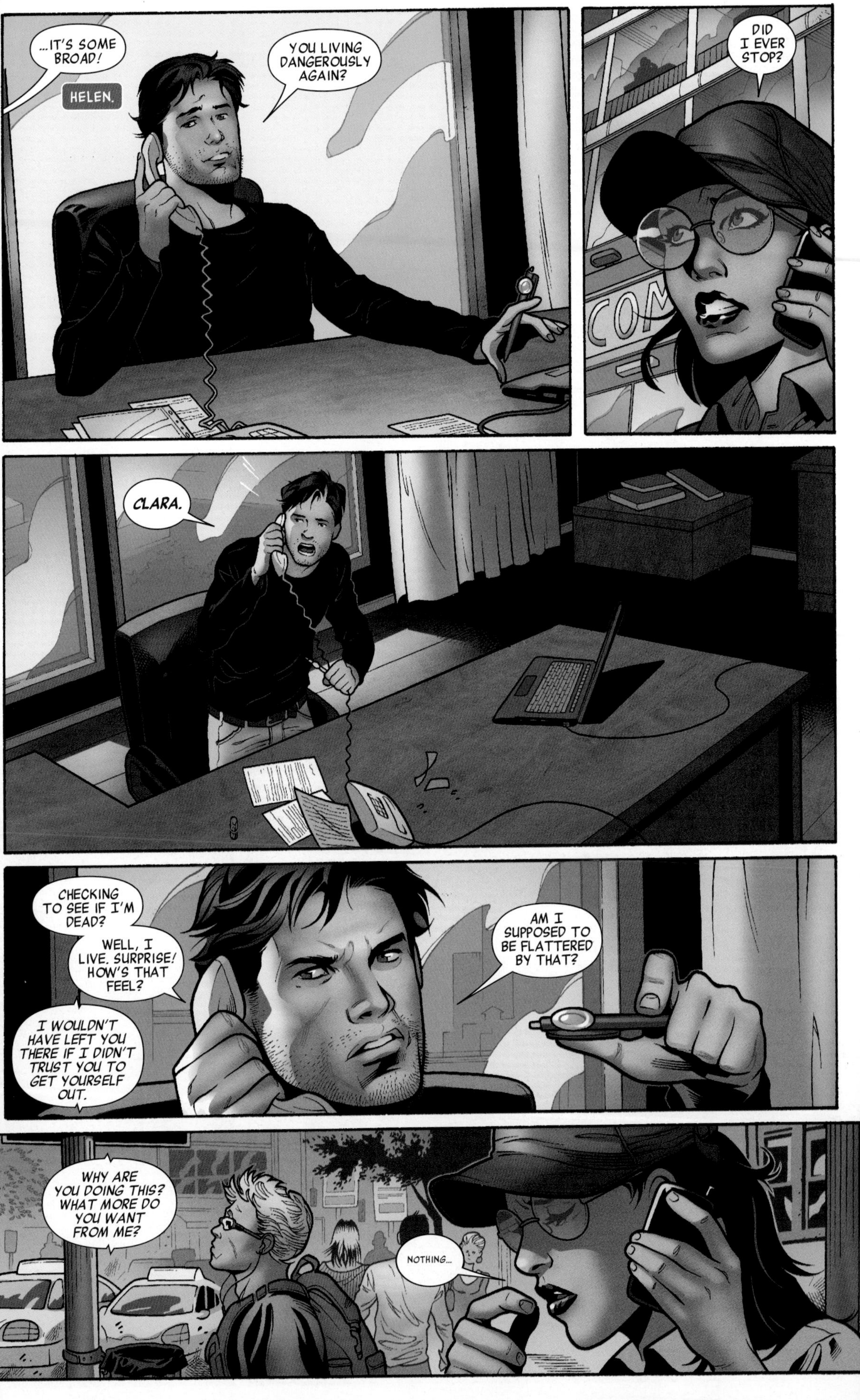
...IT'S SOME BROAD!
HELEN.
YOU LIVING DANGEROUSLY AGAIN?
DID I EVER STOP?
CLARA.
CHECKING TO SEE IF I'M DEAD?
WELL, I LIVE. SURPRISE! HOW'S THAT FEEL?
I WOULDN'T HAVE LEFT YOU THERE IF I DIDN'T TRUST YOU TO GET YOURSELF OUT.
AM I SUPPOSED TO BE FLATTERED BY THAT?
WHY ARE YOU DOING THIS? WHAT MORE DO YOU WANT FROM ME?
NOTHING...

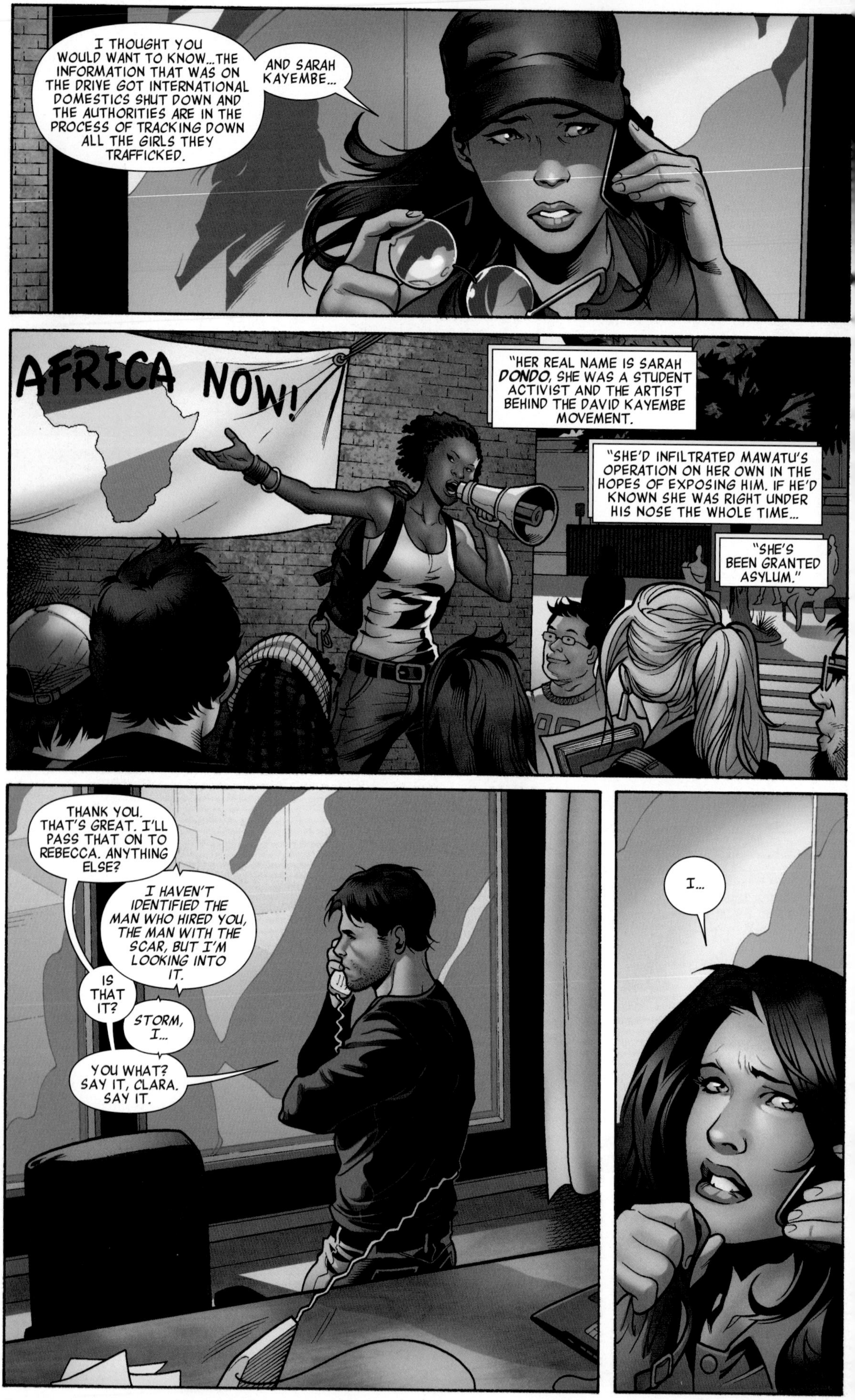
I THOUGHT YOU WOULD WANT TO KNOW...THE INFORMATION THAT WAS ON THE DRIVE GOT INTERNATIONAL DOMESTICS SHUT DOWN AND THE AUTHORITIES ARE IN THE PROCESS OF TRACKING DOWN ALL THE GIRLS THEY TRAFFICKED.
AND SARAH KAYEMBE...
AFRICA NOW!
"HER REAL NAME IS SARAH DONDO, SHE WAS A STUDENT ACTIVIST AND THE ARTIST BEHIND THE DAVID KAYEMBE MOVEMENT.
"SHE'D INFILTRATED MAWATU'S OPERATION ON HER OWN IN THE HOPES OF EXPOSING HIM. IF HE'D KNOWN SHE WAS RIGHT UNDER HIS NOSE THE WHOLE TIME...
"SHE'S BEEN GRANTED ASYLUM."
THANK YOU. THAT'S GREAT. I'LL PASS THAT ON TO REBECCA. ANYTHING ELSE?
I HAVEN'T IDENTIFIED THE MAN WHO HIRED YOU, THE MAN WITH THE SCAR, BUT I'M LOOKING INTO IT.
IS THAT IT?
STORM, I...
YOU WHAT? SAY IT, CLARA. SAY IT.
I...

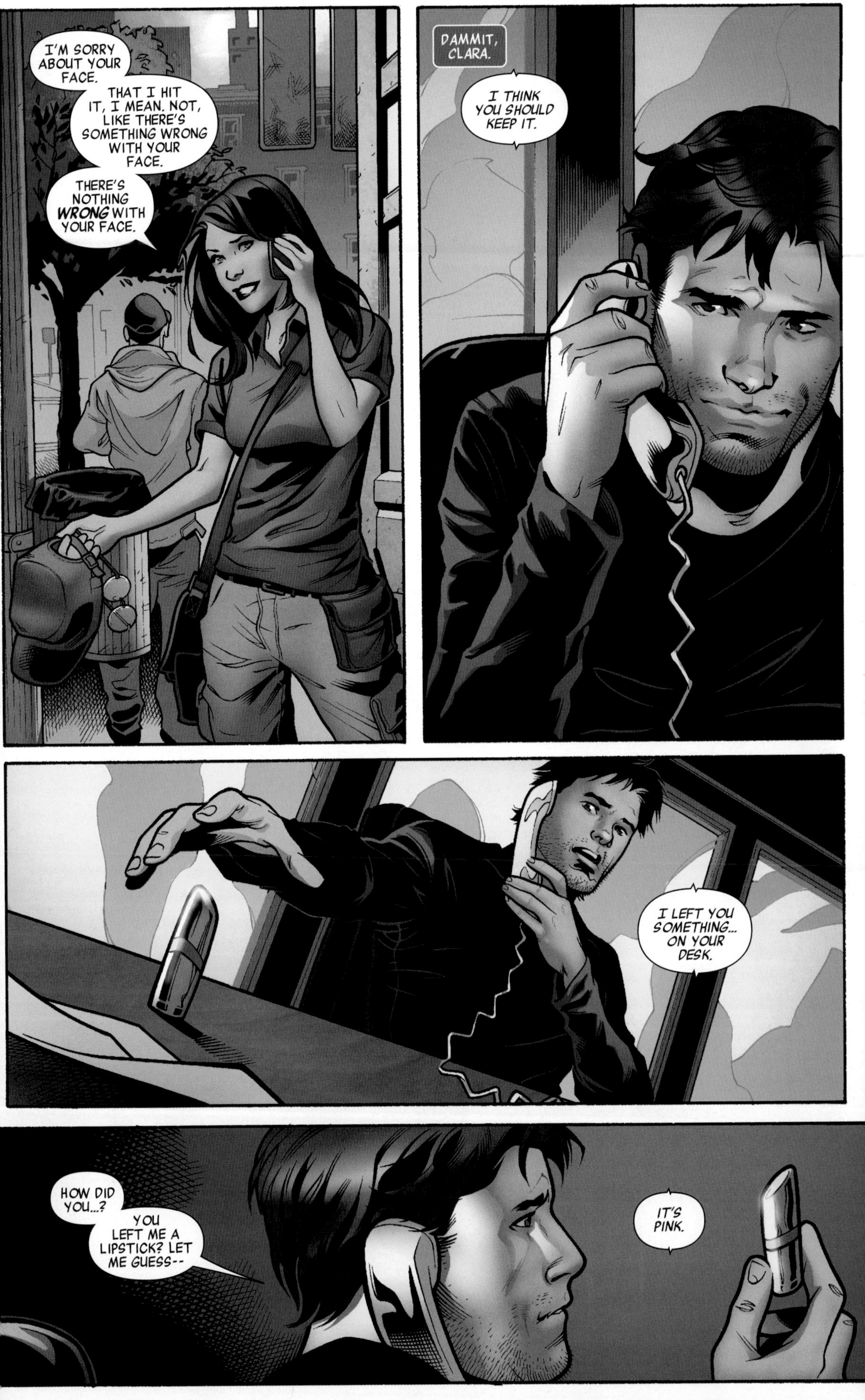
I'M SORRY ABOUT YOUR FACE.
THAT I HIT IT, I MEAN. NOT, LIKE THERE'S SOMETHING WRONG WITH YOUR FACE.
THERE'S NOTHING WRONG WITH YOUR FACE.
DAMMIT, CLARA.
I THINK YOU SHOULD KEEP IT.
I LEFT YOU SOMETHING... ON YOUR DESK.
HOW DID YOU...?
YOU LEFT ME A LIPSTICK? LET ME GUESS--
IT'S PINK.

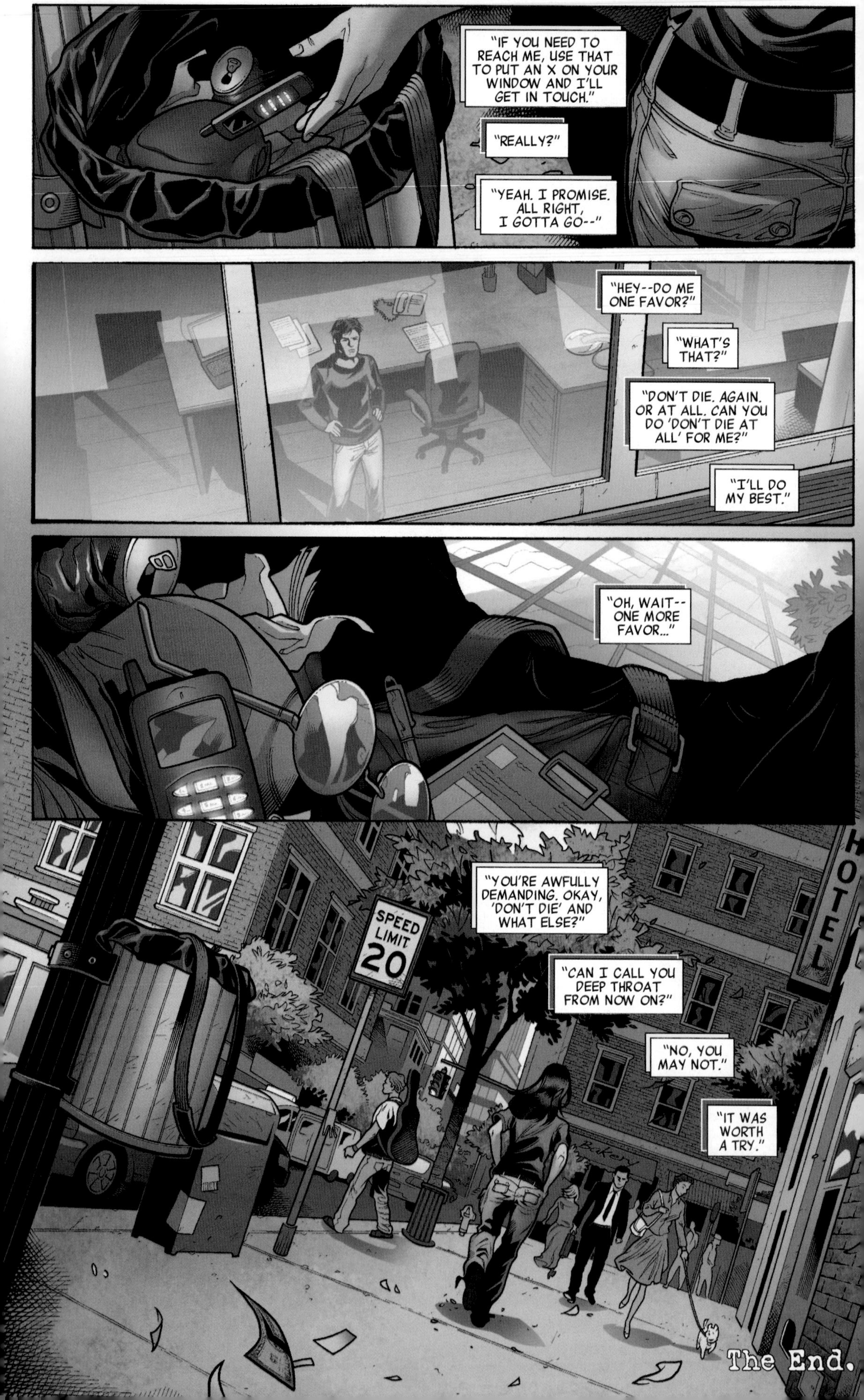
"IF YOU NEED TO REACH ME, USE THAT TO PUT AN X ON YOUR WINDOW AND I'LL GET IN TOUCH."
"REALLY?"
"YEAH. I PROMISE. ALL RIGHT, I GOTTA GO--"
"HEY--DO ME ONE FAVOR?"
"WHAT'S THAT?"
"DON'T DIE. AGAIN. OR AT ALL. CAN YOU DO 'DON'T DIE AT ALL' FOR ME?"
"I'LL DO MY BEST."
"OH, WAIT--ONE MORE FAVOR..."
"YOU'RE AWFULLY DEMANDING. OKAY, 'DON'T DIE' AND WHAT ELSE?"
SPEED LIMIT 20
HOTEL
"CAN I CALL YOU DEEP THROAT FROM NOW ON?"
"NO, YOU MAY NOT."
"IT WAS WORTH A TRY."
The End.

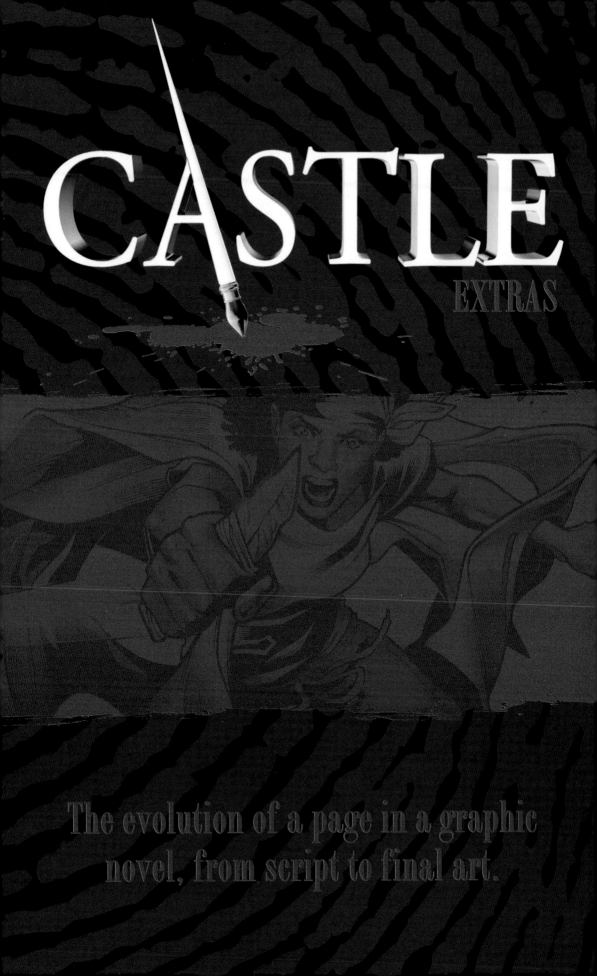

CASTLE

EXTRAS

The evolution of a page in a graphic
novel, from script to final art.

PANEL 1

Clara stands at the ledge at the edge of the building, looking over. She's clearly doing math in her head. She takes off her shoes. Storm stands about 10-15 feet back.

> **STORM**
> This is the point where you decide the heels were a bad idea?

PANEL 2

On the door. We can see the Deputy banging on the glass with the gun. The door is shaking. Clara is looking that direction.
> **FX**
> KAK KAK KAK

PANEL 3

Reverse on Clara, looking serious. Behind her, Storm doesn't quite get the severity of the situation.
> **CLARA** (SMALL)
> It's not going to hold.

PANEL 4

Clara goes up to Storm, right up to him. She puts one hand on the side of his face and pulls his head down so that they're forehead to forehead. Her other hand is down by the case that he still holds.

> **STORM**
> Um...

> **STORM**
> Are you going to hit me again?

PANEL 5

Cut back to the door. The glass breaks and the deputy's arm comes through. He's trying to reach the bar, but his arm isn't quite long enough.

> **FX**
> KRSHHHH

PANEL 6

On Clara's face as she speaks right to Storm. She almost has tears in her eyes. Not quite.

> **CLARA**
> I want you to know that I'm sorry.

> **STORM/CAPTION**
> Clara... Don't.

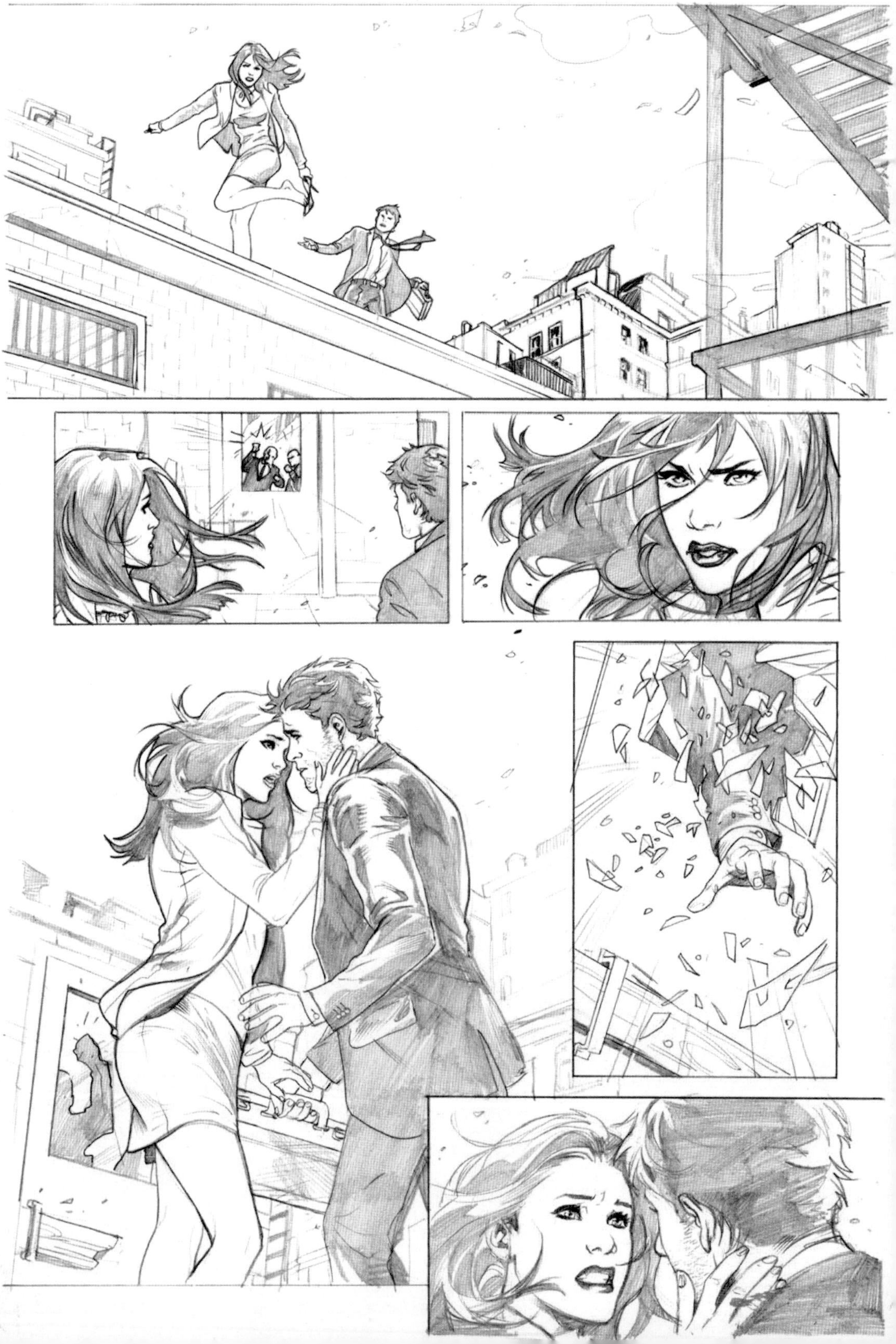

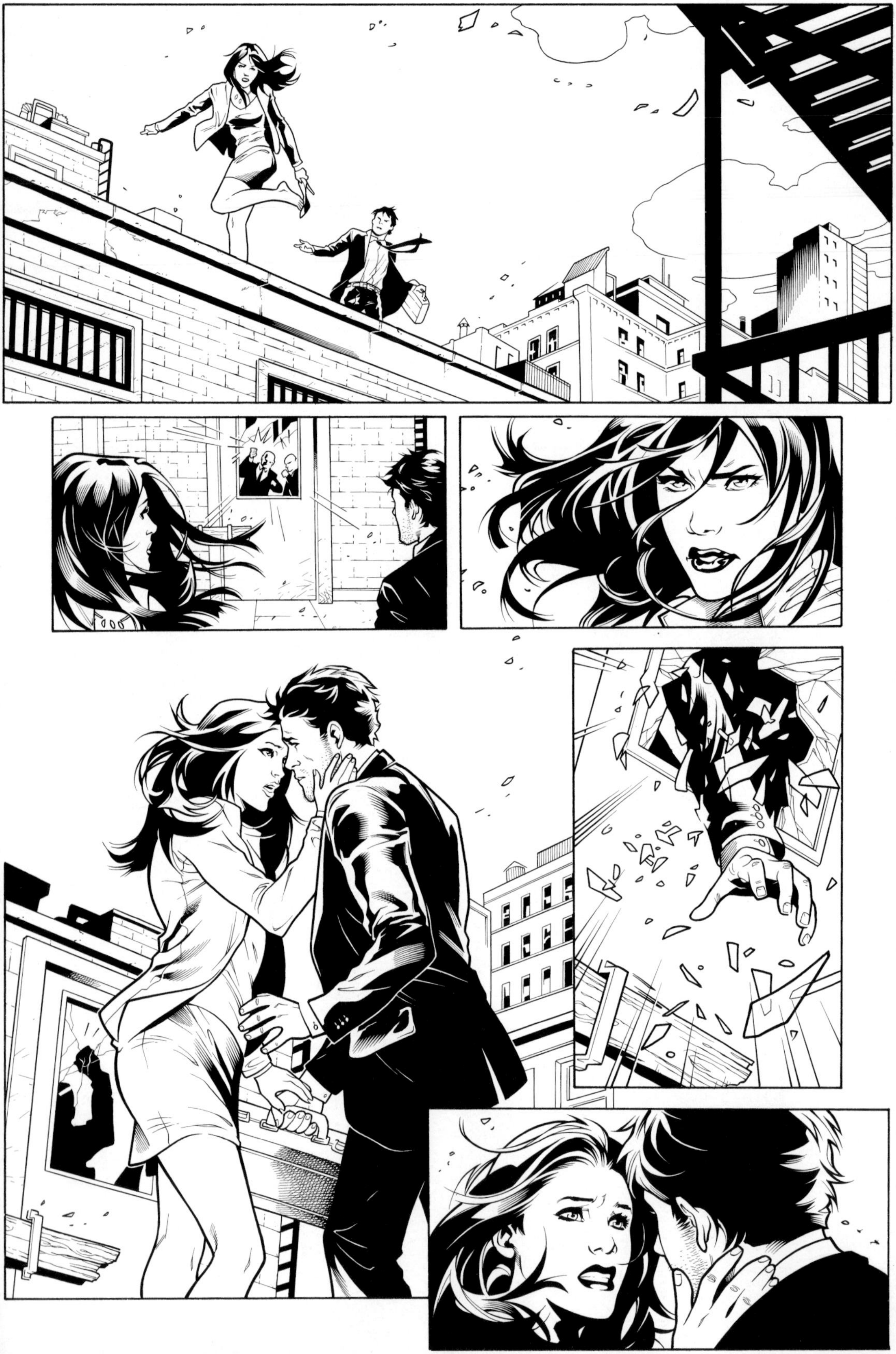

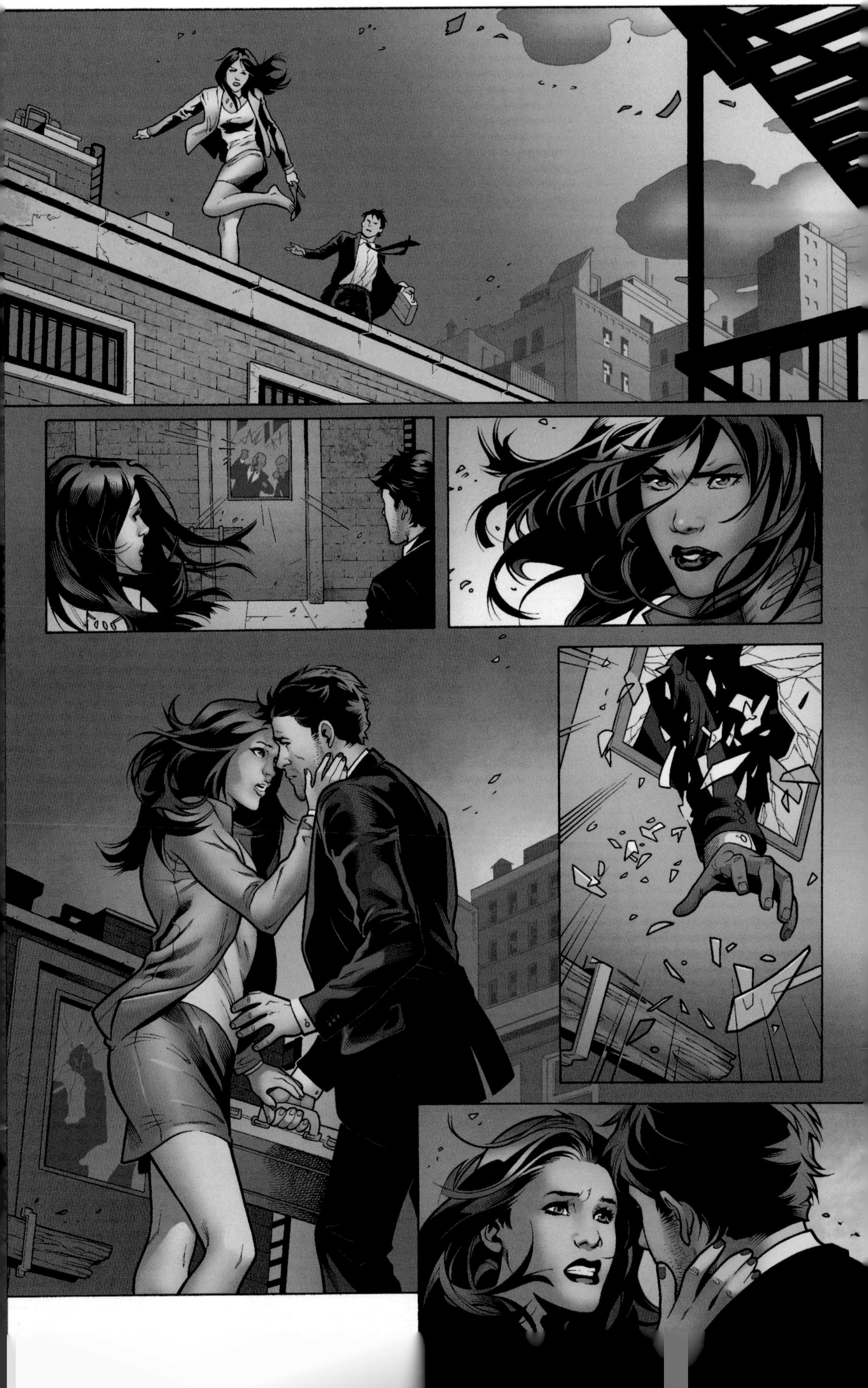

PAGE 65

PANEL 1

Storm pulls back a little bit and points to the door.

STORM
Whoa! What are you doing? You're not giving up. You don't give up. You're like... A ninja! I've seen you ninja. You can handle two guys with--

PANEL 2
They kiss.

STORM/CAPTION
Don't do this. Not now. Not like this.

PANEL 3
They're forehead-to-forehead again.

STORM
This is not how I wanted this to go. I don't want you apologize, what happened before is--

PANEL 4
Cut back to the door. The piece of wood falls out.

FX
KLUNK

PANEL 5
Back to Clara and Storm. She's got the fingers of her left hand lightly on his lips. (She's holding the drive down in her right hand.)

CLARA
This isn't about that. I'm not sorry for that...

PANEL 6
Inset. On the clasp of the briefcase. Clara's hand still holds the jump drive but she pushes the button that opens the case with her index finger.

FX
CLICK

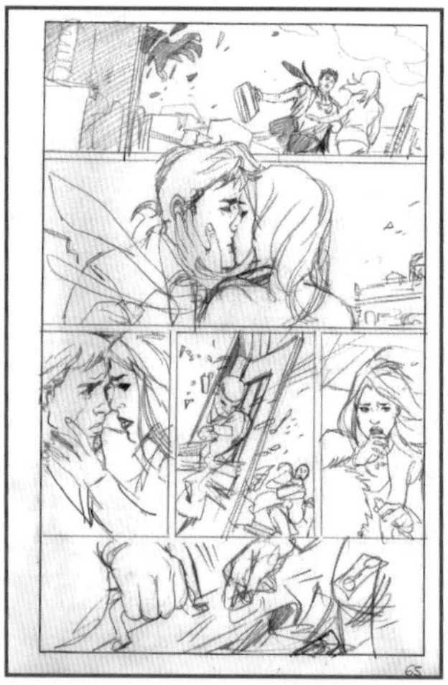

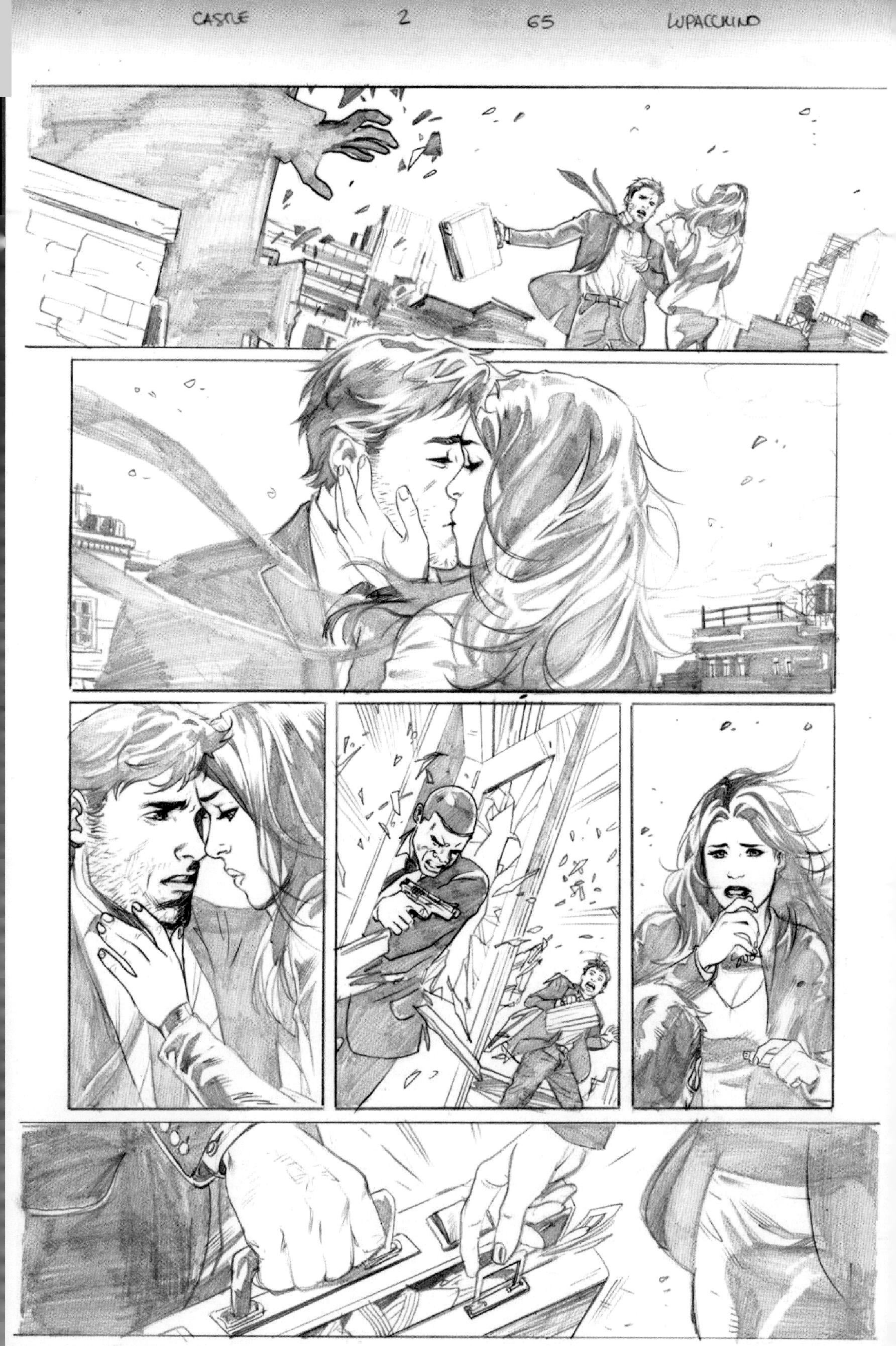
CASTLE
2
65
LUPACCHINO

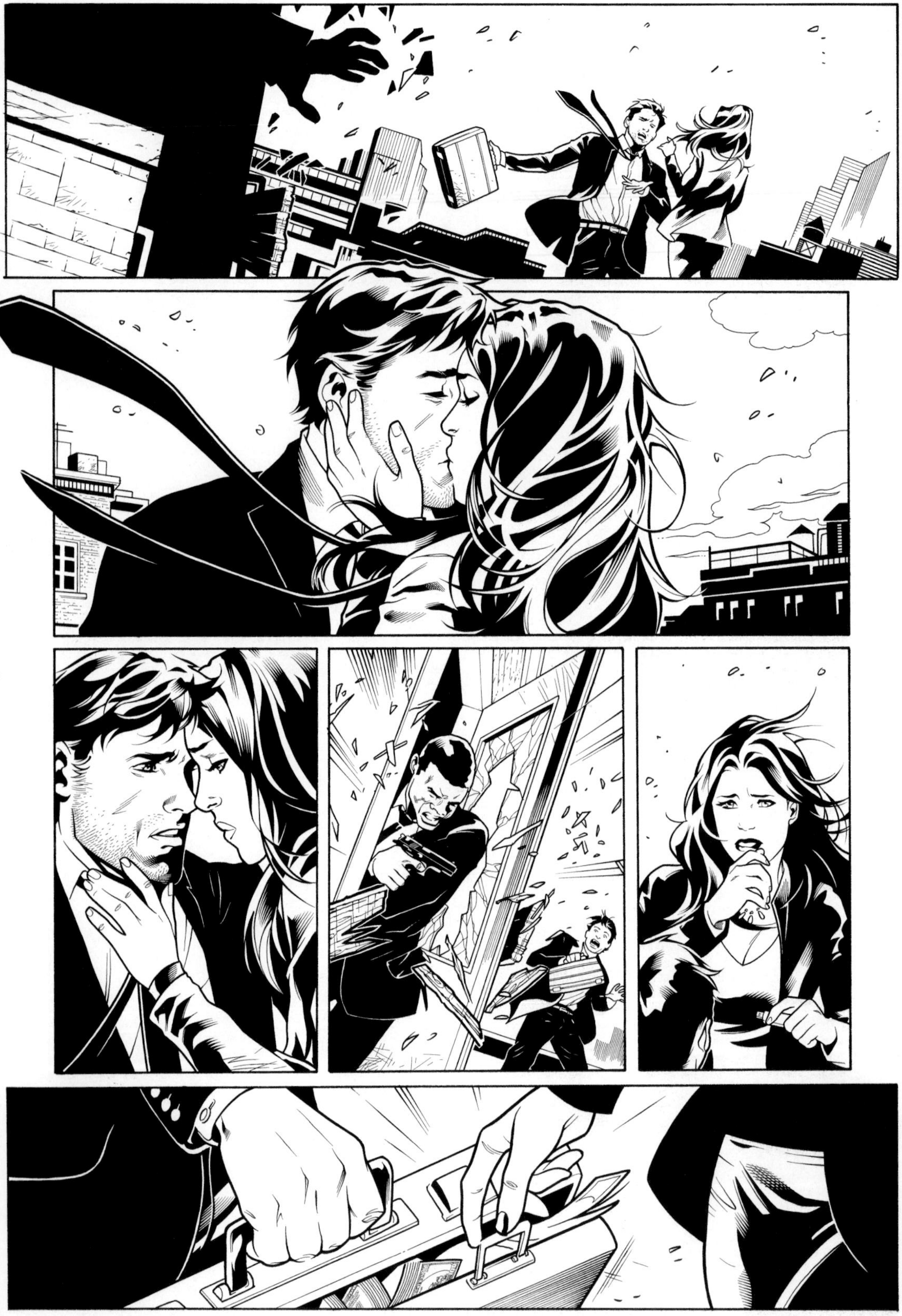

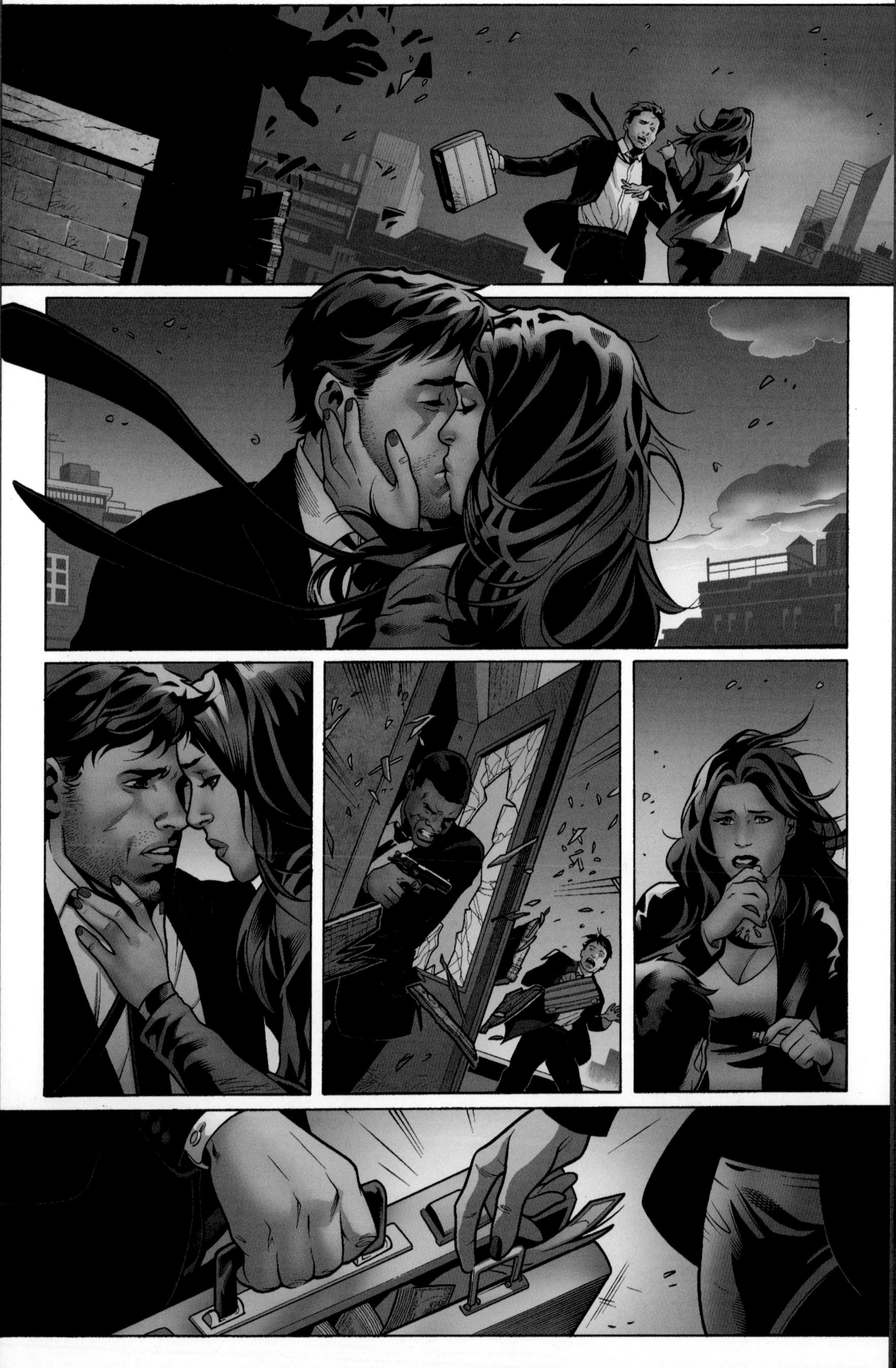

PAGE 66-67

PANEL 1

Double page spread. The rooftop as the deputy and his back up come busting through the door, their guns pulled, the case is open and all the money is lifted into the wind like blinding confetti.

Please don't hate me for making you draw a zillion $20 bills! I think it'll be bizarrely beautiful. They can even be on the waterfront so the background near sunset is gorgeous.

Clara has stepped away from Storm a little bit. Storm, the deputy and the other African are all looking at the money. Clara is looking at that building that's 18 feet across the alley.

CLARA/CAPTION
"I'm sorry for this."

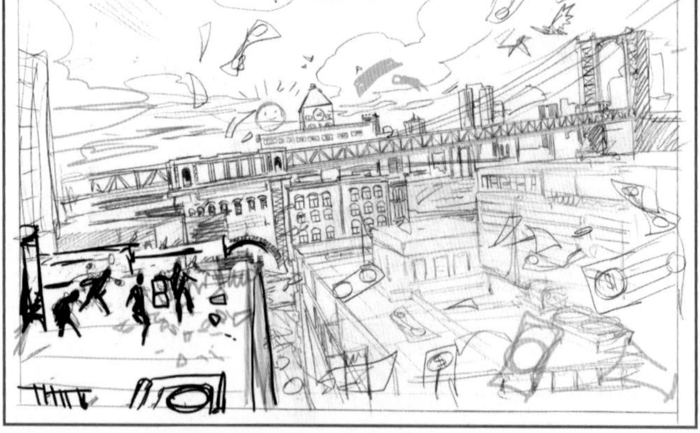

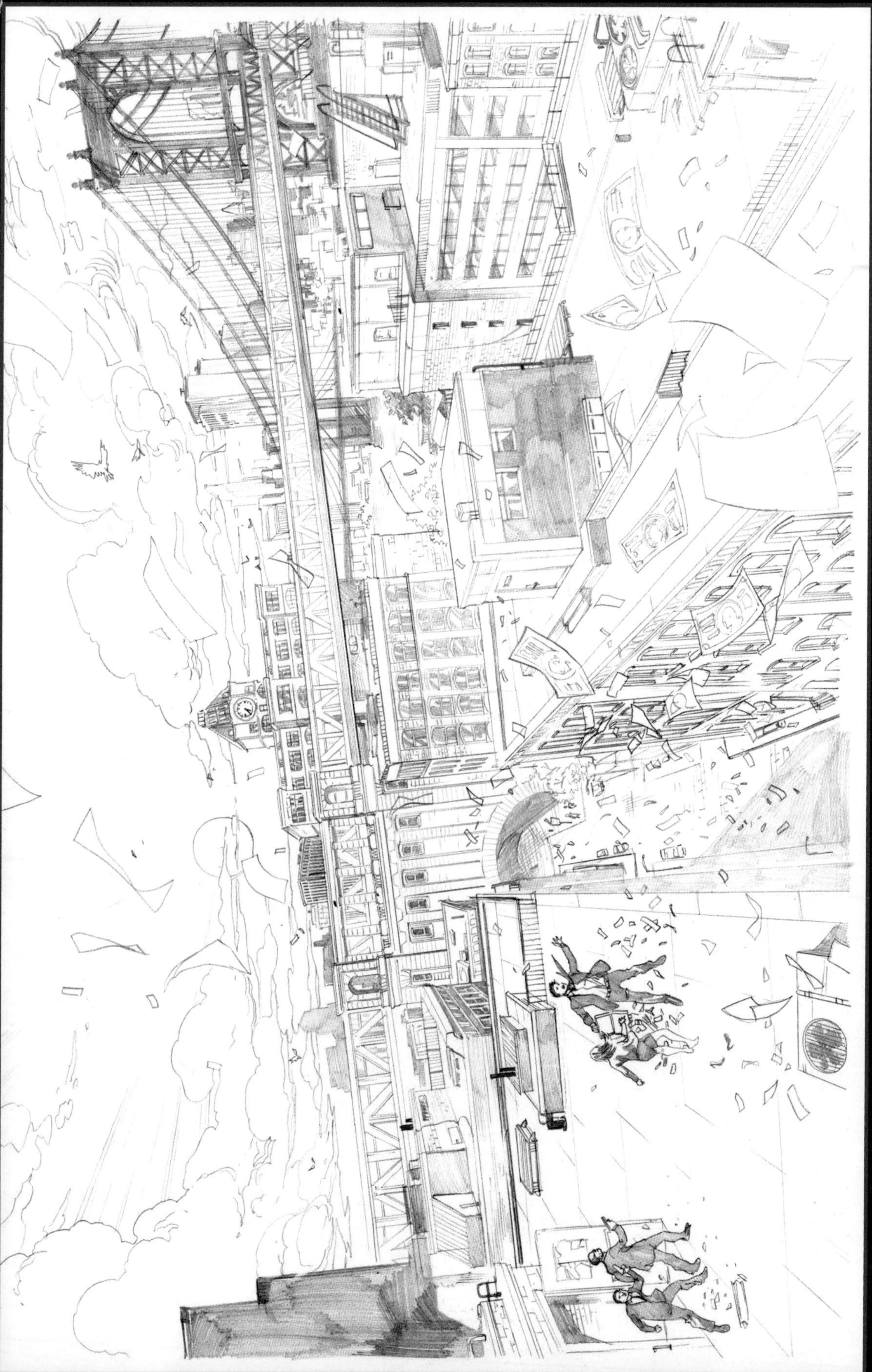

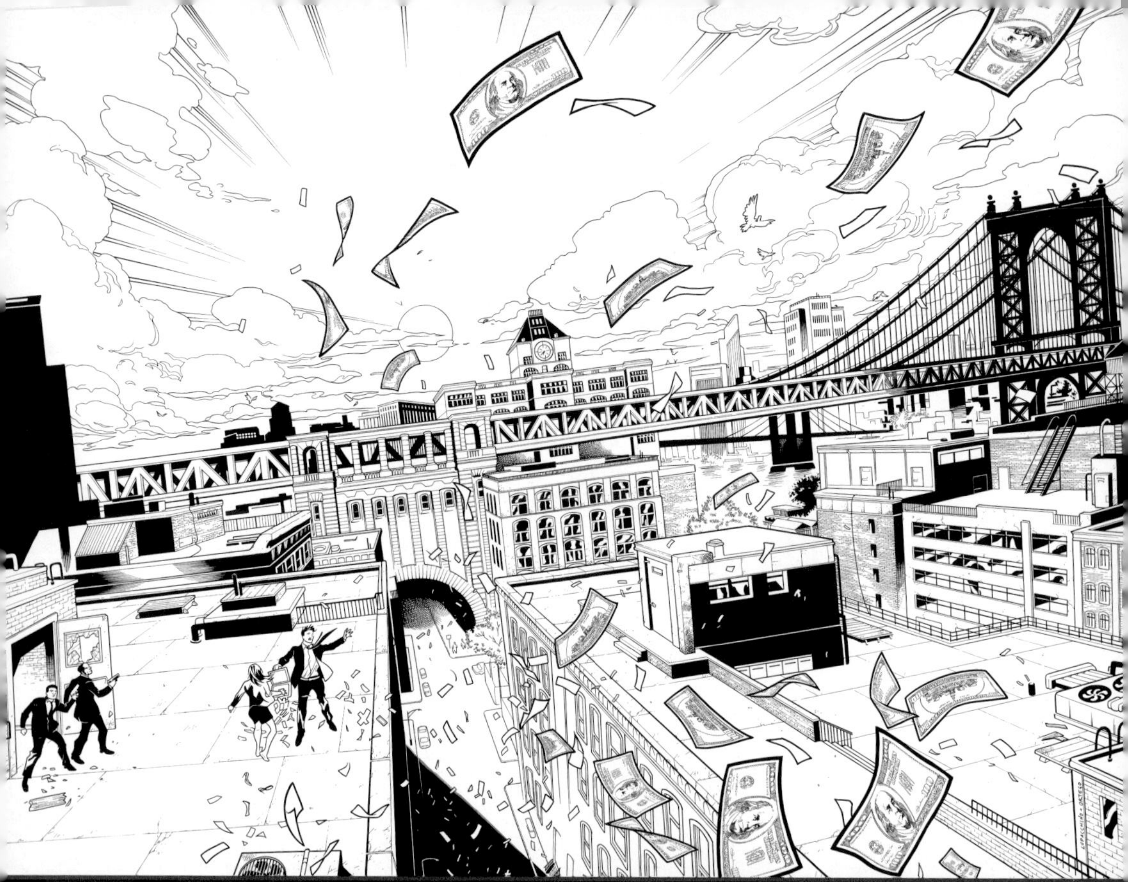
LUPACCHINO • ORTEGO

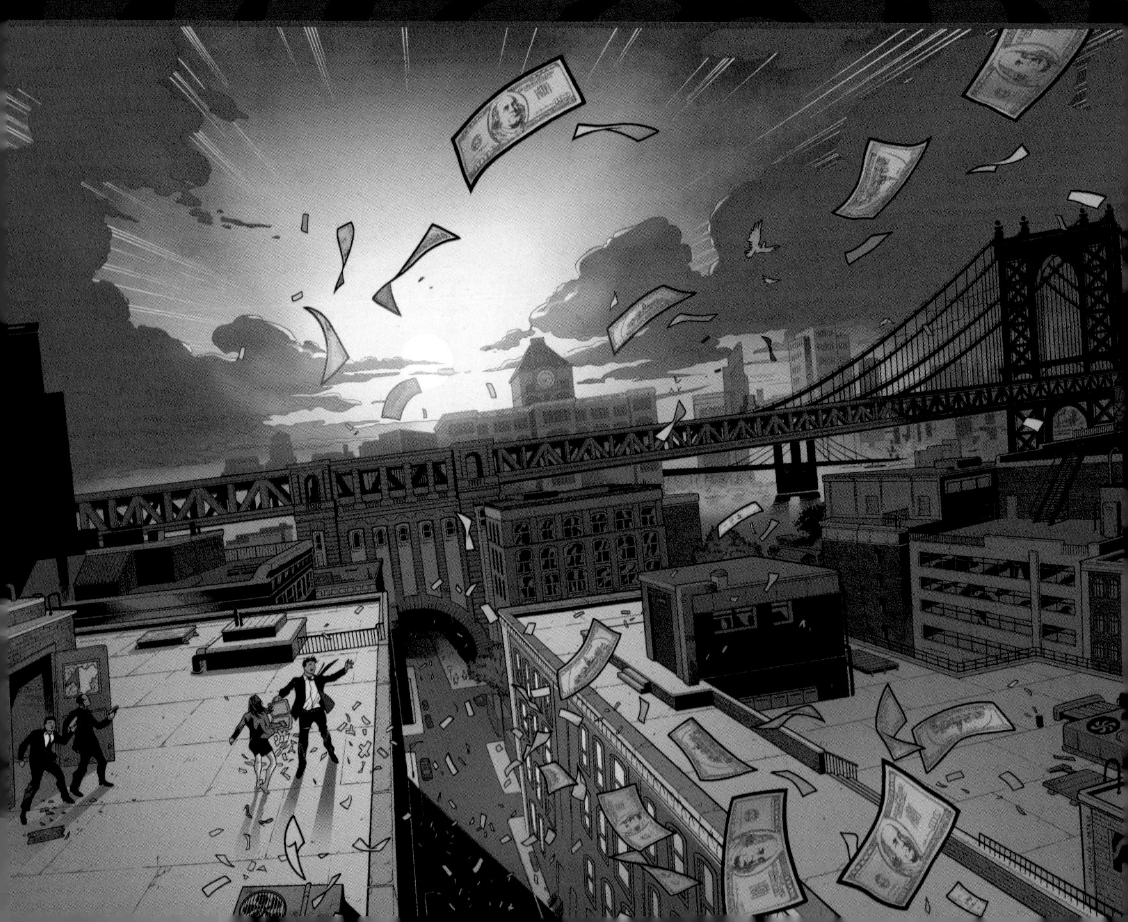

FOLLOW THE EXPLOITS OF DERRICK STORM

DEADLY STORM

While tracking down a missing husband for a desperate wife, private investigator Derrick Storm discovers there's a lot more to the job than he's been led to believe when he discovers the missing husband is actually a rogue CIA operative involved in selling national security secrets to enemy forces. He soon finds himself knee deep in international intrigue when he's recruited by the lovely and dangerous Clara Strike, a CIA agent with a penchant for trouble and adventure.

STORM SEASON

In Richard Castle's second Derrick Storm novel, the private investigator is hired to help a wealthy woman get back the money she lost to a con artist – but what should have been a routine mission quickly spirals out of control when the con artist reaches out to Storm seeking his help finding a missing woman. Haunted by a recording of the woman's scream for help, Storm investigates, and soon discovers an international conspiracy reaching further than he ever imagined – perhaps all the way to Clara Strike, a CIA agent the world thinks is dead.

A CALM BEFORE STORM

Derrick Storm is looking forward to finally getting out of the game – stocking up his cabin cruiser and heading out into the open Atlantic for good. But his plans are put on hold when, on the eve of a UN summit, the severed head of a Russian diplomat is found bobbing in the backwaters of the Hudson. Storm's CIA handler Clara Strike enlists him to crack a plot of global proportions, pitting the uncanny PI against a legion of eastern bloc mercenaries, and an ex-KGB hit man known simply as "The Fear."

STORM'S BREAK

A brutal cold snap has practically brought Manhattan to its knees, driving the island's denizens indoors. The city's homeless are driven down, into the bowels of ancient train tunnels and the concrete roots of skyscrapers. It's a world of predators and prey, and when runaway teenage girls start disappearing into this underworld, Derrick Storm isn't afraid to find out why. It doesn't take long before Storm trips to an international human trafficking ring headed by notorious Panama kingpin Marco Juarez. Teaming up with reliable and gutsy CIA agent Clara Strike, these two race to stop one of the world's most vile criminals before he destroys more innocent lives.

STORM WARNING

When Derrick Storm's close friend, attorney Sam Strummel, is murdered in cold blood in a cemetery outside of NYC, Storm launches his own investigation to bring the murderer to justice. While investigating Strummel's business dealings, Storm exposes a murder-for-hire syndicate that has just made him their next target.

UNHOLY STORM

When the daughters of four high-powered international businessmen are discovered dead in New York City, the NYPD scrambles to bring the murderer to justice. But when a fifth girl is found mutilated in a pool of her own blood, her prestigious French family hires Derrick Storm to run his own investigation and find the real killer. With limited access to evidence, Storm has only one lead – a strange symbol drawn in blood at each of the five crime scenes. While immersing himself in voodoo religion and rituals, Storm enlists the help of the beautiful and daring Clara Strike, his CIA handler. Together they uncover a deep web of deception under the guise of mysticism and devotion. And in a race against time, this most unlikely pair unlock the mystery behind a network of international assassins capable of creating a global catastrophe.

while packing his bags for a much-needed vacation, Storm gets a call from CIA Agent Clara Strike with an urgent mission. Storm must help protect the Swiss Ambassador's daughter against a formidable foe: a former KGB officer who is known for killing his victims with undetectable poison. When the mission is compromised, Clara fears that there is a mole in the CIA. In a bold move, Clara decides to put Storm undercover at Langley in order to smoke out the guilty party. Unexpectedly, Storm does more than just that; he uncovers a conspiracy that goes to the top levels of the agency and threatens Clara's livelihood.

STORM RISING

On a quest to recover a rare sapphire stolen from one of Manhattan's elite, Derrick Storm comes face-to-face with Bentley Silver: notorious jewel thief and rival womanizer. As the two men compare their conquests, they form an unlikely union in order to bring down a Parisian thief who threatens to undermine Silver's livelihood and Storm's bank account. A trail of stolen jewels leads Storm and Bentley to an underground international society, which is shrouded in secrecy and has a deadly mission.

DRIVING STORM

Storm faces his toughest case to date when CIA Agent Clara Strike asks him to clear her sister Susan's name after she's accused of murdering her husband. Strike insists that it was police incompetence and tainted evidence that led to her sister's arrest. Storm takes the case, only to realize that the police conspiracy against Susan isn't just Clara's hunch, it's a stone wall of silence even he may not be able to get past. And the closer he gets to the truth, the more danger he puts Susan in, leading Storm to a terrible choice – prove her innocence or save her life.

STORM'S LAST STAND

An ex-con out for vengeance, an old lover looking for closure, and a hardened cop hoping to find peace of mind all come crashing into Storm's life when a man they all know jumps off the Brooklyn Bridge. Or was he pushed? Now these former foes must work together to solve a crime that brings up their complicated past history and some memories better left forgotten. Storm must protect his reputation, heart, and possibly his life while unlocking the mystery behind his friend's death. In the midst of this, CIA Agent Clara Strike calls on Storm to help with what she deems, an "easy" task. But when this mission leads to Clara's abduction by MI5 agents, Storm must balance his two identities and cases while trying to save Clara's life.

STORM FALL

Storm is finally feeling like he has his life back: a few open and shut PI cases that lack any danger or intrigue and no recent calls from CIA Agent Clara Strike. But when her lack of contact begins to concern him, Storm begins to search for the woman who he has begun to care for as more than just a colleague. But what Storm unravels quickly turns his world upside down. Is Clara the CIA agent she claimed to be or a rogue spy operating outside of the law? Just when he begins to scratch the surface of the truth, his bank account is drained and a murder of a rival PI is pinned on him. Storm must take on his most challenging client yet: himself. Is this the work of Clara or one of his many enemies? Storm has to comb through his entire career as a PI and as a secret CIA operative: every criminal he put away, every crime he solved, every life he affected, in order to find out who would do this to him. Will he find the culprit pulling the puppet strings or will this be the end of Derrick Storm?

OTHER BOOKS BY THE AUTHOR

RICHARD
CASTLE
HELL HATH
NO FURY

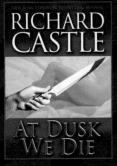

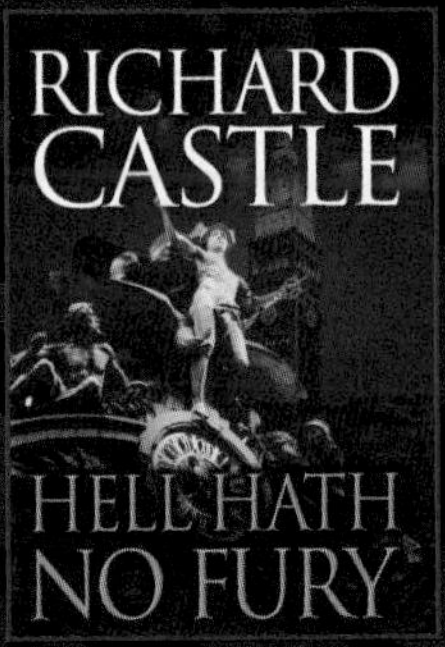

HELL HATH NO FURY

Taking a sabbatical from his college teaching job, Adam Parel has moved his family to the remote Oregon town of Jessup to finish his first novel. At first, Jessup seems ideal. Adam's wife and sons make friends quickly and there's enough quiet for Adam to get his work done. But as he researches his new hometown, Adam becomes convinced there's something sinister going on beneath Jessup's peaceful façade. People have gone missing here for decades and Adam eventually discovers the horrifying reason why: an obsessive cult that will stop at nothing to keep their sacred region "pure." As Adam struggles to escape with his family, he soon finds himself hunted by bloodthirsty fanatics for whom killing is the only way of living.

RICHARD
CASTLE
FLOWERS FOR
YOUR GRAVE

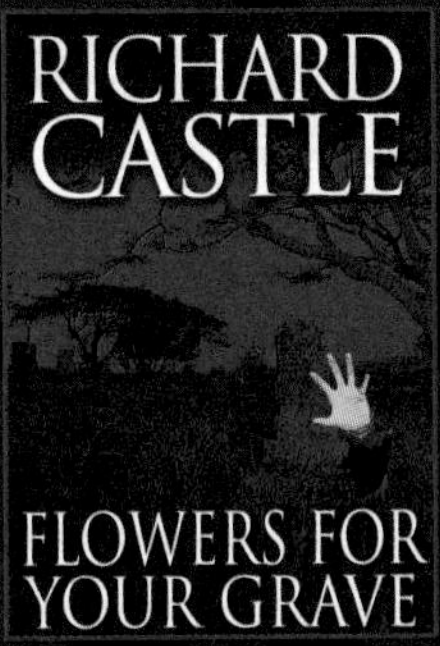

FLOWERS FOR YOUR GRAVE

Four murders in and the NYPD are still desperate for a lead on the serial killer that the tabloids are calling "The Florist." Struggling journalist Leroy Fine knows if he cracked this story he could get back everything he's lost – his job, his wife, his self-respect. So when Leroy uncovers a piece of evidence the cops have overlooked, he begins his own private investigation into the twisted and deadly world of The Florist. But as Leroy gets closer to discovering the killer's identity, he soon realizes he's put himself and everyone he loves in mortal danger. Now Leroy must decipher the Florist's riddles and unmask his identity… or end up the latest flower-covered corpse on the Ledger's front page.

RICHARD
CASTLE
AT DUSK
WE DIE

AT DUSK WE DIE

Still residing in the same tiny Texas town where he grew up, Ben Meltzer's life is a peaceful one. He runs the local drugstore and has a growing family with his high school sweetheart. So when the Satan's Creed motorcycle gang drive into town, he hardly pays them any mind. But after the entire town is ravaged by the Creed in a single night, he and his family are forced to flee for their lives and pray for the dawn. Because the Satan's Creed are no ordinary biker gang – they're ravenous vampires come to feed. As Ben attempts to keep his family safe, he quickly realizes that he must fight back – or watch as his family becomes fodder for nightmares come to life.

CASTLE
SKULL AT
PRINGTIME

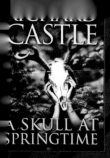

Looking for a way to pay for college after her father's death, Rachel Lyons spending the summer planting trees in the clearcut forests of remote Washingto It's a lucrative but lonely job and Rachel soon finds the monotony drainin That is, until she stumbles upon a half-buried skeleton deep in the woods – discovery that leads her to uncover an entire field of corpses. When Rachel attempts to contact authorities are thwarted, it quickly becomes clear that sl isn't alone out here. As she struggles to escape back to civilization, Rachel mu struggle to stay alive or risk becoming yet another one of the skeletons benea the dirt.

ICHARD
CASTLE
ROSE FOR
VERAFTER

A ROSE FOR EVERAFTER

At the Blessed Sacrament School for Girls, Sister Mary Grace leads her youn charges in daily Morning Prayer, asking the Lord their souls to keep. But t young women of Riverbend are starting to disappear, only to be found in shallo graves, wrapped in shrouds of white and grasping a red rose in their col dead hands. Who could be killing the town's virgin daughters? And why is h burying them alive? When Sister Mary Grace starts investigating, she discove a trail of evidence that leads from the local rectory to the upper echelons of t archdiocese – and ultimately to a secretive organization whose provenance ma be very far from godly.

New York Ledger's #1 Best Seller
ICHARD
CASTLE
HEN IT COMES
O SLAUGHTER

WHEN IT COMES TO SLAUGHTER

The neo-hippie community of Fair Haven, Vermont, had never experienced a sing murder in its nearly 40-year history – until one moonless night a week ago, whe five members of the Akin family were brutally hacked to death and found hangin from meat hooks. Suddenly, the town's tiny two-man police force – Chief Dere Olson and Deputy Ana Ruiz – find themselves thrust into a nightmare worl They wrestle with a dearth of evidence and a populace becoming more paranoi by the second as rumors abound of a scarecrow-like creature with hatchets f hands prowling the countryside. When a second family is butchered in the sam gruesome fashion, Olson and Ruiz begin to suspect that many of their townsfol are not the radical peaceniks they claim to be – the majority, in fact, harbor dar violent pasts that may finally be coming home to roost.

New York Ledger's #1 Best Seller
ICHARD
CASTLE
HEN IT COMES
O SLAUGHTER

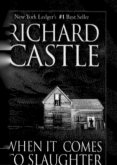

KISSED AND KILLED

Rookie detective Alexandra Jones grew up fast on the mean streets of the Bron But nothing could prepare her for the spate of murders currently plaguing th five boroughs: Someone is killing the city's richest men by cutting off the tongues and – in a final coup de grace – lopping off their privates. Jones' stree smart investigative skills soon lead her to the dark underbelly of the fashio industry, where beauty is a commodity easily bought and sold. It becomes clea that the killer is amongst those tossed aside after their youth has been used an

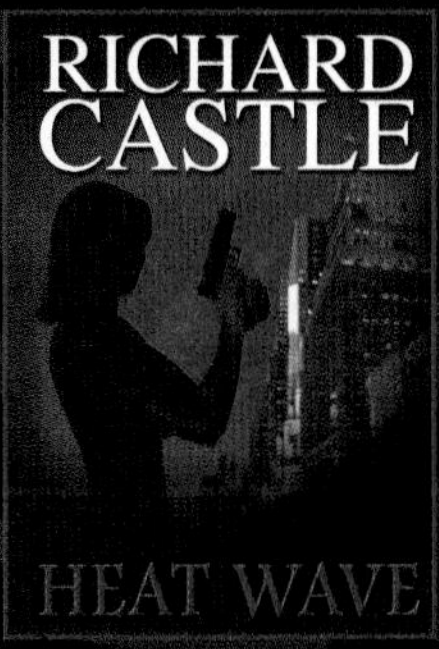
RICHARD
CASTLE
HEAT WAVE

HEAT WAVE

Mystery sensation Richard Castle introduces his newest character, NYPD Homicide Detective Nikki Heat. Tough, sexy, professional, Nikki Heat carries a passion for justice as she leads one of New York City's top homicide squads. She's hit with an unexpected challenge when the commissioner assigns superstar magazine journalist Jameson Rook to ride along with her to research an article on New York's Finest. Pulitzer Prize-winning Rook is as much a handful as he is handsome. His wise-cracking and meddling aren't her only problems. As she works to unravel the secrets of the murdered real estate tycoon, she must also confront the spark between them. The one called heat.

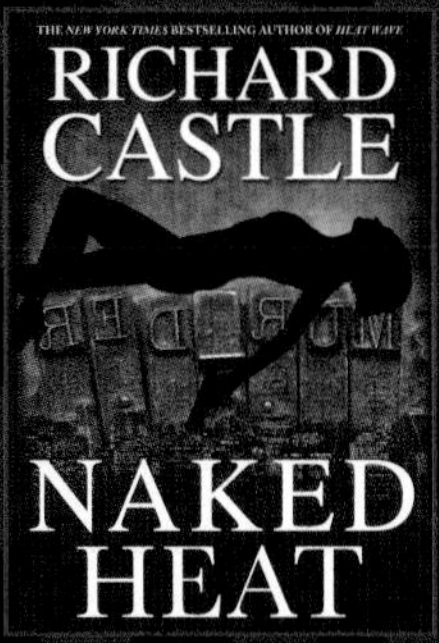
RICHARD
CASTLE
NAKED
HEAT

NAKED HEAT

When New York's most vicious gossip columnist, Cassidy Towne, is found dead, Heat uncovers a gallery of high profile suspects, all with compelling motives for killing the most feared muckraker in Manhattan. Heat's investigation is complicated by her surprise reunion with superstar magazine journalist Jameson Rook. The residue of their unresolved romantic conflict and crackling sexual tension fills the air as Heat and Rook embark on a search for a killer among celebrities and mobsters, singers and hookers, pro athletes and shamed politicians. This new, explosive case brings on the heat in the glittery world of secrets, cover-ups, and scandals.

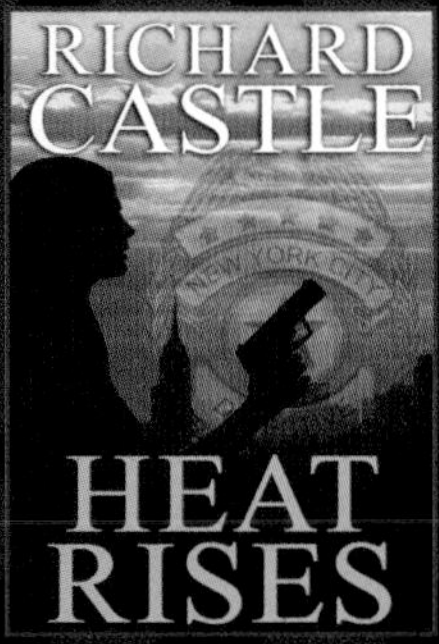
RICHARD
CASTLE
HEAT
RISES

HEAT RISES

The bizarre murder of a parish priest at a New York bondage club is just the tip of an iceberg that leads Nikki Heat to a dark conspiracy that reaches all the way to the highest level of the NYPD. But when she gets too close to the truth, Nikki finds herself disgraced, stripped of her badge and out on her own with nobody she can trust. Except maybe the one man in her life who's not a cop. Reporter Jameson Rook. In the midst of New York's coldest winter in a hundred years, there's one thing Nikki is determined to prove. Heat Rises.

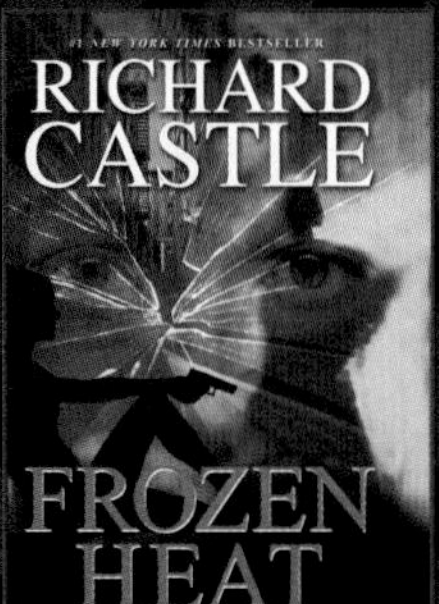
RICHARD
CASTLE
FROZEN
HEAT

FROZEN HEAT

NYPD Homicide Detective Nikki Heat gets more mystery than she imagined when she arrives at her latest crime scene. The body of an unidentified woman has been found stabbed to death and stuffed inside a suitcase left sitting on a freezer truck. A startling enough death, but an even bigger shock comes when this new homicide surprisingly connects to the unsolved murder of Detective Heat's own mother. The gruesome killing of this Jane Doe launches Heat on a dangerous and emotional investigation, rekindling the cold case that has haunted her since she was nineteen. Paired once again with her romantic and investigative partner, top journalist Jameson Rook, Heat works to solve the mystery of the body in the suitcase while she also digs into unexplored areas of her mother's background – areas Nikki has been afraid to confront before, but now must.

Facing relentless danger as someone targets her for the next kill, Heat's search will unearth painful family truths, expose a startling hidden life, and cause Nikki to reexamine her own past. Heat's passionate quest takes her and Rook from the back alleys of Manhattan to the avenues of Paris, trying to catch a ruthless killer. The question is, now that her mother's cold case has unexpectedly thawed, will Nikki Heat finally be able to solve the dark mystery that has been her demon for ten years?

Richard Castle is the author of numerous bestsellers, including *Heat Wave*, *Naked Heat*, *Heat Rises*, and the recent eBook-original trilogy of Derrick Storm shorts. His first novel, *In a Hail of Bullets*, published while he was still in college, received the Nom DePlume Society's prestigious Tom Straw Award for Mystery Literature. Castle currently lives in Manhattan with his daughter and mother, both of whom infuse his life with humor and inspiration.

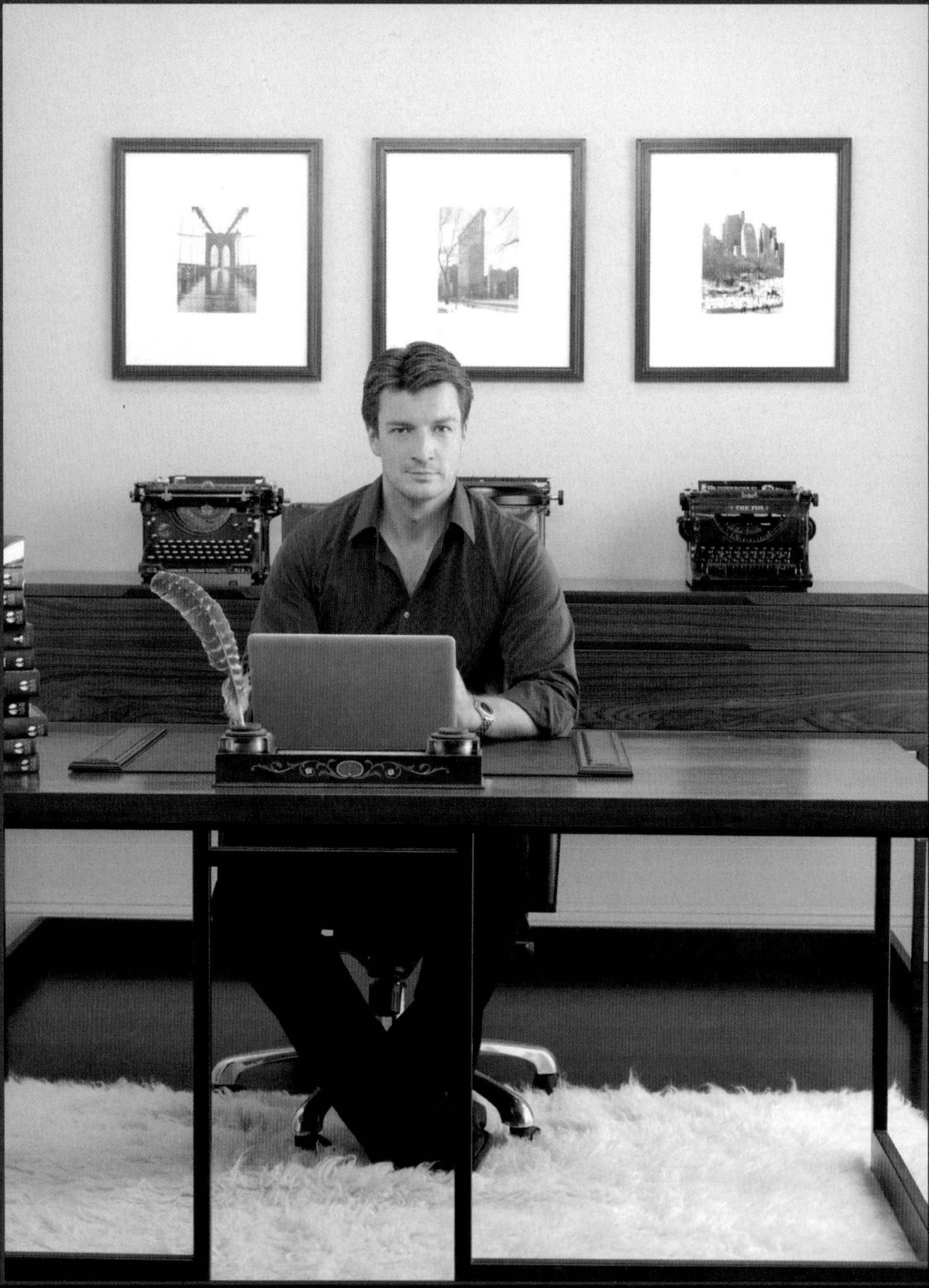

Millions of Viewers. One Official Graphic Novel. Inspired by ABC's Smash Hit CASTLE!

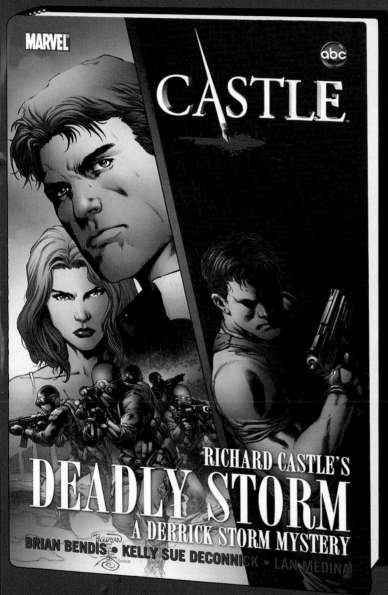

"A tense thriller that touches all the bases of a good detective yarn – an unlucky detective, a femme fatale, a seedy plot – yet with a fresh point of view and a gripping sense of action and adventure."
– *Mark L. Miller, Ain't It Cool News*

Castle: Richard Castle's
Deadly Storm
978-0-7851-5327-6

CASTLE's titular hero Derrick Storm comes to life in the pages of this all-new Marvel graphic novel. The story takes our hero Derrick Storm from the gritty world of the private eye all the way to the globe-hopping intrigue of the CIA. Eisner Award-winning Marvel writer Brian Bendis and red hot Osborn writer Kelly Sue DeConnick worked closely with CASTLE creator Andrew Marlowe to create a wall-to-wall, gritty, witty, globe-hopping detective thrill ride for fans of the hit TV show starring Nathan Fillion and Stana Katic.

RICHARD CASTLE'S
A CALM BEFORE STORM

A Five-Issue Comic Event
Beginning in 2013